PHILOSOPHY A[ND ...]
IN GURDJIEFF'S E[...]

A Modern Sufi Odyssey

VIBS

Volume 121

Robert Ginsberg
Executive Editor

Associate Editors

G. John M. Abbarno
Mary-Rose Barral
Gerhold K. Becker
Raymond Angelo Belliotti
Kenneth A. Bryson
C. Stephen Byrum
H. G. Callaway
Rem B. Edwards
William Gay
Dane R. Gordon
Haim Gordon
J. Everet Green
Heta Aleksandra Gylling
Matti Häyry
Steven V. Hicks
Richard T. Hull

Laura Duhan Kaplan
Joseph C. Kunkel
Vincent L. Luizzi
Alan Milchman
George David Miller
Jon Mills
Peter A. Redpath
Alan Rosenberg
Arleen L. F. Salles
Steven Schroeder
John R. Shook
Alan Soble
Eddy Souffrant
Tuija Takala
Oscar Vilarroya
Anne Waters

John R. Welch

Gurdjieff in 1949, the year of his death

PHILOSOPHY AND ART IN GURDJIEFF'S *BEELZEBUB*

A Modern Sufi Odyssey

Anna T. Challenger

Rodopi

Amsterdam – New York, NY 2002

The paper on which this book is printed meets the requirements of "ISO 9706:1994, Information and documentation - Paper for documents - Requirements for permanence".

ISBN: 90-420-1489-X
©Editions Rodopi B.V., Amsterdam – New York, NY 2002
Printed in The Netherlands

CONTENTS

Frontispiece		iii
Editorial Foreword		ix
ONE	Fragments of an Aimful life	1
TWO	Connections with Sufism	11
THREE	Gurdjieff's Theory of Art	31
FOUR	Travel and Transformation: *Beelzebub's Tales* within the Context of Philosophical Travel Literature	47
FIVE	The *Tales* Themselves: An Overview	67
	1. The Scenario	68
	2. The Commentaries	72
	3. Reflections	80
SIX	The Holy Planet Purgatory	83
SEVEN	A Sample of Tales	97
	1. "The Transcaucasian Kurd"	97
	2. "The Results of Some Idle Fishermen"	98
	3. "The Results of an Unwise Wager"	100
	4. "A Partial Tale about the Causes of War"	103
EIGHT	What Happens When a Master Dies? A Review of the Recent Literature	113
Notes		121
Bibliography		133
About the Author		139
Index		141

EDITORIAL FOREWORD

Plants and animals are fixed in their kind, pinned to their species. Stones, plants, and animals, they are. Only human beings can come to be. A taxonomer's category is not what makes us what we are. Of all natural beings, only human beings can either break down their species line and become unidentifiable—inhuman—or distend their species line and become what they can be—truly human. Other beings exist by fitting easily in their kind. Only human beings must make an issue of their being. Only human beings ask about the meaning of life. This is our peculiarity, the paradoxical nature of human existence. We must become what we are. We must go beyond ourselves in order to be ourselves. Being human is a task, and an achievement.

That this is so, that this task is arduous, that it must be undertaken, that nothing has meaning unless it is undertaken, constitutes the epicenter of G. I. Gurdjieff's ideas and activities, his Work. To be sure, others from Plato to Søren Kierkegaard and Martin Heidegger, from Saint Augustine to Friedrich Nietzsche, have written deeply and extensively on this theme. What distinguishes Gurdjieff from such thinkers is his unremitting way of going about the urgency of this task, his emphasis on the work involved: the effort, the hardship, the necessity of voluntary suffering. He urges us not to sentimentalize, not to remain automatic and mechanical, not to delude ourselves about our abilities and successes, not to identify with anything whatsoever, not to fall into the trance of everydayness, not to sleep at the cost of existence—to awake and be the driver, to be attentive, to self-remember, to be conscious, ceaselessly struggling toward self-transformation. More than anyone else with whom I am familiar, Gurdjieff drives home that being human comes hard to human beings. The evolution of coming to be human is not natural; it takes pains.

Another way in which Gurdjieff is different from other thinkers is the significance he places on action. He put his ideas into practice. He enacted his thoughts. Kierkegaard poked fun at G. W. F. Hegel for speaking abstractly about existence. Life, said Kierkegaard, had to be lived. But he himself only wrote treatises about it. The same holds for Nietzsche, who could hardly sustain a friendship. And Heidegger remained a professor. With the possible exception of Socrates, whom, it is worth recalling, we know only as a *dramatis persona* in Plato's dialogues, all these people have been writers and not practitioners of existence. Gurdjieff was immersed in life, and it was from within this immersion that his thought gathered its content and assumed its style. In the doing of the different tasks in life is articulated the task of becoming a human being. In the rigor of these practical undertakings, in the struggle of carrying them through, in the tension of being with others, in the contradictions of real situations, the difficulty of the endeavor for true existence strikes home. Undertakings become existential exercises—means to consciousness. This being conscious, however, is not centripetal. It is linked to the cosmos. To be awake, to be aware of ourselves, is at the same time to be aware of the workings of the universe and of the way we affect them and are affected by them. The process to consciousness, the effort to be human, and the struggle involved feed the cosmos with energies which, in turn, influence our lives, both individual and collective. In this sense, the individual struggle toward consciousness has a cosmic significance. It redeems because it preserves the universe. The universe, the Sufi claims, came into being for the sake of the Perfect Human Being. Sufi ideas such as this, grafted as they are on the existential theme of being a human being, lend Gurdjieff's work its depth and its magic, its attraction and its edifying quality.

Anna T. Challenger captures both the depth and the magic, and she presents Gurdjieff as one from whom we, too, can be instructed. Hers is not yet another book on the subject: anecdotal, impressionistic, journalistic. While acknowledging the force of Gurdjieff's teaching, she avoids the pitfalls of sentimentality and identification. She is critical in the Sufi sense of not accepting anything without having first personally realized it. And she is committed, having undertaken a labor of love in the form of personal gratitude.

Taking *Beelzebub's Tales to His Grandson* as the center, Challenger gives an account of Gurdjieff's work that is learned and extensively researched, but at the same time original, imaginative, and fresh. She comments at length on Gurdjieff's connections with Sufism, stressing in a new way the extraordinariness of Gurdjieff's methods and style, so important in a teaching tale: a combination of Socratic confrontation, Kiekegaardian indirection, and Zen austerity that conspire through humor, obliqueness, shock, illogic, and non-linearity to bring the reader face to face with his or her presumptuousness and inconsistencies, so as to clear the debris toward a way that could possibly lead to a more authentic awareness of the self.

But where Challenger breaks entirely new ground, not only in Gurdjieff studies but in the history of ideas, is the connection she establishes first between Gurdjieff and Dante Alighieri, and then between Dante and Sufism. Heeding Gurdjieff's own claim that his chapter "The Holy Planet Purgatory" is the "heart" of the *Tales* and therefore of his writing as a whole, Challenger goes on to juxtapose that chapter to Dante's *Purgatorio*, unearthing surprising parallels that complement the contents of these works. By her endeavors, Gurdjieff is enriched through Dante, and Dante is seen in the light of Gurdjieff's robust and uncompromising ways—each in his own way responding with reverence to the gift of life.

Having established Gurdjieff's connections with Dante, Challenger's research takes her beyond Dante back to Sufism, that is, back to Gurdjieff himself. She revisits *Islam and the Divine Comedy*, a book written in 1919 by Miguel Asin Palacios, a priest and Professor of Arabic Studies at the University of Madrid, to discover that the extraordinary Dante, the divine Dante, got his entire model for his famous work from Ibn 'Arabi, a proto-sufist, who wrote some twenty-five years before Dante's birth. Challenger's research, however, is not done for its own sake; it is not archeological, but genealogical, establishing links as well as contrasts. Unlike Ibn 'Arabi's and Dante's Satan, Gurdjieff places Beelzebub at the center of his *Tales*. Beyond good and evil, he takes seriously the antagonism necessary for the evolution of the process of becoming human. And he brings home that this antagonism, the struggle of the higher and the lower, the tension between Heaven and Hell, are right here, on Earth.

As is well-known, Gurdjieff composed piano music, put together theatrical performances, wrote stories, and directed dancing groups. He took art seriously. Challenger responds to this seriousness with a chapter on Gurdjieff's views on art. At a time when the idea of *art pour l'art* was rampant, he took a different stance. Art is not for its own sake, but for the sake of humanity. Closer to Leo Tolstoy than to Eduard Hanslick, and against the subjectivism that apotheosizes the creator, for Gurdjieff art serves a function: the fulfillment of our spiritual needs, the creation of consciousness.

Challenger, however, does not only give us a much needed presentation of Gurdjieff's theory of art and the influence of that theory on several artists. She goes on to place Gurdjieff's *Tales*, his philosophical literary art, in the larger context of some of the greatest works of literature. She does this not to present her own aesthetic, but to link the theme of travel, central to the *Tales*, with that of the epics of *Gilgamesh*, Homer's *The Odyssey*, Miguel de Cervantes' *Don Quixote*, Dante's *Divine Comedy*, Voltaire's *Candide*, and Thomas Mann's *The Magic Mountain*. This is a veritable *tour de force*.

Gurdjieff lamented the fact that he had not studied more of the classics. Challenger does it for him, and in doing so she articulates his thoughts as he might have seen them reflected in the peregrinations and embodied in the actions of the heroes of these great works, the core of these thoughts being the transformation of the being of human beings. Travel, Challenger is aware, is analogous to living or to experience or to the experience of living; it involves an estrangement and an alienation of the ordinary self and then a return to an extraordinary one. We *are* only in this return. By abandoning the familiar and living in what is alien, we come to ourselves. This movement of alienation and return is completable but never completed. Only in our becoming are we more than what we are. Not accidentally does Nikos Kazantzakis begin his *Odyssey* with Odysseus' restlessness in Ithaca, his itching, as Herman Melville would put it, for things still unknown.

Nenos Georgopoulos
University of Macedonia

One

FRAGMENTS OF AN AIMFUL LIFE

Aim for knowledge.
If you become poor, it will be wealth for you.
If you become rich, it will adorn you.

—El-Zubeir, son of Abdu Bakr (twelfth-century Sufi), "Riches"

Numerous books giving accounts of G. I. Gurdjieff's life, based on the little that is known of it, have been published during the last few decades, and the Peter Brook film *Meetings with Remarkable Men* (1979) offers a visual and narrative rendition of Gurdjieff's early years prior to his appearance in Europe, as based on Gurdjieff's partly autobiographical book of the same title. Readers familiar with Gurdjieff's teaching are aware of the futility of trying to construct any typical biography of his life, the prospect having been compared with trying to capture the identity of Proteus or to chronicle the life of Moses. I therefore offer only the following brief sketch as an overview.

Born in the city of Alexandropol, Armenia, in 1877 according to his passport, or possibly as early as 1866 according to other accounts, Gurdjieff was the eldest of several children born to Georgios Georgiades, a Greek by birth, and to an Armenian mother (the family name was changed at some point for political reasons). Combined circumstances of geography and family background yielded in Gurdjieff a facility with languages: he spoke Greek, Turkish, Armenian, later Russian, and eventually acquired a working facility with several European languages. This factor later served to give him first-hand access to various schools of thought and enabled him to disseminate his teaching among an international following of students.

When he was still a boy, around eleven or twelve years old, his family moved to Kars in northeastern Turkey. Here, he first attended Greek school, then took lessons at the Russian municipal school, and later, at the suggestion of Father Borsh—dean of the Russian Academy—the young Gurdjieff was taken out of school and privately educated by the dean himself, as well as by other tutors selected at the dean's discretion. From these teachers, he received a rigorous education in geography, history, anatomy, physiology, mathematics, Russian, Scriptures, and other subjects. Father Borsh and Gurdjieff's father were apparently the two strongest influences during his formative years. He refers to the dean as "my unforgettable tutor, my second father."[1] This man, who was considered a spiritual authority in the region surrounding Kars, tried to cultivate Gurdjieff for the priesthood, the dean's conception of this vocation being that it demanded a holistic understanding of body and soul. Priests, according to Borsh, should be educated to carry out all the duties of a medical physician so that physical illnesses could be attended to with both spiritual and physiological attunement. Although Gurdjieff records that he had other ideas for his future, he did pursue studies to become a physician-priest. Years after Father Borsh's death, when Gurdjieff found himself in the vicinity of Kars, he had a funeral service performed over his teacher's grave. In *Meetings with Remarkable Men*, he pays tribute to Borsh's profound effect on his life: "Rest in peace, dear Teacher! I do not know whether I have justified or am justifying your dreams, but the commandments you gave me I have never once in all my life broken."[2]

Gurdjieff's father was a bard who possessed "the soul of a true poet."[3] He also worked as a carpenter after the move to Kars, having lost the family fortune as a result of a cattle plague. Gurdjieff writes of his father's influence: "by his constant conversation with me and his extraordinary stories, [he] greatly assisted the arising in me of poetic images and high ideals."[4] The chapter "My Father" in *Meetings with Remarkable Men* resounds with feelings of deep love, respect, and gratitude toward a man who possessed a valuable lived wisdom, was a conscientious family person, and behaved honestly and straightforwardly in his dealings with others; a person who embodied and practiced the ideals he espoused, and whose relationship to his first-born son was like that of an older brother. Gurdjieff laments his father's pointless and untimely death at the hands of the Turks during a mania of human psychosis (in the form of the Turkish attack on Alexandropol in 1917) in which Georgiades was fatally wounded while trying to defend the family property. Both Gurdjieff's father and Father Borsh were worthy in Gurdjieff's value system of the appellation "remarkable"—a title designating one "who stands out from those around him by the resourcefulness of his mind, and who knows how to be restrained in the manifestations which proceed from his nature, at the same time conducting himself justly and tolerantly towards the weaknesses of others."[5]

At some point during these early years, Gurdjieff formulated what he would later refer to as "the idée fixe of my inner world,"[6] which was to discover the significance and purpose of organic life on earth, in particular of human existence. Having been deeply influenced by his father's ability as an ashokh or storyteller to recite from memory hundreds of stories from antiquity, including the *Gilgamesh* epic and the Sufi tales *A Thousand and One Nights*, Gurdjieff became convinced that the answers he sought could be found in the ancient traditions. He therefore left Kars and embarked on a twenty-year search for understanding, which took him through countries of the Middle East, Central Asia, and to India and Tibet. The apex of this search seems to have been his contact with the Sarmoun Brotherhood, an organization that John G. Bennett understood to be connected with the Khwajagan Sufis of Central Asia.[7] From his contact with the Sarmoun, Gurdjieff apparently gained the quintessential response to his burning query about the purpose of human existence and of organic life on Earth: the Theory of Reciprocal Maintenance. But for the most part, the existential content of these twenty years remains speculative.

In 1913, Gurdjieff appeared in Moscow, prepared to pass on to others the fruits of his twenty-year-long odyssey, or, as he expressed it, "to actualize in practice what I had taken upon myself as a sacred task."[8] While in Russia, he met and married Countess Julia Ostrowska, a lady-in-waiting in the court of Tsar Nicholas II, with whom he remained until her death from cancer in 1926. From the time of his arrival in Moscow until his death in 1949, he selflessly devoted the whole of his extraordinary energies to transmitting to others via every conceivable means the understanding about human existence that he believed he had acquired during his searching years.

The second half of Gurdjieff's life, from 1913 to 1949, can be roughly divided into three phases. The first encompasses the years 1913 to 1924, during which Gurdjieff was intensely involved in conveying to large numbers of students both the theoretical and the practical aspects of his teaching. During these years, he made a number of attempts to establish his Institute for the Harmonious Development of Man—in Moscow, Berlin, Tashkent, Tiflis, and Constantinople—each time being forced to abandon his chosen location due to unstable political conditions. In each of these cities, Gurdjieff purchased or rented property, bought necessary equipment, recruited students, and created the best possible conditions for what in his opinion constituted "harmonious development." His intention was to create "conditions in which a man would be continually reminded of the sense and aim of his existence by an unavoidable friction between his conscience and the automatic manifestations of his nature."[9] Gurdjieff's Institute for the Harmonious Development of Man finally took root in Fontainebleau, France, in 1922, with the purchase of the two-hundred-acre Prieuré des Basses Loges, chateau of the widow of Maitre Laborie, and payment for Laborie's services as defense lawyer in the famous Dreyfus trial.

Activity at the Institute flourished for the first two years. A distinguished following of international students—among them a large nucleus of well-known professionals, including Thomas de Hartmann, Alfred Orage, Alexandre de Saltzmann, and for a time Jean Toomer and Kathryn Mansfield—engaged themselves in work and study for fourteen or more hours each day (Mansfield being exempted from the rigorous regime due to her illness). The practical work included learning trades, such as carpentry or shoemaking, and performing various manual jobs, such as building a Russian bath, taking care of farm animals, cooking for large numbers of people, and gardening. The chateau had been unoccupied for eight years, so the task of restoring and maintaining the grounds was itself laborious. Gurdjieff also taught sacred dances, which he had learned at schools in the East; these were practiced in the evenings after dinner. Performances of these movements were eventually staged at the Théâtre des Champs-Elysées in Paris and at Carnegie Hall in New York. All physical tasks were carried out in conjunction with exercises in attention and Self-Remembering, and all work was perceived as a means rather than an end—a means to the development of Consciousness, Will, and Individuality. Various aphorisms were inscribed on the Prieuré walls to serve as reminders of the Institute's purpose, sayings such as, "Looking backwards, we only remember the difficult periods of our lives, never the peaceful times; the latter are sleep, the former are struggle and therefore life,"[10] and, "The worse the conditions of life the more productive the work, always provided you remember the work."[11]

This thriving activity at the Prieuré came to a sudden halt on 8 July 1924, when Gurdjieff's Citroen collided, at the speed of ninety kilometers per hour, with a tree on the road between Paris and Fontainebleau. Gurdjieff barely survived the accident. He was unconscious for several days and incapacitated for a number of months. And the effect of his condition on life at the Prieuré was one of sudden paralysis. C. S. Nott, a leading pupil of Gurdjieff's at the time, recorded his impressions of this period: "It was as if the mainspring of a great machine had broken. . . . The force that moved our lives was gone."[12] As Gurdjieff regained consciousness and began the agonizing process of recovery, he was forced to bear witness to the process of involution at work within the walls of the Institute for which he had sacrificed so much and striven for years to establish—involution in the form of the deterioration of conditions, both financial and existential, which were the immediate consequence of his inability personally to manage affairs and consciously to direct the forces at work there. He had to acknowledge what was for him a devastating realization: that the Institute for the Harmonious Development of Man had failed insofar as not a single pupil, nor even all of his students collectively, possessed the inner resources required even temporarily to sustain the momentum of life he had set into motion. This school, even in the temporary absence of its teacher, was no longer a school in the living sense of the word; apart from the consciousness of the master, it was reduced to an estate that housed so many separate entities engaged in solitary and unrelated tasks. What then was the point, if the purpose of existence there depended completely on the consciousness of one person?

On 26 August 1924, Gurdjieff announced the liquidation of the Institute and began to consider other ways in which he might transmit his teaching. Of this critical juncture in his life, he wrote, "Since I had not, when in full strength and health, succeeded in introducing in practice into the lives of people the beneficial truths elucidated for them by me, then I must at least, at any cost, succeed in doing so in theory before my death."[13] In the fall of 1924, he embarked on a new phase of work: that of transmitting his teaching via the relatively more static form of the written word. Activity at the Prieuré did eventually resume, but it never again achieved the fervor experienced during those first two years. After 1924, Gurdjieff embarked upon the second phase of his work, which would remain his key focus until 1935: he turned his attention to writing.

Gurdjieff first attempted to convey his ideas by means of short scenarios intended for the cinema or theater. These included four pieces entitled *The Cocainist, The Chiromancy of the Stock Exchange, The Unconscious Murder,* and *The Three Brothers*. The last of these is thought to have been inspired by Fyodor Dostoyevski's *The Brothers Karamazov* (1880), the three Karamazov brothers being dominated by intellect (Ivan), emotion (Aloysha), and body (Dimitri), as were the three brothers of Gurdjieff's scenario.[14] Another early piece by Gurdjieff was the ballet *The Struggle of the Magicians*. Then, within months of having written these initial experimental pieces, he hit upon a plan for the overall format his writings would take. He intended to write three works, each with a separate purpose. In the first, he wished to destroy in people their convictions about what he considered to be the false and illusory reality in which most people live their lives. In the second, he proposed to demonstrate different valid ways of perceiving reality. And in the third, he would share with others the ways he had discovered of touching or merging with these different realities. Gurdjieff proceeded to write these texts, which were eventually published under the titles (1) *Beelzebub's Tales to His Grandson*, or *All and Everything*, (2) *Meetings with Remarkable Men*, and (3) *Life is Real Only Then, When "I Am."* One additional written work, *The Herald of Coming Good*, was published in 1933, but within one year Gurdjieff withdrew it from circulation. (It has since been reprinted by Samuel Weiser in 1971.) Those copies that had already been distributed were, whenever possible, collected and destroyed. The "good" the pamphlet heralded referred to Gurdjieff's forthcoming writings.

Gurdjieff began writing *Beelzebub's Tales* in December 1924, and had from the start hit upon a cosmic framework for his ideas and a unique narrator in the guise of Beelzebub, the fallen angel, who had to redeem his offenses to God through his own conscious labor and intentional suffering. The task of actually expounding upon his system of thought within the confines of a literary structure proved extremely arduous for him: "To write my book for conscious man would be easy," he mused; "but to write for donkeys—very difficult."[15] The first version of the *Tales*, which cost its author "three or four years of almost unceasing day and night work,"[16] had to be discarded when Gurdjieff recognized in the response of his uncomprehending audience that he had "buried the dog [not bone] too deep." No one could grasp his intended meaning. He was forced, therefore, in spite of poor health, to rewrite *Beelzebub* from the beginning—a task that took him until the end of 1929.

Most of Gurdjieff's writing was done either in the animated atmosphere of Paris's Café de la Paix (his favorite "office") or in Fontainebleau's Café Henri IV. The manuscript was dictated or written down in Armenian or Russian, the Armenian sections translated into Russian, then the whole translated into English, all under the author's supervision and by those students most seasoned in his ideas. The well-known editor Alfred Orage, who moved in literary circles frequented by writers such as T. S. Eliot, Ezra Pound, e. e. cummings, Dylan Thomas, and Kathryn Mansfield, and whom T. S. Eliot considered "the best literary critic of that time in London,"[17] did most of the editing of Gurdjieff's manuscript. During the height of activity at Fontainebleau, Orage gave up his prestigious position as owner and editor of the London weekly review *The New*

Age, considered one of the best publications of literature and ideas in England at the time, to go to the Prieuré and work. To the amazement of the literary world, Orage shifted his role from revered literary critic to chief disseminator of Gurdjieff's ideas in New York, engaging his energies in raising large sums of money for the publication of *Beelzebub's Tales*. At one point, Orage, desiring to see Gurdjieff's magnum opus published, used his literary connections to arrange a meeting in New York between Gurdjieff and Alfred A. Knopf. But when asked by Knopf whether he would be interested in publishing *All and Everything*, Gurdjieff responded, to Orage's chagrin, by telling Knopf he could have his (Gurdjieff's) book only after Knopf had "cleaned [his] house" (rid his publishing house of all trash).[18]

In 1930, the first copies of the second version of *Beelzebub* were produced in mimeographed form—more than one hundred copies were distributed among students who studied it and read it aloud at gatherings. Gurdjieff continued to revise the manuscript for several more years, during which time he also completed his "Second Series," *Meetings with Remarkable Men*, plus what is extant of *Life Is Real*. All three works were published posthumously: *Beelzebub's Tales* in 1950 by Harcourt, Brace in New York and by Kegan Paul in London; *Meetings with Remarkable Men* in 1963 by Dutton in New York and by Kegan Paul in London; *Life Is Real Only Then, When "I Am"* in 1975 by Triangle Publications in New York. Gurdjieff's desire had been that, upon publication of *Beelzebub's Tales*, an unlimited number of free copies of the book should be made available, and he urged his students to carry copies wherever they went and to offer public readings from it when possible. In a letter dated January 1949, Gurdjieff wrote, "I intend that the first series of my writings shall be made available without payment to all who are in need of their help."[19] In fact, after his decision in 1948 to publish the *Tales*, enough money had been raised to pay for the free distribution of thousands of copies. Nevertheless, upon his death it was distributed through commercial channels.

During these same years, Gurdjieff also composed, in collaboration with the Russian pianist Thomas de Hartmann, over three hundred pieces of music. Some of their musical compositions correspond to chapters of Gurdjieff's written work and are intended to create emotional states that parallel the intellectual ones evoked by his writings. Other pieces are religious in nature or express themes connected with life in the East. Many bear titles reminiscent of Sufi life and thought.

The year 1935 marks the beginning of the third and final phase of Gurdjieff's work. He wrote nothing after May 1935, when "The Outer and Inner World of Man," the final chapter of *Life Is Real*, had been completed. By 1939, the Institute at Fontainebleau had been sold and Gurdjieff had moved into a small apartment on Rue des Colonels Renard, Paris. Here, an international array of students—primarily French, British, American, and some Russian—would gather daily to listen to long readings from *Beelzebub's Tales*, to partake of sumptuous meals that had been personally prepared by Gurdjieff, and to listen to his haunting musical compositions as he played on the harmonium. Sometimes, over one hundred people would crowd into his small apartment to take part in these daily rituals. Gurdjieff now sought from among his followers persons who might internalize the message of *Beelzebub* and carry on his work.

Gurdjieff's teaching during this last phase of activity took on a more personal tone. Meals were prepared and served twice daily in the Paris apartment: lunch from around 1:30 P.M. and dinner at around 10:00 or 11:00 P.M. These "banquets" were highly ritualistic. Each person seated at Gurdjieff's table had a special function to perform. The directeur was responsible for the entire meal going smoothly, and for offering the "Toast of the Idiots." To the directeur's left was the verseur (pourer of liquids), who was responsible for remembering what each guest was drinking so that glasses would be filled promptly and correctly; and so on around the table.

The "Science of Idiotism," Gurdjieff's primary rubric for discussion and his instructional method during these meals, was a ritualistic teaching technique he had learned during a stay at a Sufi community, and he claimed it was an ancient tradition. The term "idiot," he explained, has two meanings. The meaning attached to it by ancient sages was "one who attempts to be oneself." The other definition the term has acquired designates a "simpleton" or "madperson." A human being who is himself or herself, or who even aspires to achieve a level of reality beyond that of illusion, appears to those who live an illusory existence to be insane—as Plato beautifully illustrates in his Allegory of the Cave. Everyone who acts upon the decision to strive to realize his or her spiritual potential becomes an idiot in both senses of the term, insofar as the person who attempts to be authentic appears by ordinary standards to be a lunatic. According to Gurdjieff's "Science of Idiotism," twenty-one gradations of reason exist, ranging from human beings to God—eighteen of which are realizable on a human plane—and for each he had a particular title (Zigzag Idiot, Hopeless Idiot, Enlightened Idiot, and so on). Every person seeking Reality is an idiot at some level on the scale of reason. The ultimate aim of each idiot on the path of spiritual evolution is to reach the level of Idiot #18, and each step up the ladder involves a spiritual death and resurrection. Gurdjieff's guests were asked to locate their own gradations of reason on the scale of idiotism, and at evening meals he would propose individual toasts to the assorted idiots present, while elaborating on the characteristics corresponding to each. On the occasion of a toast, all present would wish with all their being that the idiot under consideration would succeed in achieving the death and rebirth requisite for ascent to the next level of idiotism. Fixed rituals were associated with these toasts, all of which were accompanied by alcohol, which the Sufis claimed increases the power to wish. Conversation at mealtime was cherished by the guests, as each moment offered precious opportunities for learning.

Gurdjieff personally prepared all the meals for these daily gatherings. He was considered an autocrat in his own kitchen, and his dishes were notoriously exotic and delectable. Ezra Pound recorded a painterly description of one of the master chef's soups: "Gurdjieff made a Persian soup, bright yellow in colour, far more delicate—you might say Piero della Francesca in tone, as compared with borscht (tinted Rembrandt)."[20] Pound confessed that he could have become a disciple of Gurdjieff on the basis of his cooking. But the preparation of food was, like everything else, a means of instruction. Students looked on as Gurdjieff prepared various dishes, and if he happened to be called away to speak with a visitor, as frequently happened, his students would be left to complete the dish, or the entire meal, in all exactitude from memory.

Meals were typically followed by Gurdjieff's performances on the harmonium, a ritual described by Elizabeth Bennett in her journal of 1949:

> Gurdjieff was truly hospitable and took great trouble, even when he was very ill, to see that his visitors were given the most considerate treatment. Part of the entertainment offered to them was provided by his music. He played one of those little hand organs so popular in the Near East, the instrument placed on his knees, one hand for the keyboard and the other working the bellows. On this he performed the most moving and unearthly music, which he varied to suit any occasion.[21]

The tremendous output of energy required for a man now in his eighties personally to prepare and serve food on a daily basis for large numbers of people, having done grocery shopping in the mornings; to discourse for hours on end about the human condition, focusing daily on selected topics suitable to the needs of his audience; to follow these lengthy, ritualistic meals twice daily with musical performances—all combined with the ponderous concerns surrounding the financing of such a lifestyle—epitomizes the super-efforts Gurdjieff required of others. By making gargantuan efforts, he was embodying the bottom line of his teaching: to live life such that when we die, we die like human beings, not like animals. Just twenty days before his death, one guest, upon completing the luncheon ritual, remarked that Gurdjieff looked tired; perhaps they should not return that evening for dinner, she suggested; perhaps he should rest. "No, no; come half past ten";[22] he couldn't lie around all day like an idiot!, he retorted. Though an idiot he surely was, like all the other idiots in his flat who had gambled more conventional lives to seek ever-higher levels of understanding. He would not relent until the last possible moment.

In addition to the ritualistic life carried on within the Paris apartment during those final years, frequent outings also took place to the French countryside—to Dijon or Vichy, for example, or to the Caves of Lascaux, where Gurdjieff would pontificate on the age and meaning of the cave drawings; sometimes rides to Switzerland to swim at the foot of a glacier, caravans of cars weaving colorfully through the French or Swiss countryside. Impressions are the third vital food necessary for human survival, after material food and air, he insisted, and the impressions should be constantly flowing, fresh, and ever-changing. The "Science of Idiotism" was carried on wherever the entourage stopped to eat—whether by the roadside or at a hotel restaurant—and the readings of *Beelzebub's Tales* continued.

Gurdjieff's methods of teaching during this last span of years assumed a different style from the earlier years at Fontainebleau. Circumstances were not so contrived as they had been in previous years; the master did not, as formerly, attempt to "create" or "manifest" conditions in which a person would invariably come into conflict with his or her ego or conscience. Now he taught through everyday situations—cooking, eating and drinking, playing music, and visiting beautiful and interesting sites. Polish theater director Jerzy Grotowski attributes this change in Gurdjieff's style to a deepening awareness on his part of the limitations of most human beings:

> Paradoxically, the younger Gurdjieff—it seems to me—expected so much from others that he finally realized that there were no real people around him, because he demanded everything. Afterwards there is another Gurdjieff, the old one. Does he demand less? No, he does not demand less, but the way of demanding has changed. . . . Perhaps I am wrong, but I see there an extraordinary change of attitude consisting of a greater skepticism about human beings, and, at the same time, a very special, very exacting tolerance. And I don't think it is just a question of age.[23]

Grotowski's analysis makes sense. A number of people from the earlier years had been alienated from Gurdjieff by what they considered to be the excessive and unnecessary harshness of his demands. A number of others who had most revered him were abruptly cut off and sent away when Gurdjieff felt they were too identified with him or were draining his energy reserve by making his life too easy, even though it seems they could have provided great help over the years, and good company. For example, he exhibited profound disappointment in people after the car accident in 1924. On the other hand, many pupils stood by him throughout the years, claiming all along to understand his methods and ways. Certainly, whenever one phase of work had served its purpose—a purpose that often he alone seemed to understand—Gurdjieff would abandon it to begin something new. Perhaps in this last phase he was playing yet another role for purposes of his own evolution. Whatever the reason, during the Paris years he adopted the role of servant, of doing for others, and reverted to simple, everyday circumstances as his tools for instruction.

Gurdjieff died at the Armenian Hospital in Paris on 29 October 1949. He is buried in the cemetery at Avon near Fontainebleau, as are his mother, wife, brother, and Kathryn Mansfield, all of whom died while at the Institute. His grave is marked by two uninscribed monoliths, one for his wife and one for himself. On the occasion of his death, American architect Frank Lloyd Wright, who had befriended Gurdjieff, recorded in his diary that Gurdjieff seemed to "have the stuff in him of which our genuine prophets have been made. And when the prejudice against him has cleared away, his vision of truth will be recognized as fundamental."[24]

Beelzebub's Tales is a highly unconventional piece of literature, through which the author relentlessly tries to break down our habitual ways of looking at life and to bring about in us a complete reorientation toward the world. Gurdjieff once said, "I have very good leather to sell to those who want to make shoes out of it."[25] The payment he requested was not money, but sacrifice: conscious labor and intentional suffering. Struggling to understand the levels of meaning of *Beelzebub's Tales* requires just such payment, this writing being part of the "good leather" he offered for sale. The *Tales*, Gurdjieff deemed, were his soldiers in a fight for a new world. Their main theme could be summed up by one of his favorite sayings: "Two things have no limit: the stupidity of man and the mercy of God."[26]

Two

CONNECTIONS WITH SUFISM

> My heart has opened unto every form:
> it is a pasture for gazelles,
> a cloister for Christian monks,
> a temple for idols,
> the Ka'ba of the pilgrim,
> the tables of the Torah,
> and the book of the Qur'an.
>
> —Ibn 'Arabi (thirteenth-century Sufi), "Interpreter of Desires"

As indicated in Chapter One, the twenty years of G. I. Gurdjieff's life prior to his arrival in Moscow remain, to a great extent, a mystery. *Meetings with Remarkable Men* is, at least on one level, semi-autobiographical, although Gurdjieff records that the deeper purpose of the book was to supply "the material required to create the feeling of a new world."[1] Information pertaining to Gurdjieff's life is scattered throughout his other writings as well, but his purpose in recording stories that stemmed from personal experience was always primarily didactic, not autobiographical. So he brazenly wielded an artist's license to bend fact for illustrative purposes. Similarly, at times he would go out of his way deliberately to obscure information regarding his personal life, preferring to discourage personality worship and unconscious imitation on the part of his students, for the purpose of preserving the most fruitful teacher-pupil relationship. His first priority was his teaching. Thus, to speak with authority about many details regarding his life and travels is nearly impossible.

Several attempts have been made to reconstruct the two decades of Gurdjieff's life during which he traveled and studied, accumulating the knowledge and understanding that would serve as the foundation of his teaching. The most extensive of these attempts is John G. Bennett's *Making a New World*. Although Bennett admits that "Gurdjieff did not make the task [of reconstructing the events of his life] easy," he goes on to add, "It would be impossible to reconstruct either the routes or the chronology of his journeys, if he had not also mentioned historical events that can serve as landmarks."[2] Bennett confronted the confusion surrounding Gurdjieff's traveling years and, making use of his knowledge of history, his fluency in Turkish, his lengthy travels in the regions where Gurdjieff had lived and studied, and his association with Gurdjieff and his ideas, he pieced together a hypothesis about the course of Gurdjieff's wanderings and the sources of his teaching. Of primary importance is Bennett's overall conclusion regarding the most significant influence informing Gurdjieff's world-view and philosophical stance. Bennett concludes that "Gurdjieff was, more than anything else, a Sufi."[3]

Gurdjieff undoubtedly drew upon a number of schools of thought and synthesized apparently diverse ideas in the process of creating his own vision. As a child, he had been deeply influenced by the ancient legends that his father would recite as a professional bard—in particular the Assyrian and Babylonian legends of Gilgamesh's quest for immortality. Later, Gurdjieff educated himself extensively in neurophysiology and psychology, and he writes of having intensively studied Indian philosophy, ancient Armenian literature, and the works of Pythagoras and Saint Basil the Great. Different aspects of his teaching have been traced to Zoroastrianism, Buddhism, Hinduism, Christianity, and Islam. Whatever the diverse avenues of knowledge he pursued and to which he was exposed, however, the focus of his research was always, in his own words, "to understand clearly the precise significance, in general, of the life process on earth of all outward forms of breathing creatures and, in particular, of the aim of human life in light of this interpretation."[4] Gurdjieff devoted his life to this end, searching for answers in all possible areas of study, in particular striving to penetrate the world's religious traditions and to fathom the esoteric dimension of each.

In the following passage, Bennett comments on Gurdjieff's continued thirst for knowledge and on his insistence on following his own path in life:

> Gurdjieff, to the end of his life, was totally receptive to new ideas and new impressions, and in his youth must have been a joy to the Sufi communities and individuals whom he met in his travels. He must also have been a trial, for he makes no secret of his self-willed determination to do things his own way, and of his disregard of all convention.[5]

Underlying Gurdjieff's "self-willed determination to do things his own way," we can recognize a fundamental principle of his philosophy: insistence on critical thinking and on accepting from potential sources of knowledge only what can be personally verified as true. He likewise discouraged his students from accepting anything he said on the basis of "faith." On the wall of the Prieuré was inscribed the saying: "If you have not a critical mind your staying here is useless."[6] Perhaps in part Gurdjieff's healthy critical disposition toward all doctrine made him sympathetic to the path of Sufism, for it is the Way of the Sufi—as understood in its broadest sense—that appears to have been the most prevalent influence on his methods and thought. Bennett correctly surmises, "The Sufi origin of his teaching was unmistakable for anyone who had studied both."[7] Consequently, we may move back and forth with ease between Sufism and Gurdjieff's teaching without a need for re-orientation.

Unearthing supporting evidence with which to justify Gurdjieff's connection with Sufism is not difficult. He openly acknowledged his association with the Sufi path and attributed a number of his teaching methods, such as the use of sacred dances and music, to Sufi sources. In a 1923 prospectus advertising dance performances by Gurdjieff and his students at the Théâtre des Champs-Elysées in Paris and at Carnegie Hall in New York, he credits several Sufi orders as sources: the Naqshbandi, Qadiri, Qalander, Kubravi, and Mevlevi. Titles of some of his musical compositions read: "Sacred Reading from the Koran," "Sayyid Song and Dance," "The Bokharian Dervish Hadjii-Asvatz-Troov," "Sayyid No. 1," "Sayyid No. 7," and "Sayyid No. 9." A chapter of *Beelzebub's Tales to His Grandson*, also titled "The Bokharian Dervish Hadjii-Asvatz-Troov," portrays this title character, an aspiring Sufi, as a rare breed of Earth-being who is sympathetic toward and capable of understanding Beelzebub. One untranslated sentence from *Beelzebub's Tales* remaining in the original Turkish is the Sufi saying: "*Dooiyninishi, pakmazli pishi, geyann purnundah pussar eshahi dishi*"[8] ("The affairs of the world are like a spiced dish; who eats it grows asses' teeth").[9]

Of the different Sufi orders Gurdjieff mentions in connection with his sacred gymnastics, the one most noted for its use of music and dance is the Mevlevi, founded by Jelaluddin Rumi, its members known as the Whirling Dervishes. Rumi found in dance a unique satisfaction and depth of expression. "There are many roads which lead to God," he wrote; "I have chosen the one of dance and music";[10] and "A secret is hidden in the rhythms of music. Should I reveal it, it would upset the world."[11] One legend relates that when his own beloved master, Shams of Tabriz, died, Rumi could not stop dancing. Through dance he found the means of expression for his deepest emotions and insights. The dervish dances are said to contain the secret of existence, as implied in a poem by the classical Turkish poet Divan Mehmed Tchelebi, which takes the form of a dialogue: the narrator asks his interlocutor, "What is the secret of the whirling dance of the Mawlawis, oh my friend?" And he is told: "You have to go back to where you came from. It is the secret of the origin and of the return."[12] The dance of the Mevlevi symbolizes this going from and toward the Source, as well as the yearning that constitutes the interim that is human existence. Music, Rumi believed, serves to deepen our yearning for our origin: "We are all part of Adam, we have heard these melodies in paradise."[13] Human beings are nothing more nor less than lutes, Rumi poeticized in a musical metaphor. When we are empty—devoid of manifestations of egoism—we sound forth beautiful music; when full, we produce no music, but rather disharmony and discord.

As Gurdjieff cites the Mevlevi order as a source of his sacred gymnastics, his purposes in teaching dance must have coincided with those of the Whirling Dervishes. In fact, P. D. Ouspensky records that he and Gurdjieff once attended a performance of the Mevlevi in Constantinople and that Gurdjieff took the occasion to explain how the whirling of the dervishes is, among other things, a demanding mental exercise based on a complicated number system, like the movements he had taught Ouspensky and others in Essentuki.[14] Thomas de Hartmann also recalls having accompanied Gurdjieff to performances of the Whirling Dervishes, and he writes of these Sufis' spectacular music and dance.[15] Part of Gurdjieff's dance repertoire included the Mevlevi "Stop Exercise," wherein, at a signal given by the sheikh, the dervishes instantly stop whirling, their bodies and facial expressions abruptly arrested, fixed in the positions they held at the moment of the signal. One purpose for the use of this exercise is to insure the ongoing lucidity of the dancers, not permitting them to succumb to states of intoxication created by the frenzy of the dance. Gurdjieff used the same exercise as a method for self-study. When his dancers suddenly found themselves frozen in odd grimaces and unfamiliar postures, and received "snapshots" of themselves that were unflattering and alien to their comfortable self-images, their self-perspectives broadened and became more representative and authentic. As a result, everyday patterns of gestures and movements, accompanied by their parallel emotions and thoughts, would undergo a process of deconstruction.

The breaking down of fixed postures and gestures as a method of self-study was a key purpose behind Gurdjieff's use of movements in general; the "Stop Exercise" highlighted and crystallized what the gymnastics as a whole aimed to achieve. In ordinary life, every person is limited to a handful of mechanical movements and gestures, each of which is connected with unconscious ways of thinking and feeling. Gurdjieff intended the movements to break the cycle of mechanical motions by forcing the dancer to move abnormally, and in so doing to expand his or her array of emotions and thoughts. All the movements serve also to heighten the level of attention, requiring intense efforts of the intellectual center—concentration being divided into several directions at once—so a dancer cannot afford even a momentary lapse of consciousness. At the same time, Gurdjieff's use of music was intended to stimulate the emotional center so that, as a whole, his sacred gymnastics engaged the intellect, the emotions, and what he called the moving-instinctive center, together with the will, in a collective effort of consciousness.

Gurdjieff's dances had other dimensions as well, apart from their usefulness as tools for self-study; they were art in motion—an objective artform that embodied truths for those who could understand their symbolism. Like the dance of the Mevlevi, which speaks of our origin and return—the white robes of the dancers symbolizing the shroud; their black coats the tomb; their high felt hats the tombstone; their thrusting off of the black coats a rebirth; their whirling the motions of the planets; their upturned right hand an appeal for divine grace from above; their downturned left hand a giving of that grace to the Earth after having warmed it by the love of their hearts[16]—so Gurdjieff's dances embodied symbolic knowledge about the fundamental laws governing the universe. And Gurdjieff was deeply interested in what Rumi called the secret of music that could upset the world. In the chapter of *Beelzebub's Tales*, "The Bokharian Dervish Hadjii-Asvatz-Troov," this Asian dervish is characterized as a highly conscious human being who has dedicated life to the study of the science of vibrations, in particular to the power inherent in the vibrations of the musical octave. Gurdjieff unmistakably identifies himself with this character by having the dervish tell his (Gurdjieff's) own story about the tragic loss of his young wife to cancer—a loss that could have been prevented had he (Hadjii-Asvatz-Troov/Gurdjieff) not been rendered unconscious for an extended period of time as a result of a near-fatal accident, and this at a critical time in his wife's illness. Had it not been for the unfortunate accident, Hadjii the dervish (and through him Gurdjieff) grieves, he could have saved his wife's life with his knowledge of the science of vibrations. The Bokharian dervish's passion for understanding the "secrets" of musical vibrations was Gurdjieff's own.

Gurdjieff's interest in music was not only theoretical. He composed a large number of musical scores in collaboration with the famous Russian pianist Thomas de Hartmann, whose ballet "The Pink Flower" was performed at the Imperial Opera by the most famous Russian dancers of the time—among them Anna Pavlova and Vaslav Nijinsky—with Czar Nicholas II in attendance. De Hartmann lived with Gurdjieff from 1917 to 1929, and during those years the two men jointly composed hundreds of pieces of music, many of them for purposes of supplying the necessary emotional force to the movements; others to accompany Gurdjieff's ballet, *The Struggle of the Magicians*. De Hartmann called their collaborative music "a waking up music,"[17] in that it engages the listener in a struggle for higher consciousness. De Hartmann provides a memorable account of one collaborative creative act on the part of the two artists:

> Once as I was watching [the movements] and playing the piano, as usual, Mr. Gurdjieff gave me a little piece of paper on which he had written an upper voice as an embellishment. It became impossible to play all the parts with two hands. So he told Madame de Salzmann to play the lower part and me the upper part, and this became the dance of the dervishes. The more the pupils entered into the movement, the more exciting it became, full of a magical force characteristic of all orders of dervishes. It was very interesting to edit and rewrite the music of this dance; this had to be done at once according to Mr. Gurdjieff's instructions, which showed the main melody in the left hand one sixth lower. Here it was amazing how the accompaniment, the little high voice, and the lower sixth were blended to form a whole. Soon after that Mr. Gurdjieff brought me

another little piece of paper with unusual flats in the key signature. The melody, with a monotonous beat in the bass, ran from beginning to end. This was the big dervish movement. When it was performed at the Théâtre des Champs-Elysées in Paris, Mr. Gurdjieff told some musicians in the orchestra to add a second voice, very soft, built on the same scale. This added tone was to represent the dervishes who were not active in the movement but who in a very low monotonous voice were saying their prayers. Now the whole thing became strikingly effective.[18]

Ouspensky likewise recalls a collaborative artistic effort involving the formulation of lyrics for the dervish song that accompanied Act One of *The Struggle of the Magicians*:

Sometimes I worked with him for entire days and nights. One such night in particular remains in my memory, when we "translated" a dervish song for "The Struggle of the Magicians." I saw Gurdjieff the artist and Gurdjieff the poet, whom he had so carefully hidden inside him, particularly the latter. This translation took the form of G. recalling the Persian verses, sometimes repeating them to himself in a quiet voice and then translating them for me into Russian. After a quarter of an hour, let us say, when I had completely disappeared beneath forms, symbols, and assimilations, he said: "There, now make *one line* out of that." . . . G. continued and again after a quarter of an hour he said: "That is another line."[19]

In this manner of intense combined effort, the "Song of the Dervish" was born.

In 1923, Gurdjieff delivered a lecture at Fontainebleau in which he made a significant reference to Sufism. After elaborating on some ancient doctrines, he told of one doctrine that has existed down to the present time, but which is not recognized by other religions. In distinguishing Sufism from other religious doctrines, he underscored the Sufi emphasis on critical thinking and self-verification. A section of his lecture reads:

The majority of religions breathe, act and live according to holy writ, commandments and precepts. At the same time a teaching existed of wise men who tried to realize for themselves every religion, and all legends and all doctrines dispassionately. They did not blindly submit. Before accepting anything, they beforehand realized it for themselves. Whatever they could realize for themselves, they accepted. What they could not, they rejected. In this way a new religion was formed, although the material of which it was formed was adopted from other religions. The doctrine I am speaking of is the teaching of the Sufi. . . .[20]

Sufism has been defined as "the inner teaching of Islam," "Islamic mysticism," or, metaphorically speaking, "the central and most powerful current of that tidal wave which constitutes the Revelation of Islam."[21] The Sufis claim to be the "Friends of God," a privileged class spoken of in the Koran, the inner message of which they interpret as having been specifically addressed to them. At the same time, Gurdjieff describes Sufis as a people who study all religions, thereby formulating a new "doctrine" that emerges from the meeting place of the revealed religions. The two definitions are not contradictory; they consider Sufism on different levels. The Koran itself maintains the unity and identical source of all religions; and Islam perceives itself, not as a new religion, but as the last in a chain of great religions addressed to humankind. One of a number of passages from the Koran that alludes to Christianity is: "You will find that the best friends of the believers are those who say: 'We are Christians.'" The non-exclusive nature of Islam as expressed in this passage, which is representative of the Koran's overall emphasis on the unity of religions, seems to point to a nearly equivalent esoteric meaning of each, making the inner teaching of Islam more or less parallel to, for example, esoteric Christianity.

The key to the inner unity of religions of which Gurdjieff spoke is to be found in the term "esoteric," which designates a level of understanding as fundamentally different from the "exoteric" as three dimensions differ from two (to use a helpful analogy of Martin Lings).[22] The ordinary, exoteric interpretation is relatively superficial; the esoteric embodies the quintessential dimension of depth. So, the many ostensible differences between the beliefs and practices of Orthodox Moslems and Orthodox Christians, for example, are significantly fewer if we consider for comparison a Sufi Saint and a Christian Saint, such as Rumi as compared with Saint Francis of Assisi (St. Francis died when Rumi was nineteen, and they were known for a number of common traits). The additional dimension of depth claimed by Sufism, provoked Hakim Sanai of Afghanistan to assert: "Everyone in the ordinary world is asleep. Their religion—the religion of the familiar world—is emptiness, not religion at all."[23] But as the spiritual traveler progresses along his or her chosen path, converging toward the center of the circle from its circumference, the more closely does one religion resemble another, and the final destination of each line of convergence is the center point of the circle—Reality, or corresponding Self-Knowledge. "Muslim, Hindu, Christian, Jew, and Sikh. Brothers in a secret sense . . ." reads one line from a Sufi song.[24] The end point of Sufism is the Perfected or Completed Human Being, supporting Frithjof Schuon's observation that "esoterism is without a country and it establishes itself wherever it can."[25]

Many beautiful passages of Sufi poetry exist, together with a multitude of interesting teaching tales, attesting to the expansive, all-embracing vision of the Sufis, while others parallel esoteric Christianity and Sufism. "The hermitage of

Jesus," poeticizes Rumi in an abstruse metaphor, "Is the Sufi's table spread."[26] Jesus is regarded as the Perfected Human Being, and therefore as the Perfect Sufi. He is said to "stand at the head of the Sufis," having been conceived by Holy Spirit, whereas Mohammed had a physical father. But Mohammed also represents a Completed Man, as does each of the great prophets. While the path of Jesus involved struggling with solitude, however, that of Mohammed was to live within the community of ordinary humanity, making his way more akin to the philosophy of Sufism. This "difference within sameness" is perhaps one way of understanding Rumi's metaphor—the "hermitage," or "way," or "dwelling place" of Jesus (solitude) being that "tablespread" upon which the Sufi engages in communal living. Both are fashions of being in this world "as a traveler and a passerby"; only the mode of travel differs.

Like Rumi, Shaikh Jonaid of Bagdad (d. 910), another of the great masters, defined Sufism in terms of religious comprehensiveness and elasticity. The Sufi, he wrote, is one

> whose heart, like Abraham's, has become immune from attachment to the world and complies with God's command; and whose submission is that of Ishmael, and whose sorrow is that of David, and whose poverty is that of Jesus, and whose yearning is that of Moses engaged in prayer of supplication, and whose sincerity is that of Mohammed.[27]

According to Islamic belief, the greatest of the prophets who have intervened in human affairs during times of acute spiritual crises have been Moses, Jesus, and Mohammed. The message of Mohammed holds a privileged position only in that it is the most recent of the messages addressed to humankind. Ibn 'Arabi's system of thought, too, as put forth in his *Meccan Revelations*, synthesizes classical Sufi doctrine with elements of Christianity, Gnosticism (Self-Knowledge is equivalent to Knowledge of Reality), and Neo-Platonic philosophy (the Creation is the manifestation of the Emanation of God). According to 'Arabi, the Sufi serves as the best conduit between God and the world by residing on the border between light and shadow, or, in Rumi's terminology, by "going back and forth across the doorsill where the two world's touch."[28] In this respect, the Sufi is in the best position to reveal God, or, more emphatically, to realize God. In fact, 'Arabi makes the radical claim, also put forth in Christianity's *Pistis Sophia*, that it is for the sake of the Perfected Human Being that the Universe came into being. According to this claim, it is the realized Sufi alone who preserves the existence of the Cosmos. When we consider such passages and concepts in conjunction with Gurdjieff's description of Sufism as a synthesis of the inner meanings of all religions, it becomes apparent that, although Sufism can simplistically be defined as Islamic mysticism, linking Sufism exclusively with Islam is misleading. The

Sufis seek Truth wherever it can be found, and Gurdjieff was, according to his own definition, a self-styled "Seeker after Truth"—perhaps the best definition of a Sufi.

Having considered the all-embracing nature of Sufism on the level of doctrine, we can return to and consider its definition as "Islamic mysticism" on a level that lies outside the sphere of doctrinal meaning. If esoterism embodies the existential equivalent to the third dimension of depth, then perhaps we can profit by considering this spatial analogy in relation to the Sufi's altered, more dynamic relation to time—the fourth dimension. As mentioned earlier, the Revelation of Mohammed is accepted by Moslems as the last in the chain of revelations addressed to humankind, so its message is considered the most relevant to the present era of history. And if the Sufis are the "Friends of God" of which the Koran speaks, then they are most closely attuned to the inner message of the latest revelation. Mohammed supported this interpretation of "God's Friends" by saying: "He who hears the voice of the Sufi people and does not say [Amen] is recorded in God's presence as one of the heedless." Along the same lines, Rumi wrote, "Let the one who wants to sit with God sit with the Sufis."[29] The term "revelation" has been defined as "a confrontation of time with Eternity,"[30] and the Sufis claim to reside on the border between light and shadow, or at "the doorsill where the two worlds touch."[31] Their existential relationship to time, then, is both qualitatively and quantitatively different from that of the average person living out life on the exoteric plane. In fact, the spatial images used by 'Arabi and Rumi to indicate the "place" of residence of the Sufi indicate that the realized Sufi exists in relation to time at that brink where time confronts Eternity—where Revelation takes place.

If the Revelation of Islam is, then, in some significant respect distinguishable from other revelations, its uniqueness is perhaps bound up with the dimension of time. The Revelation recorded in the Koran is addressed to a period in history (seventh-century A.D. and onward), which is characterized by increasing corruption, and its message is infused with a sense of urgency because of the increasing degeneracy of the times. Mohammed is "the Prophet of the Hour," a harbinger of foreseeable doom, who heralds the "Pull of the Hour": "Naught is left of this world but trial and affliction"; "No time cometh upon you but is followed by a worse." Mohammed also said that every verse in the Koran has both an "outside" and an "inside" message, the "inside" being intended specifically for the "Friends of God." If the way of Sufism has its foundation in a synthesis of revelations, then integral to that synthesis is the spirit of urgency at the heart of the Koran—the message of which bears a heightened significance for the Sufis as the Friends of God. With an ominous tone of urgency, the Koran is a call to commitment and action; it exhorts humanity to call itself to account before it is called to account. The Sufis respond to that call with accelerated spiritual development, enabling them to "travel through time" with hastened speed toward the time-place of Revelation. The Sufis call themselves the "Sons and Daughters of the Moment"—situated in God's Present. Gurdjieff referred to time as the "Unique Subjective," its "pull" varying in relation to our own momentum. The spiritual momentum that characterizes the Sufi way of life is the deepest response to the Koranic injunction: "Die before you die."

Of the alternative paths within Sufism that lead in the direction of Reality, I previously linked Gurdjieff with the Mevlevi Order in his use of sacred dances and other practices initiated by Rumi. A more overarching correspondence between his teaching and a specific Sufi school, however, is recognizable in the Naqshbandi Order, a descendant of the Khwajagan of Central Asia, the general perspective and emphases of which find strong expression in Gurdjieff's teaching. Several indications point to the Naqshbandi as a key source of Gurdjieff's ideas and practices. In *Meetings with Remarkable Men*, for example, Gurdjieff writes of having made a pilgrimage to Mecca and Medina in the company of dervishes for the purpose of gaining "a more thorough knowledge of the fundamental principles of the religion of Mohammed"[32] and "perhaps finding answers there to the questions [Gurdjieff] considered essential."[33] He found these cities disappointing and void of what he sought, however, and concluded that the heart of Islam was in Bokhara, "where from the beginning the secret knowledge of Islam had been concentrated, this place having become its very center and source."[34] The region of Bokhara served as the center of the Khwajagan Sufis—whom many consider to be the founders of Sufism—and of their successors, the Naqshbandi, until the end of the nineteenth century. (Only after the death of Khaja Bahaudin Naqshband in 1389 did the Khwajagan Order adopt the title "Naqshbandi.") Bennett was convinced that Gurdjieff had drawn heavily on this source for his teaching. Having spent a number of years in Central Asia conversing in Turkish with dervishes there, Bennett concluded: "I became convinced from my own contacts with . . . the Naqshbandi Brotherhood, that [Gurdjieff] had adopted many of their ideas and techniques."[35] Likewise, Idries Shah, a popular twentieth-century Sufi who has written a plethora of books on Sufism and has served as a disseminator of Sufi ideas in the West, points out the same parallel in his *Way of the Sufi*:

> G. I. Gurdjieff left abundant clues to the Sufic origin of virtually every point in his "system"; though it obviously belongs more specifically to the Khajagan (Naqshbandi) form of the dervish teaching. In addition to the practices of "the work," such books as Gurdjieff's *Beelzebub* . . . abound with references, often semi-covert ones, to the Sufi system.[36]

That Bennett and Shah independently reached the same conclusion regarding the affiliation of Gurdjieff's teaching with the Naqshbandi evinces an unusual arrangement agreed upon by the two men, who met for the first time in 1962. Shah appeared then in England with the prospect of locating former students of Gurdjieff and completing the education that Gurdjieff had begun to instill in them before his death. Shah sought out Bennett, who had established a school in the Gurdjieff tradition, and told Bennett that he had been sent by his own teacher to supply former students of Gurdjieff with the additional knowledge and methods needed to complete their education. After screening Bennett's three hundred or so students, Shah assumed responsibility for the half who were in a position to benefit from his instruction. Shah also requested that Bennett donate to him all of the property connected with his school so that it could be used to further Sufi studies in the West. Bennett did so, voluntarily relinquishing to Shah all of his property at Coombe Springs, a school that Bennett had worked twenty years to develop and which at the time was valued at over one hundred thousand British pounds.[37]

The Naqshbandi Sufis and Gurdjieff both refer to their teaching as the "Fourth Way," a term that designates a method of spiritual growth effected by means of a balanced development of the physical, emotional, and intellectual faculties in conjunction with the Will. This emphasis on balanced development distinguishes the Fourth Way from other paths of spiritual transformation, such as the ways of the faqir (physical mastery), the monk (emotional devotion), and the yogi (development of intellectual prowess)—all of which concentrate on mastering a single faculty—as well as from any methods of spiritual practice that call for forms of asceticism or withdrawal from the world. The Fourth Way cultivates all human faculties simultaneously and harmoniously, and its followers pursue spiritual transformation by means of fashioning themselves through interaction with the world. Fourth Way adherents recognize that playing a significant role in society demands greater sacrifice and requires a more concentrated state of presence than does seclusion, and that constructive interaction with the world carries the added benefit of contributing to the welfare of others. The Naqshbandi therefore work outwardly at useful tasks, such as craftmaking, while inwardly worshipping God. They also, like Gurdjieff, make use of shocks and surprises as methods of awakening, and they teach the necessity of voluntary suffering on the path of spiritual evolution. These Sufis recognize that the friction integral to human relationships and interaction affords the best possible "work material"—the "pulling and hauling" of life creating the most intensive conditions within which to struggle against the manifestations of egoism and mechanical behavior.

A concise summary of the Khwajagan teaching left by a Sufi master of the twelfth century—Abdulhalik Gujdvani—reads like a summary of parts of Gurdjieff's teaching, emphasizing his concepts of Self-Remembering, the importance of Aim, and the dangers of Identifying with anything other than the inner 'I.' "Be present at every breath," Gujdvani recorded; "Keep your intention always before you"; "In all of your outward activity remain inwardly free"—sayings that could have been found inscribed on the Prieuré walls in Fontainebleau.

The silent worshipping of God in the heart is the practice of the *dhikr*, one of eleven principles on which the Naqshbandi Order is based. A response to a number of Koranic injunctions to call upon and remember God often—such as "The heart is healed by the permanent remembrance of God" and "Is it not through remembering God that a heart can rest in peace?"—the *dhikr* is the practice of repeatedly invoking God's name in an attempt to achieve a state of continual remembrance, to convert the practice of *dhikr* into the state of *dhikr*—of sustained awareness of the Divine. This act has a cleansing effect on the heart, Sufis claim, purifying it of the accretions that accumulate in times of forgetfulness.

Probably the single most important message and practice of Gurdjieff's legacy has to do with the importance of what he called "Self-Remembering." He taught that we are not conscious, as we suppose, but live in a state of perpetual sleep, and that this is the case because we are almost always absent to ourselves. A state of forgetfulness defines our existence. To remember ourselves is to recall, in a profound sense, that we exist, to pull ourselves to consciousness—a state in which life has a very different sense and feel. The *dhikr* of Sufism is the Self-Remembering of Gurdjieff, for, as he quotes his father as saying, "If there is 'I' in one's presence, then God and Devil are of no account."[38] Without extricating ourselves from lethargy to a sense of "I Am," we can make no progress in the direction of Objective Consciousness, but blindly and mechanically live the cyclically repetitious live(s) of, for example, the main character of Ouspensky's novel *The Strange Life of Ivan Osokin*, repeating the same mistakes and patterns of behavior over and over again.

Also linking Gurdjieff to the Naqshbandi Sufi Order is the popular legendary figure Mullah Nassr Eddin, or Nasrudin, a Khwajagan Sufi who is the hero of hundreds of Sufi teaching stories, as well as a central figure in *Beelzebub's Tales*. In the Islamic world, Nasrudin is known as the master of paradox, a figure perceived as either the wisest of men or the most foolish, depending on his interlocutor's interpretations of his actions and sayings. Nasrudin is reputed to have said, "I am upside down in this life"; he is noted for turning conventional thinking on its head and calling into question everything that "goes without saying." The stories of the Mullah are used in certain dervish orders as a teaching tool to illustrate the limitations of the rational mind; one Sufi order in Pakistan uses only Nasrudin jokes and stories as its instructional material. Idries Shah remarks on this point, "The Sufis, who believe that deep intuition is the only real guide to knowledge, use [Nasrudin] stories almost like exercises."[39] Meditating on their "illogic" can effect a breakthrough into higher levels of understanding than that afforded by the rational mind.

Gurdjieff introduces Nasrudin into *Beelzebub's Tales* as "a very wise three-brained being" from Asia, "whom they called there 'Mullah Nassr Eddin,'" and one who "for every situation great and small in the existence of the beings there . . . had an apt and pithy saying."[40] Because these sayings were full of insightful truths about life on Earth, Beelzebub came to adapt them as guidelines for living a fruitful and comfortable existence on the planet. During the course of relating his tales about Earth life to Hassein, Beelzebub frequently calls to mind Nasrudin's observations on the human condition, most of which concern the inconsistency of human behavior and the inability of the intellect to arrive at a sound understanding of life. By means of humor and indirection, Nasrudin presses the point that our entire being must be involved in experience if life is to be qualitatively worthwhile.

In addition to adding humor and numerous examples of illogic to Beelzebub's tales, Nasrudin serves as Gurdjieff's representative of the popular or lived wisdom that he always respected. In Chapter One of the *Tales*, Gurdjieff declares, "I [am] a follower in general not only of the theoretical—as contemporary people have become—but also of the practical sayings of popular wisdom which have become fixed by the centuries."[41] Nasrudin is Gurdjieff's embodiment of practical, down-to-earth, commonsensical thinking, offering such advice as, "You cannot jump over your knees, and it is absurd to try to kiss your own elbow," a saying which Beelzebub interprets in one critical situation as, "When an event is impending which arises from forces immeasurably greater than our own, one must submit."[42]

Michel Waldberg, in *Gurdjieff: An Approach to His Ideas*, points out the similarity between the role played by this Sufi figure as a character in *Beelzebub's Tales*, and that enacted by Gurdjieff as author of the book. Nasrudin is the Master of the Way of Blame, playing the role of fool or madman, or any necessary role for the purpose of aiding the disciple in recognizing his or her own behavior in that of the master. Gurdjieff, both in life and as author of the *Tales*, assumed the role of Master of the Way of Blame to illuminate for us our own shortcomings. Waldberg elaborates on this method of instruction:

> When he assumes this role, the master is a mirror. A mirror in which the disciple sees himself. He caricatures and exaggerates what "is not working" in the disciple, feigns anger, arrogance, and if necessary lecherousness, and is therefore disconcerting, because the disciple has a long way to go before realizing that the hateful person the master is showing him is himself.[43]

In *Beelzebub's Tales*, Gurdjieff's chief motive is to create in his readers an awareness of their inconsistent, contradictory natures, while correspondingly arousing in them a deep sense of longing for the possession of authentic Selfhood. He uses this caustic Sufi character to help him achieve his purpose.

Two typical Nasrudin tales are the following:

It is noon on a blazing hot day. In the town square the perspiring Mullah, covered in dust, is down on his hands and knees looking for something in the sand.

One of Nasrudin's neighbors sees him, comes up to him and asks: "What have you lost?"

"My key," says the Mullah, who goes on scrabbling in the sand while his neighbor squats down to help him look.

After a few minutes the sweating, panting neighbor asks: "Are you sure it was here that you lost your key?"

"No," says the Mullah. "It was at home."

"Then why are you looking for it here?" asks the exasperated neighbor.

"My dear fellow," Nasrudin exclaims in surprise, "because here there is more light!"

And again:

A philosopher, having made an appointment to dispute with Nasrudin, called and found him away from home. Infuriated, he picked up a piece of chalk and wrote "Stupid Oaf" on Nasrudin's gate.

As soon as he got home and saw this, the Mullah rushed to the philosopher's house.

"I had forgotten," he said, "that you were to call. And I apologize for not having been at home. Of course, I remembered the appointment as soon as I saw that you had left your name on my door."[44]

We enjoy humor as our initial response to these stories because we bring to bear a logical mindset in our encounter with them. The confrontation of the logical and the illogical induces laughter. This use of humor is another Sufi tool for expanding the mind's understanding, a tool of which Gurdjieff makes extensive use and on which Shah comments: "As a shock-applier and tension-releaser and an indicator of false situations, humor, certainly to the Sufi in traditional usage, is one of the most effective instruments and diagnostic aids."[45] Humorous stories are designed to illuminate, according to a person's reactions, that person's mental blocks and false assumptions, with the further prospect of helping to dissolve them.

Gurdjieff employs humor for like purposes. By means of Nasrudin's commentaries and Beelzebub's harangues against humanity, Gurdjieff manages to depict in a darkly humorous way his portrayal of the human condition, with its prejudices, exaggerated sense of self-worth, and false imaginings. And as with Sufi literature, by highlighting these qualities he affords the possibility for their dissolution. André Breton described the particular kind of humor used by Gurdjieff (and Nasrudin) as "black," distinguishing it from silliness, skeptical irony, and pleasantry without gravity, regarding black humor as the "mortal enemy of sentimentality."[46] Indeed, he considered using excerpts from *Beelzebub's Tales* in his *Anthology of Black Humor*. Along similar lines, Waldberg likened Gurdjieff's humorous critique of humanity to what Charles Baudelaire called the "absolute comic"—humor that produces an explosive effect and evokes a state of vertigo. Vertigo is produced in the *Tales*, he says, by Gurdjieff's portrayal of the dizzying heights of human stupidity and corruption. Waldberg rhetorically asks, "But how do you make men aware of their own monstrosity?"; "And what weapons require polishing in order to wake them from the presumptuous sleep which they call their life?"[47] His answer is, of course, humor, an important tool in Gurdjieff's battle against unconsciousness.

At the same time, not all of Gurdjieff's tales depend on the device of humor for illuminating the reader. Many tales to Hassein are related in a serious, even grave tone, evoking reactions different from those triggered by laughter. Beelzebub's more sober reminiscences of Earth life are more akin to the traditional Sufi teaching tale, a literary form employed, as always with Sufi art, for the purpose of transmitting kinds and levels of knowledge that defy direct transmission. All stories are designed to break down fixed thought patterns and to reveal ever more subtle levels of perception and understanding. Their primary objective is less to convey morals or to pass on messages as it is to expand the mind's capabilities by enabling it to function elastically. Shah refers to Sufi teaching tales as "conscious works of art, devised by people who knew exactly what they were doing for people who knew exactly what could be done with them."[48]

To exemplify the different levels of interpretation that can be revealed in a single tale, Shah alludes to the famous "Elephant in the Dark" story from the literatures of the masters Sanai and Rumi. In this story, several blind men come upon an elephant, and each defines it according to his own perception of a single part, so that one claims the elephant is a snake, another a fan, another the trunk of a tree, and so on. Regarding the tale's different interpretive possibilities, Shah writes,

> This story, on the lowest possible level, makes fun of the scientists and academics who try to explain things through evidence which they can evaluate, and none other. In another direction, on the same level, it is

humorous in as much as it makes us laugh at the stupidity of people who work on such little evidence. As a philosophical teaching it says that man is blind and is trying to assess something too great for assessment with inadequate tools. In the religious field it says that God is everywhere and everything, and that even though man gives different names to what seem to him to be separate things, these things are in fact only parts of some greater whole which he cannot perceive.[49]

And the story has inner dimensions that these interpretations do not begin to touch.

Gurdjieff employs a similar multi-dimensional, muti-layered structure in the hundreds of tales he has Beelzebub relate to Hassein. All of the properties and layered themes Shah mentions in reference to "The Elephant in the Dark" can be located also in Gurdjieff's tales: his harsh criticism of scientists and academics for their overly intellectual and myopic approach to life; his repeated claims that humanity is blind and asleep, living out existence in a disconnected, fragmented way; and his use of humor to allow us to distance ourselves from and laugh at our own stupidity. Throughout all, we find his vindication that God is everywhere and everything. And all such "messages" are of secondary importance to the preeminent point: the self's confrontation with the self; the dissemblance of false realities to create new openings in which to build something real. Akin to the structure of much Sufi literature, including the Koran, the format of *Beelzebub's Tales* is not linear; its stories are scattered throughout the whole of the work, rather than relayed in single episodes. The English literary critic Alfred Orage likened the framework of the *Tales* to "an onion with an almost infinite number of skins. You peel off a few, and then you realize that underneath there remains skin after skin, meaning after meaning."[50] In truth, this analogy is misleading in the sense that it presumes a symmetry of structure; whereas, rather than building up in a concentric pattern, Beelzebub's tales meander in and out of one another, a thread being dropped at one point, picked up at another, dropped again, and resumed pages or chapters later. This non-linear narrative approach obviously demands more of the reader, requiring more attention and effort than would a straightforward narrative, and reminding us of another dimension that Gurdjieff's tales, the Koran, and much Islamic literature have in common—that they are offered in the tradition of oral literature, intended for recitation in public and in groups. In this sense, they can truly be thought of as cyclical, validating Orage's claim on a different level that they follow an onion-like pattern: the reading of the text is never complete, but always begins again where it leaves off. With continued oral repetition, the scattered stories and themes acquire a sense of continuity, which they would lack with a single silent reading. And the spoken sounds, the rhythm of the words, the cadences of the passages, the ebb and flow of the repeated images, permeate the listener on levels other than those effected by comprehension—like a musical background that prepares for a receptive ambiance within which the mind can do its work.

Gurdjieff chose the literary framework of interwoven teaching tales as the artistic medium through which to fashion the legacy of his understanding about human existence. He evidently believed that this genre, given its oral tradition, best enabled him to retain the "lived" quality that was essential to his teaching. Waldberg alludes to this point when he records of Gurdjieff's writings, "In the work he left behind, he does not appear as a philosopher, but as a storyteller . . . It is always through myth and legend, fable and story, apologue and parable . . . always in a 'living' manner that he offers his teaching."[51] Although the Sufis warn against the limitations of the written word, they still recognize the value of an artful story as a teaching instrument, as Rumi testifies in one of his recorded sayings: "A tale, fictitious or otherwise, illuminates truth."[52] Gurdjieff was also wary of the written word, but he ultimately had no choice but to convert his dynamic teaching into some comparatively static form—the interweaving of tales evidently providing the most elastic, pliable platform for the preservation of this living teaching in the physical absence of the teacher.

In addition to the above-mentioned similarities between *Beelzebub's Tales* and Sufi literature—emphasis on illogic; non-linear structure and oral nature; pointed use of humor; and multidimensionality—we can recognize that both literatures are grounded on similar underlying principles. In Chapter One of the *Tales*, Gurdjieff states his categorical refusal to make use of what he calls "bon ton literary language";[53] that is, his refusal to craft a finely tuned style, to give emphasis to the aesthetic, to wield language in a carefully wrought way. Rumi, too, specifies of Sufi literature, "The Sufi book is not literacy and letters."[54] Neither Gurdjieff nor the Sufi is concerned with impressing, entertaining, or providing pleasure to the reader. The sole motive is awakening, a distinction calling for a literature considerably different from that to which most of us have become accustomed. Sufi writings are a means to an end—the end of jolting the reader from sleep and providing the possibility for radical transformation.

A fundamental premise of Sufism is that we as human beings have far greater potential than we imagine; that we are infinitely perfectible and capable of achieving immortality, although this is a remote goal that can be approached only through intense and sustained effort. In our present state, we exist as raw material that remains to be fashioned and honed through interaction with the world. In the course of this interaction, our objective should be to overcome manifestations of mechanical behavior and to struggle against all forms of egoism. The result can be the creation in ourselves of something permanent and capable of surviving death. El-Ghazali, an eleventh-century Sufi master, wrote of this ultimate goal of Sufism: "The purpose of the exercise of . . . Sufism . . .

is to gain an eternally durable existence."[55] And Rumi alludes to the relative conditions of human durability: "It is reasonable to be afraid of dying, but . . . a stone is not so frightened as a clod is."[56] All Sufi practices, exercises, disciplines, and artforms, are directed toward the end of a permanent existence, which was likewise the ultimate goal of Gurdjieff's teachings and writings. He conceived of immortality as a potential state that is realized only rarely, when an individual is able to accomplish a complete transformation of being through conscious effort and suffering. Bennett writes of this conviction of Gurdjieff's: "Gurdjieff is emphatic in his assertion that man who does not fulfill his cosmic duties by his own 'conscious labors and intentional sufferings' loses his immortal soul and after death is 'destroyed forever,'"[57] a doctrine Bennett links to the Sufi schools of Central Asia. Our reality, however, in contrast to our potentiality, is that most of humanity exists in a state of sleep and unfulfillment, completely unaware of the purpose or stakes of existence. Sanai of Afghanistan, teacher of Rumi, recorded such a summary of the human condition: "Humanity is asleep, concerned only with what is useless, living in a wrong world."[58] Gurdjieff's writings abound with references to our condition of slumber and forgetfulness, the lamentable state of being that results in our inverted value system, causing us to perceive "a fly as an elephant and an elephant as a fly."[59]

The ultimate aim of perfection and immortality is remote, and along the path of spiritual evolution are different stages that vary in name and number depending on the tradition—whether the seven valleys traversed by the thirty birds in Farid-Ud-Din Attar's *Conference of the Birds*, or the twenty-one levels of Idiotism evoked nightly by Gurdjieff at his communal dinners. The journey is an optional one, but not to embark on it is to do nothing of consequence with life. It can begin only with the awakening of an unquenchable thirst for the real, with "the cry of the craving soul," in a line from Rumi. This is the journey that Beelzebub has been on for centuries, resulting in his acknowledgement by the host of archangels; that Dante Alighieri narrates in the *Divine Comedy*, at the end of the *Purgatorio* section, in which he is told by Virgil: "Lord of yourself I crown and mitre you";[60] and it is the same journey Mohammed makes in his Night Journey and Ascension. Hassein is only beginning such a journey, Beelzebub having succeeded in awakening within his grandson the necessary craving for understanding that the journey demands. Insofar as this travel is voluntarily undertaken, for those who choose it, it becomes a goal to which all lesser goals must be renounced. Sufi literature, then, has no other objective than to aid seekers on the path of spiritual evolution—by awakening the craving, by removing disillusions, and by pointing the way to higher states of being, depending on the place of the seeker. "Sufism has two main objectives," wrote Mevlevi, founder of the Mevlevi dervishes, in "The Sufi Quest": "to show the man himself as he really is, and to help him develop his real, inner self, his permanent part."[61] Sufi literature is one tool for achieving these objectives.

Sufism's first objective, according to Mevlevi, is to enable us to see ourselves as we really are and not as we imagine ourselves to be; that is, to enable us to look squarely at ourselves without our usual buffers, to confront our emptiness, and then to have the fortitude not to give way to despair but to recognize our inner lack as something that can be built upon. Many people, Gurdjieff warned, find this confrontation too devastating and cannot bear to let go of buffers. Others never get beyond the point of despair. But for those who have the fortitude to avoid despair or to convert it into a source of strength, the possibility remains of building up the real, permanent part that is the second of Mevlevi's objectives. Kathryn Mansfield, in a letter written at Gurdjieff's Institute, expresses the attitude of one who has developed strength from a feeling of inner emptiness. She writes, "What can one do with life when one has lost all illusion? It is as though a farmer said, 'They have removed all the weeds from my field—what can I do with it now?'"[62] Gurdjieff, in his life and in his literature, held to the above two Sufi objectives that Mevlevi outlines in defining the Sufi quest.

To build requires effort, the inherent value of which is conveyed through this brief Sufi tale:

> Someone said to Bahaudin Naqshbandi: "You relate stories, but you do not tell us how to understand them." He replied, "How would you like it if the man from whom you bought fruit consumed it before your very eyes, and left you only the skin?"[63]

The greatest value of a tale lies in the struggle for understanding that it demands, and in the inner friction that struggle creates, rather than in the storyline itself, or in the themes or messages conveyed. Gurdjieff held to this view, as the complexity of *Beelzebub's Tales* attests. For only extreme efforts can lead us to a more conscious understanding of ourselves and the world, Gurdjieff tells us in his chapter subtitled "A Warning." Ordinary efforts are by the way. Along these same lines, Rumi instructs, the "degree of necessity determines the development of organs in man . . . therefore, increase your necessity."[64] Gurdjieff requires out-of-the-ordinary efforts of his readers in order to create an opportunity for growth.

Despite the measures he took to conceal information regarding his past, Gurdjieff's debt to Sufism is evident. When he spoke of places he had been and people with whom he had studied, it was often in the context of stories that contained obvious exaggeration and contradiction, most likely with the purpose—in accord with Sufi tradition—of discouraging identification, of shifting the focus from himself to his teaching. But given all the obscurity surrounding his searching years, Gurdjieff's connection with Sufism is undeniable. Recognizing the Sufi influence on his major literary work can help to shed light on its meaning and purpose, while acknowledging such influence in no way confines our interpretation of *Beelzebub's Tales* or excludes other influences.

Three

GURDJIEFF'S THEORY OF ART

We gave advice in its proper place,
Spending a lifetime in the task.
If it should not touch anyone's ear of desire,
The messenger told his tale, it is enough.

—Muslih-uddin Sa'di (thirteenth-century Sufi), *The Rose Garden*

Because literature for G. I. Gurdjieff, as for the Sufis, is inextricable from philosophy, it is appropriate in considering *Beelzebub's Tales to His Grandson* to address some fundamental philosophical questions, the answers to which help put Gurdjieff's writings into perspective. Among the issues to be addressed, one of primary importance is to define what constitutes literature for Gurdjieff, or what, according to his aesthetics, distinguishes literature from non-literature, art from non-art.

Unraveling this distinction involves comprehending some of Gurdjieff's fundamental ideas about human beings and their place in the world. I have already proposed that Gurdjieff's primary philosophical stance is that of Sufism, and his philosophy of art supports this contention. At the core of his aesthetics is the position that no form of artistic expression possesses value in itself; no art is appreciable for its intrinsic value alone. Because of his premises concerning the meaning and purpose of human existence, all "art" for Gurdjieff, and consequently all literature as an art-form, must be functional or didactic. The value of an art work resides in its potentiality to transform or metamorphose the art appreciator. Insofar as a work of literature, a piece of music, a painting, or any other potential art form aids human beings in the process of their spiritual evolution, that object or activity earns the designation "art" for Gurdjieff and possesses what he refers to as "soul."

Gurdjieff's use of terminology to espouse his aesthetics and other branches of his philosophy frequently involves supplying old terms with new meanings. Consequently, we are forced, when approaching his writings temporarily to abandon old associations of key words used in his discussions. Such is the case with the terms "soul," "objective" and "subjective," and "conscious" and "unconscious." "Subjective art," for example, in Gurdjieff's terminology, refers to most of what is commonly interpreted as art. Most twentieth-century art in its various forms, according to his standards, would fall into this category. But subjective art is not authentic art for him; instead, it is the result of mechanical, unconscious human activity, and most of humanity, according to Gurdjieff, is unconscious. For the same reason, he refers to subjective art as "soulless," in that it results from little or no consciousness on the part of the would-be artist.

In his introduction to *Meetings with Remarkable Men*, Gurdjieff asserts that contemporary civilization is unique in history in its massive production of soulless, pseudo-art.

On the other hand, "objective art" is authentic art, in that it results from deliberate, premeditated efforts on the part of a conscious artist. In the act of creation, the true artist avoids or eliminates any subjective or arbitrary input, and the impression of such art on those who experience it is always definite. To the degree that objective art is the result of consciousness, it inherently possesses "soul." As one example of soulful art, Gurdjieff cites the paintings of Leonardo da Vinci; as another, he refers to the Taj Mahal. Both constitute objective works of art.

In a speech about art delivered to a group of students in Moscow in 1916, Gurdjieff broached an explanation of his aesthetic terminology and of his division of art into categories. The speech was delivered in Russian and translated into English by P. D. Ouspensky:

> I do not call art all that you call art, which is simply mechanical reproduction, imitation of nature or of other people, or simply fantasy or an attempt to be original. Real art is something quite different. . . . In your art everything is subjective—the artist's perception of this or that sensation, the forms in which he tries to express his sensation and the perception of these forms by other people. . . . In real art there is nothing accidental. . . . The artist *knows* and *understands* what he wants to convey, and his work cannot produce one impression on one man and one impression on another, presuming, of course, people on one level.[1]

Every aspect of the creation and effect of objective art is premeditated and definite.

Gurdjieff anticipates the unsympathetic response that his criteria for art predictably arouse, and the question of whether such deliberate and controlled creation is really creation at all. He also anticipates the argument regarding whether the elimination of the subjective element in art is, in fact, desirable. Does not the subjective contribution of the artist—his or her individuality—instead enhance an artwork with added dimension and significance?

Gurdjieff's response to such questions draws a resolute distinction between what most people accept as art and the criteria that he demands it fulfill. He claims that most people, rather than measuring art by the consciousness that it represents, measure it instead by its unconsciousness. People are in the habit of admiring the elusive, indefinite, or mysterious quality that they take for granted as an essential component of an act of artistic creation, without which, they assume, we are dealing with craft, perhaps, or some other type of product that is inferior to art. In contrast, Gurdjieff measures artistic merit solely by the level of consciousness an artwork represents. Again, he explains: "You say an artist creates; I say this only in relation to objective art. In relation to subjective art I say that with him 'it is created.' You do not differentiate between these, but this is where the whole difference lies."[2] Subjective art involves no creative act on the agent's part; instead, something "is created" in or through the agent who serves as a vehicle for "creative" activity: "This means that he is in the power of ideas, thoughts and moods which he himself does not understand and over which he has no control. They rule him and they express themselves in one form or another."[3] When these moods have taken some accidental form, they just as accidentally produce an effect on the art appreciator, depending again on personal moods, tastes, and habits. In the making of subjective art, everything about the creative process and its effect on the perceiver is accidental, whereas with objective art the artist is the sole responsible agent of creation: "He puts into the work whatever ideas and feelings he *wants* to transmit. And the action of this work upon men is definite."[4] Each person responds to authentic art according to his or her level of understanding, but nothing is arbitrary about its creation or transmission. The true artist determines and controls the process of creation from start to finish, including thoughts, feelings, and the projection of energies, all of which are generated from within.

For us to regard Gurdjieff's aesthetics sympathetically, we need to consider his ideas about art within the context of his larger body of thought. In particular, two key points in his philosophy of art must be highlighted and linked to his larger world-view. One is that, despite the forcefulness with which Gurdjieff distinguishes conscious and unconscious art, he readily acknowledges that these antithetical categories exist largely on a theoretical level. The situation regarding individual works of art is more complex, in that tangible artworks almost inevitably embody both subjective and objective elements. Given this reality, each is relatively valuable artistically according to the level of understanding it represents.

This premise—that the worth of art is relative depending on the degree of consciousness it represents—presupposes that artists are of relative worth depending on their levels of understanding. The notion of relativity applies to art insofar as it applies foremost to artists and to human beings in general. Gurdjieff holds that people differ drastically from one another in respect to their levels of consciousness, and consequently they produce art that belongs to varied levels. Addressing a group of students in Moscow, Gurdjieff explains the distinction he recognizes among human beings:

> At the moment it is not clear to you that people living on the earth belong to very different levels, although in appearance they look exactly the same. Just as there are different levels of men, so there are different levels of art. Only you do not realize at present that the difference between these levels is far greater than you might suppose. . . .[5]

Gurdjieff's perception that we vary according to levels of understanding may appear a common observation. Where he perhaps differs from others in this notion is in the degree to which he maintains that we differ. In one of his lectures, to illustrate his understanding of the difference he perceives among human beings, Gurdjieff uses the analogy of the difference between the essence of a mineral and a plant, of a plant and an animal, and of an animal and a human being. The essence of two people, he asserts, can vary in quality more than that of a mineral and an animal. The range that exists among human beings makes them equivalent at times to different species.

In Gurdjieff's terminology, "being" refers to the essence of a thing—to what something is "essentially." He contends that in Western culture only a person's knowledge is valued, while a person's being is treated as inconsequential. Yet being or essence is at least as important as knowledge, and levels of knowledge and being must be compatible for comprehension to result. The relation of being to knowledge is important for the artist because the production of objective art depends on the understanding that results from their harmonious relation. He explains the relevance of this balance:

> Especially in Western culture it is thought that a man may possess great knowledge—be an able scientist, make discoveries, advance science, and at the same time he may be, and has the right to be, a petty, egoistic, caviling, mean, envious, vain, naïve and absent-minded man. . . . And yet it is his being. And people think that his knowledge does not depend on his being. People of Western culture put great value on the level of a man's knowledge but they do not value the level of a man's being. . . . They do not understand that a man's knowledge depends on the level of his being.[6]

The level of knowledge depends on that of being because a concept or idea can be understood only to the degree that a person's essence is prepared for it. Two people with different qualities of essence will understand the same idea quite differently; the level on which they can *know* something is directly related to the level of their being.

When knowledge and being are not at compatible levels, understanding becomes distorted and efforts put forth to achieve a result are ineffectual or harmful in their consequences. Gurdjieff explains, for example, what can result from a predominance of knowledge:

> If knowledge gets far ahead of being, it becomes theoretical and abstract and inapplicable to life, or actually harmful, because instead of serving life and helping people the better to struggle with the difficulties they meet, it begins to complicate man's life, to bring new difficulties into it, new troubles and calamities which were not there before.[7]

If an unproportional amount of knowledge does not result in harmful consequences, it at the very least becomes stagnant, for the person whose essence is inferior to knowledge is unable to achieve constructive results with the knowledge he or she possesses: "If knowledge outweighs being, a man knows but *has no power to do*. It is useless knowledge. On the other hand, if being outweighs knowledge, a man *has the power to do* . . . but [he] does not know what to do."[8] That person's essence remains aimless. Either form of imbalance results in empty or distorted efforts. Positive consequences, or objective art in this case, can result only from a harmonious balance of knowledge and being.

All the differences that strike us about people, then, can be explained according to their levels of understanding. As a result of this difference, people interpret the world and respond to it in diverse ways: "Men seem to us to vary so much because the actions of some of them are deeply conscious while the actions of others are completely unconscious. The question is complicated because both types of actions can be seen in one man."[9] Human beings, depending on the compatibility of their knowledge and essence, span a vast continuum ranging from unconscious to highly conscious.

The levels of understanding that exist among human beings are reflected in all their activities: as many levels of art, language, religion, and other human endeavors exist as do levels of understanding. For example, on one level art may manifest as crude and imitative, on another as sentimental, on another as intellectual, constructed art, and so on. Or, on one level religion may exist as ceremony and sacrifice, on still another as faith and adoration, on another as based on philosophical or theological ideas, and on another it may involve conscious efforts to live according to the precepts of Christ or Buddha. All the manifestations of our lives can be divided into categories based on the degree of consciousness invested in every action.

Within Gurdjieff's theory of levels of consciousness, movement from one level to another, higher level can occur only as a result of intentional efforts, or of "conscious labor" and "intentional suffering," in his terminology. The term he uses to refer to movement from lower to higher levels is "conscious evolution"—a form of evolution that has nothing to do with Charles Darwin's "natural" evolution. Conscious evolution requires intentional efforts to evolve, and the only alternative is degeneration:

> Everything in the world, from solar systems to man, from man to atom, either rises or descends, either evolves or degenerates, either develops or decays. But nothing evolves mechanically. Only degeneration and destruction proceed mechanically. That which cannot evolve consciously—degenerates.[10]

When we fail to make conscious efforts to evolve, we are mechanically carried downward in a process of devolution or degeneration—the only movement that takes place without deliberate interference. Making conscious efforts means forcing ourselves to act against the forces of inertia that result mechanically from the opposing forces of nature. When we succumb to inertia, the laws of nature carry us downward in consciousness and understanding. Only through conscious efforts can we resist this process of degeneration: "If you make conscious efforts, Nature must pay. It is a law,"[11] says Gurdjieff, describing the relationship of human beings and nature. All intentional efforts to force movement in an upward direction and against the laws of nature result in the evolution of human consciousness.

The concept of conscious evolution leads us to Gurdjieff's second key premise about art—that it must be functional. The function of art and of the artist is to intervene and to assist in the process of conscious evolution. To aid us in our upward movement toward higher understanding and to help us struggle against the opposing forces of nature is the sacred purpose and obligation of art.

To achieve this end, objective art must be multi-dimensional, lending itself to diverse levels of interpretation so that a single work simultaneously satisfies the needs of people at different levels of understanding. In its attempt to achieve harmony in the art appreciator, objective art must address itself to all aspects of a human being simultaneously, not making unproportional demands on the intellect, for example, without requiring equivalent efforts from the emotional and sensory powers. Such art has the power to aid conscious evolution in a number of ways. It may strive to educate us about our place and role in the universe, or provide objective knowledge about the laws of nature to which we are subject, educating us regarding which of those laws we might transcend or better use to our benefit. It may arouse in us a greater degree of spiritual awareness and sense of being-obligation, or force us out of a state of sleep or stupor. It may attempt to break down fixed patterns of thought so that we experience more refined and extraordinary perceptions. Whatever form objective art assumes, its purpose is to help the upward flow of consciousness against the current of mechanical life.

It was Gurdjieff's opinion that Eastern art has remained truer to this purpose than has Western art:

> I studied Western art after studying the ancient art of the East. To tell you the truth, I found nothing in the West to compare with Eastern art. Western art has much that is external, sometimes a great deal of philosophy; but Eastern art is precise . . . it is a form of script.[12]

Ancient art was not for liking or disliking but for understanding, and each person exposed to it understood according to his or her ability. But now this purpose of relating and preserving knowledge has been disassociated from art, and what falls under the rubric of art is a barely recognizable imitation of what art once was. According to Gurdjieff's aesthetics, talent is irrelevant to art, which should be concerned only with knowledge and objective truth.

Just as Eastern art more closely accords with objective art, so too was ancient art more substantial than most of what is produced by contemporary civilization. In his Introduction to *Meetings with Remarkable Men*, Gurdjieff addresses the issue of contemporary literature as representative of contemporary art in general, and he illustrates its difference from the literature of other epochs. His observations are credited, in part, to a speech delivered by a learned Persian on the subject of literature. In the guise of the Persian sage, Gurdjieff declares,

> To sum up everything that has been said about the literature of our times, I cannot find better words to describe it than the expression 'it has no soul.' Contemporary civilization has destroyed the soul of literature, as of everything else to which it has turned its gracious attention. . . . I have all the more grounds for criticizing so mercilessly this result of modern civilization, since according to the most reliable historical data which have come down to us from remote antiquity, we have definite information that the literature of former civilizations had indeed a great deal to assist the development of the mind of man; and the results of this development, transmitted from generation to generation, could still be felt even centuries later.[13]

To illustrate the different quality and substance that some ancient literature possessed, Gurdjieff relates an old Persian tale, "The Conversation of Two Sparrows." In the story, an old sparrow converses with a young sparrow and lamentfully muses about the lack of substantial, nutritive food, which had been available in former times. Now the sparrows are hungry, for no real food is to be found. The food of which the sparrows speak is the sustenance, or being-food, that literature once provided, but which is quite scarce in modern literature and art:

> Once upon a time, on a cornice of a high house, sat two sparrows, one old, the other young. They were discussing an event which had become the "burning question of the day" among the sparrows, and which had resulted from the mullah's housekeeper having just previously thrown out of a window, on to a place where the sparrows gathered to play, something looking like left-over porridge, but which turned out to be chopped cork; and several of the young and as yet inexperienced sparrows had sampled it, and almost burst.
>
> While talking about this, the old sparrow, suddenly ruffling himself up, began with a pained grimace to search under his wing for the fleas tormenting him, and which in general bred on underfed sparrows; and having caught one, he said with a deep sigh:

"Times have changed very much—there is no longer a living to be had for our fraternity. In the old days we used to sit, just as now, somewhere upon a roof, quietly dozing, when suddenly down in the street there would be heard a noise, a rattling and a rumbling, and soon after an odour would be diffused, at which everything inside us would begin to rejoice; because we felt fully certain that when we flew down and searched the places where all that had happened, we would find satisfaction for our essential needs.

"But nowadays there is plenty and to spare of noise and rattlings, and all sorts of rumblings, and again and again an odour is also diffused, but an odour which it is almost impossible to endure; and when sometimes, by force of old habit, we fly down during a moment's lull to seek something substantial for ourselves, then search as we may with tense attention, we find nothing at all except some nauseous drops of burned oil."[14]

The tale refers to the old horse-drawn vehicles and to present-day automobiles: even though automobiles produce all the more noise and rumblings and stink than did the horses of former times, they offer nothing at all when it comes to the feeding of sparrows.

The purpose of the analogy, of course, is to illustrate the difference between contemporary literature and the literature of former epochs, between contemporary art and some ancient, more objective art. Even though both ancient and modern art may have some motives and ideals in common, the outcome is somehow quite different:

In the present civilization, as in former civilizations, literature exists for the purpose of the perfecting of humanity in general, but in this field also—as in everything else contemporary—there is nothing substantial for our essential aim. It is all exterior; all only, as in the tale of the sparrow, noise, rattling, and a nauseous smell.[15]

Contemporary literature has somehow become misdirected, in Gurdjieff's estimation. As in the tale, it is bypassing our essential needs and leaving us spiritually unfulfilled. Modern writers place unnecessary emphasis on "externals," such as elements of style, because they lack understanding of art's true significance—to contribute to the perfecting of humanity.

An example of literature of a different order is *A Thousand and One Nights*, the title of which in Arabic means *Mother of Records* (a work of literature that the Sufis claim is of Sufic origin and content). Gurdjieff describes the effect of such literature on an audience of listeners:

I myself have seen how hundreds of illiterate people will gather round one literate man to hear a reading of the sacred writings or the tales known as

Thousand and One Nights. You will of course reply that the events described, particularly in these tales, are taken from their own life, and are therefore understandable and interesting to them. But that is not the point. These texts—and I speak particularly of the *Thousand and One Nights*—are works of literature in the full sense of the word. Anyone reading or hearing this book feels clearly that everything in it is fantasy, but fantasy corresponding to truth, even though composed of episodes which are quite improbable for the ordinary life of people. The interest of the reader or listener is awakened . . . by the author's fine understanding of the psyche of people of all walks of life round him. . . .[16]

If literature is to be "literature in the full sense of the word," or objective art as the above work is purported to be, then what is required is a high level of understanding on the part of the writer—understanding of the true significance and responsibility of literature, as well as of the psyche or essence of all types of people.

The situation regarding contemporary writers and artists is the opposite, however, because the majority of them lack either the correct motives or the understanding requisite for the production of objective art. Their aims are often egoistic, and the "divine impulse of conscience" has atrophied in them. In *Beelzebub's Tales*, Gurdjieff expresses the opinion that of all contemporary Earth beings, artists are most vulnerable to the diseases of pride, self-love, vanity, and other comparable diseases. Contemporary artists, because they are for whatever reason idolized and exalted by the public, acquire false notions about themselves and their abilities, making them less capable than ever of producing art that contributes to the perfecting of the human race.

Gurdjieff's contention that contemporary artists are incapable of fulfilling the spiritual needs of humanity has been taken seriously by some twentieth-century artists and has led to a re-evaluation of their obligations as artists and of their personal potential to fulfill those obligations. Two famous writers who heeded Gurdjieff's call for a new kind of artist were the American writer and poet Jean Toomer and the New Zealand-born writer Kathryn Mansfield. Both were strongly attracted to Gurdjieff's ideas and spent time with him at the Institute in Fontainebleau. Toomer was involved with Gurdjieff and his work for over fifteen years, conducting his own study groups on Gurdjieff's ideas in New York's Harlem and in Chicago. Toomer raised $15,000 toward the publication of *Beelzebub's Tales*. Mansfield died at Gurdjieff's Institute and is buried near him in a cemetery in Avon, near Fontainebleau.

Toomer and Mansfield were accepted literary artists before their encounters with Gurdjieff's ideas, but through his influence they came to adopt different ways of thinking about art and about their roles as artists. Records of their personal struggles to become something "more" are preserved in Mansfield's diary and in the letters written before her death at the Institute, as well as in Toomer's diaries, in his letters, and in his later writings. Their reflections on literature and the task of the writer take Gurdjieff's theoretical ideas on the subject to the most basic level of lived experience, and demonstrate that the intense struggle involved in creating greater art is commensurate with a struggle to create a different self.

Under Gurdjieff's tutelage, Toomer saw differently his obligation as a writer and felt the incongruity of claiming to be an artist without having in his possession a consolidated self. He found that the objective art of which Gurdjieff spoke required flashes of objective consciousness, and that to achieve such flashes and to expand their duration, a great inner unity was needed, a high degree of self-mastery. Having arrived at this understanding, Toomer immersed himself completely in the study and practice of Gurdjieff's ideas, offering as his explanation at the time: "One must become a man before he can become an artist."[17] He expressed what he came to recognize as a syndrome common to most of humanity: "The open conspiracy: 'Let's do outside things; inside things are too difficult.'"[18] With Gurdjieff, Toomer took a radical turn toward "inside things" and strove hard to become a "man."

Gorham Munson, in his essay "The Significance of Jean Toomer," published in 1928 in Munson's book *Destinations*, pays homage to Toomer's serious attempts to live up to his new vision of the artist. In this essay, Munson writes of the potential of the new sort of artist that Toomer represents, while praising Toomer for setting a precedent for all artists. Any artist who feels deeply the grave responsibility that his or her gifts entail, declares Munson, is forced to seek answers to the fundamental questions, such as "What is the function of human beings?" and "What is the world?" Munson writes, "The significance of Jean Toomer lies in his strenuous attempts to answer these questions."[19] He presents Toomer as an artist to be emulated:

> Shortly after writing *Cane*, he [Toomer] formed two convictions. One was that the modern world is a veritable chaos and the other was that in a disrupted age the first duty of the artist is to unify himself. Having achieved personal wholeness, then perhaps he would possess an attitude that would not be merely a reaction to the circumstances of modernity, merely a reflection of the life around him, but would be an attitude that could *act* upon modernity, dissolve away the remainder of an old slope of consciousness, and plant the seeds for a new slope.[20]

At Gurdjieff's Institute in France, Toomer found what he considered the best method for his quest. He wrote from Fontainebleau, "I am. What I am and what I may become I am trying to find out."[21] With Gurdjieff's help, Toomer returned to the most preliminary questions, convinced that a true artist could only be one who had come to understand at least the basics of the human condition. This deep authenticity on Toomer's part prompted Munson to declare him a symbol for all artists: "He is a dynamic symbol of what all artists of our time should be doing if they are to command our trust," Munson wrote. "He has mastered his craft. Now he seeks a purpose that will convince him that his craft is nobly employed."[22] Toomer's search for understanding was a search without an end, Munson acknowledged, but through the search itself he was bound to experience an inner fusion that could only lead to greater profundity—and therefore to greater art.[23]

Mansfield's association with the Gurdjieff Institute is interesting, since she spent the last months of her life absorbing and recording the impressions created by Gurdjieff. Her letters and diary entries at the time testify to the different quality of life she sensed while surrounded by others with aims similar to hers. "If I were allowed one single cry to God," she wrote, "that cry would be: I want to be REAL!"[24] Here, she found kindred spirits who were overwhelmed by the same desire—people who were "truly themselves," she wrote, "and not playing a part behind a mask."[25] Her personal writings are rich with eloquent and moving descriptions of the life she observed around her at the Institute, and some who were there with her recorded her more memorable conversations. Ouspensky wrote of one conversation that he had with Mansfield shortly before her death. "We sat in the evening in one of the salons," he recorded, "and she spoke in a feeble voice which seemed to come from the void."[26] She described her feelings about the environment Gurdjieff had created:

> I know that this is true and that there is no other truth. You know that I have long since looked upon all of us without exception as people who have suffered shipwreck and have been cast upon an uninhabited island, but who do not yet know of it. But these people here know it. The others, there in life, still think that a steamer will come for them tomorrow and that everything will go on in the old way. These already know that there will be no more of the old way. I am so glad that I can be here.[27]

In a letter to her husband she uses the same shipwreck-castaway figure:

> I'll tell you what this life is more like than anything: it is like *Gulliver's Travels*. One has, all the time, the feeling of having been in a wreck and by mercy of Providence got ashore—somewhere.... Simply everything is different. Not only languages, but food, people, music, methods, hours—all. It's a real new life....[28]

Her true education, she claimed, was just beginning at age thirty-four.

Although she continued to record her impressions in private correspondence while at the Institute, Mansfield wrote nothing for publication during this period. Her feelings about literature were shifting, and she found herself increasingly critical of her own writings, as of most literature. "I confess present-day literature simply nauseates me," she wrote to a friend, "excepting always Hardy and the other few whose names I can't remember. But the general trend of it seems to me quite without any value whatever."[29] Her own stories, she felt, contained something false and narrow, even "evil," and they reminded her of birds bred in cages. "There is not one that I dare show to God,"[30] she told Alfred Orage.

The changes taking place in Mansfield's feelings about literature were not just the result of exposure to a different philosophy of literature represented by Gurdjieff's thought, but were more the result of inner changes taking place in Mansfield. "I cannot express myself in writing just now," she wrote of this interlude in her life; "the old mechanism isn't mine any longer, and I can't control the new."[31] The months with Gurdjieff were months of transformation and metamorphosis for her, and one result of her changing perceptions was that she came to expect something different from literature. In a conversation, she described her shifting world-view:

> I'm aware . . . of a recent change of attitude in myself, and at once not only my old stories have come to look different to me, but life itself looks different. I could not write my old stories again, or any more like them: and not because I do not see the same detail as before, but because somehow or other the pattern is different. The old details now make another pattern. . . .[32]

Had Mansfield lived to incorporate this "different pattern" into future stories, her approach to writing, she indicated before her death, would have been quite different.

Orage, the English editor and critic, who was a close friend of Mansfield, was also present at the Institute during her three-month stay. He had published her first story in his magazine *The New Age* when Mansfield was twenty-one, and it was he who introduced her to Gurdjieff. During the months together at Fontainebleau, they often conversed on the subject of literature, and their conversations were recorded and later published by Orage as "Talks with Kathryn Mansfield." Here, Orage relates how he and Mansfield had often discussed the phenomenon of their disappearing interest in literature. "What has come over us?" she asked Orage. "Are we dead? Or was our love of literature an affectation, which has now dropped off like a mask?"[33] Then, shortly before her death, she attempted to articulate for Orage what had come to her as a revelation: she had understood that a different approach to literature was possible. Among her deepest and last insights were these:

> Suppose that I succeed in writing as well as Shakespeare. It would be lovely, but what then? There is something wanting in literary art even at its highest. . . . The greatest literature is still only mere literature if it has not a purpose commensurate with its art. Presence or absence of purpose distinguishes literature from mere literature, and the elevation of the purpose distinguishes literature within literature. That is merely literary

that has no other object than to please. Minor literature has a didactic object. But the greatest literature of all—the literature that scarcely exists—has not merely an aesthetic object, nor merely a didactic object, but, in addition, a *creative* object: that of subjecting its readers to a real and at the same time illuminating experience. Major literature, in short, is an initiation into truth.[34]

Speaking of her writing, she said that through it she had been nothing more than a camera, always recording and representing, but never *creating*: "And, like everything unconscious, the result has been evil."[35] She said that her new plan was to widen the scope of her camera, and then to employ it for the conscious purpose of representing life as it appears to a *creative* attitude.

This idea—of employing a creative attitude in writing—seemed to Mansfield the key to a new literature. The term "creative," whatever else it may have meant for her, referred primarily to an active rather than a passive attitude on the part of the writer—an active attitude employed to evoke an active response in the reader. Orage asked her to explain what she meant by "creative attitude," and she replied:

> You must help me out, Orage, if I miss the words. But I mean something like this. Life can be made to appear anything by presenting only one aspect of it; and every attitude in us—every mood . . . has only one aspect. Assuming that this aspect is more or less permanent in any given writer . . . he is bound to present only the correspondent aspect of life, and, at the same time, to do no more than present it.[36]

She continues later in the conversation:

> An artist communicates not his vision of the world, but the attitude that results in his vision; not his dream, but his dream-state; and as the attitude is passive, negative, or indifferent, so he reinforces in his readers the corresponding state of mind. Now, most writers are merely passive; in fact, they aim only at representing life, as they say, with the consequence that their readers for the most part become even more passive . . . What I am trying to say is that a new attitude to life on the part of writers would first *see* life different, and then *make* it different.[37]

Orage does not attempt to interpret Mansfield's last insights; perhaps it is impossible to decipher the vision that lies behind her words. He says only that she was full of ideas for stories based on a new creative principle, and that until her death at Fontainebleau she remained radiant with her new insight about literature.

Although the details of her vision may remain obscure, two points about her connection with Gurdjieff remain clear. One is that she went to the Institute with the realization that to write better, she must somehow become "more" or "better" herself—and Gurdjieff, she believed, could help her to do this. The second is that her final understanding of what constituted greater literature was catalyzed by the conditions and atmosphere created by Gurdjieff and based on his ideas. Furthermore, this understanding coincided with Gurdjieff's views: the artist is under an obligation to achieve some degree of consciousness, and art should serve to help others do the same.

An obvious question is: "Is *Beelzebub's Tales*, then, art?"; and concurrently, "Is Gurdjieff, then, in the final analysis, an artist?" Many respectable critics, writers, and artists respond with a resounding "Yes." Others could be cited who deny the status of "artist" to Gurdjieff. The question is approachable only if we evaluate Gurdjieff on his own terms. He was a man who possessed the objective consciousness he considered prerequisite for the artist. His laborious efforts spent writing and revising *Beelzebub's Tales* were made with the aim of striking a chord in our being that might move us along the path of conscious evolution. Gurdjieff considered *Beelzebub's Tales* an objective work of art—a legominism through which truths about human beings and the world could be preserved and passed on to future generations. Through this work, he said, he wished to declare war on the world as it is and to begin the germination of a new world through the creation of a new consciousness. Michel Waldberg considers *Beelzebub's Tales* "one of the most perfect expressions of an art form addressed not only to the mind, but to the heart and body too."[38] Frank Lloyd Wright thought of Gurdjieff as a great artist, and he set down as his final judgment of Gurdjieff that in him "we have for the first time a philosopher distinguished from all others, [but] Gurdjieff was not only an original philosopher; he was a *great artist*." "I often hear his music," wrote the architect; "It is from another world."[39] James Moore, author of *Gurdjieff and Mansfield*, responds to the question of Gurdjieff as artist with ambiguity, insofar as the effect of *Beelzebub's Tales* will not be known until some future time. He says of these writings that they resemble the Sphinx, whose "vision is directed far off, as if piercing the very depths of space."[40] What we lack as yet, concludes Moore, and what we need before evaluating *Beelzebub's Tales*, is someone to make clear its meaning and to uncloud its obscurity. But where, he asks, "is the new Oedipus who will stand between these paws and travail to unlock this riddle?"[41] Until such an interpreter appears, Moore concludes, we have no way of knowing whether and to what extent *Beelzebub's Tales* is an objective work of art.

Having considered at length Gurdjieff's theory of art, including his assertion that objective art has always a specific and determined effect on the participant, depending on that person's level of understanding, we must conclude that Gurdjieff's artistry, as embodied in *Beelzebub's Tales*, demands extraordinary efforts on the part of the reader in order to evoke the author's hoped-for response. The question about Gurdjieff as artist, therefore, is perhaps too linear and two-dimensional to apply to a work like the *Tales*, and the inapplicability of linear thinking to Gurdjieff and the *Tales* is perhaps a clue to Mansfield's idea about "creative" literature. *Beelzebub's Tales* is objective art to the degree that we, as readers, permit it to be in the act of our diligent and conscious participation in this work. To the extent that we bring consciousness to bear in our active engagement with this literary work, each of us becomes the Oedipus who stands between the Sphinx's paws. There can be no other, external Oedipus to explain the riddles. The "artistic" dimensionality of *Beelzebub's Tales* varies according to each reader's level of being and the compatibility of his or her essence and knowledge. The aim of a book is to instruct, observed the Sufi poet Rumi; yet, it can also be used as a pillow.

Four

TRAVEL AND TRANSFORMATION: *BEELZEBUB'S TALES* WITHIN THE CONTEXT OF PHILOSOPHICAL TRAVEL LITERATURE

> This travel is not comparable to the ascent of
> Man towards the Moon,
> No, but to the ascent of the sugarcane
> to the sugar.
>
> —Jelaluddin Rumi (thirteenth-century Sufi), *Mathnavi IV*, 553–554

> I often regretted having begun too late to give
> the legends of antiquity the immense significance
> that I now understand they really have.
>
> —G. I. Gurdjieff, *Meetings with Remarkable Men*

The theme of travel—of voyages out and back, of flights of the body or the imagination or the spirit—has been employed as an organizing principle in literature at least since the first recorded epic poems. The hero or heroine ventures outside the realm of ordinary experience and comes face to face with the unknown and the extraordinary. In the process, he or she gains experience, deeper insight, and wisdom. On one level, the journey from place to place supplies a central metaphor for life and death and applies to all humanity, as, in the words of Henry David Thoreau: "Going from—toward: it is the journey of everyone of us." On a more subtle and interesting level—the allegorical—the hero or heroine of a travel tale represents that segment of humanity that is moving forward on the path of conscious evolution. Here, the physical and the metaphysical blend; the outward journey coincides with inner transformation; the change in external conditions is accompanied by spiritual metamorphosis and rebirth. The central character, in response to experience gained and obstacles overcome, moves toward the essence of his or her own individuality—as the sugarcane ascends to the sugar.

The nature of the hero's travels away from the status quo environment takes on many interesting variations in the history of literature, and is embodied in literary forms ranging from the epic poem to the philosophical tale to the modern novel. I first present a few examples of famous heroic journeys in the history of literature, offering a general Gurdjieffian interpretation of some basic themes, and then place G. I. Gurdjieff's philosophical and literary work, *Beelzebub's Tales to His Grandson*, within the framework of philosophical travel tales, the allegorical significance of which is the central character's metamorphosis of being.

Consider, for example, the epic of *Gilgamesh*, which was discovered in the mid-nineteenth century, the Sumerian version of which has been dated at around 2700 B.C.[1] This poem recounts the legendary journey of the beautiful and heroic Gilgamesh, fifth King of Eurech after the great flood. From the opening of the tale, Gilgamesh is described as a wise man and a wanderer—the two attributes being interdependent: "This was the man to whom all things were known; this was the king who knew the countries of the world."[2] However extraordinary his wisdom may be, Gilgamesh lacks the critical knowledge of the secret of immortality. His mother is a goddess who bequeathed him divine beauty and courage, but his human father endowed him with a mortal nature. Upon the death of his dearest friend, Enkidu, Gilgamesh internalizes the fact of his own mortality, and asks: "How can I rest, when Enkidu whom I love is dust, and I too shall die and be laid in the Earth forever?"[3] In search for an answer to this ultimate question, Gilgamesh embarks on a journey that takes him to the ends of the knowable Earth.

Having heard legend of one human being who was granted immortality by the gods, Gilgamesh wanders over the world in search of the garden of the sun in the Land of Dilman—residence of the immortal Utnapishtim—in order to discover the secret of eternal life. To reach his destination, of course, he must travel where "no man born of woman" has traveled before: to the great mountains that guard the rising and setting of the sun, which are guarded by deadly giant scorpions; through twelve leagues of total darkness in the body of the mountains; to the unearthly landscape of the garden of the gods—bedecked with rare gems, agate and pearl, and lapis lazuli leaves that hang heavy with rare fruits—and then across the vast ocean to the river of death, a journey that has been made only by the Sun. Finally, his body broken with exhaustion, his face scorched by heat and cold "like the face of one who has made a long journey,"[4] Gilgamesh reaches his destination and stands before the once mortal Utnapishtim to pose his burning question: "Tell me truly, how was it you came to enter the company of the gods and to possess everlasting life?"[5]

This section of the epic is the most fragmentary, but we can gather the following from its extant content. Utnapishtim at first tries to dissuade Gilgamesh from his search: "There is no permanence. Do we build a house to last forever?"[6] But as Gilgamesh will not be deterred, Utnapishtim reveals the advice given to him by the god Ea, which enabled him to overcome death: "Tear down your house and build a boat," he was told; "abandon possessions and look for life, despise worldly goods and save your soul alive. Tear down your house, I say, and build a boat."[7] Then, to determine the extent to which Gilgamesh might qualify for immortality, Utnapishtim puts him to a test: he instructs Gilgamesh to prevail against sleep for six days and seven nights. But no sooner has Utnapishtim completed giving him instructions, and while Gilgamesh still sits listening before him, "a mist of sleep like soft wool teased from the fleece drifted over him." "Look at him now," Utnapishtim says to his wife; "the strong man who would have eternal life, even now the mists of sleep are drifting over him."[8] Utnapishtim offers the following comment regarding the state of sleep: "The sleeping and the dead, how alike they are, they [the sleeping] are like a painted death."[9]

Finally, at the request of Utnapishtim's wife, Gilgamesh is offered a second chance to demonstrate his ability to survive death: Utnapishtim tells him another secret of the gods—of a thorny plant that grows at the bottom of the deepest waters and that is capable of restoring to men their lost youth. But Gilgamesh once again proves incapable of the challenge; although he is able to retrieve the plant from the bottom of a deep channel, a serpent snatches it from him as he bathes in a pool. The serpent immediately sloughs its skin in an act of self-renewal; Gilgamesh, however, is left to make the long journey home to Eurech, where he engraves his story in stone. He returns to his kingdom a wiser, but still mortal man.

How are we to interpret Gilgamesh's long and hazardous journey away from Eurech, which only leads him home again with the certain knowledge of his own mortality? Are we to gather that Gilgamesh fumbled his two opportunities to gain a possible but extremely difficult-to-attain immortality? Utnapishtim's own story would seem to support this interpretation. The advice he received from Ea had to do with sacrifices that must be made in life and with the establishment of proper priorities (for example, being *in* the world and not *of* it, with spiritual needs weighed more heavily than material ones) as prerequisites for achieving immortality, neither set of conditions of which, perhaps, Gilgamesh is capable of meeting. The test of sustained wakefulness imposed by Utnapishtim calls for greater efforts than Gilgamesh can muster. And finally, the plant of self-renewal is lost because its possessor must exercise constant vigilance—which Gilgamesh, in a moment of carelessness, fails to exercise against the serpent. Perhaps the price of immortality is greater than Gilgamesh can pay. Or is the point instead that Gilgamesh's difficult journey drives home to him the reality of his own limited nature—that it teaches him humility in the face of the gods and reminds him that even the greatest kings must finally lie down in death? Although the second alternative is undoubtedly part of the point—a lesson that all of us must inevitably learn—I will pursue the first line of interpretation, since it is more in keeping with Gurdjieffian thought. More specifically, I am interested in Gilgamesh's inability to remain awake when instructed to do so, and with Utnapishtim's equation of a state of sleep with death.

Gilgamesh falls asleep, as stated, while Utnapishtim is yet completing his instructions to remain awake, and the duration of time Gilgamesh sleeps is six days and seven nights—the exact amount of time he was instructed to remain awake. Gilgamesh sleeps for the duration of the test. If we consider, allegorically, his inability to remain awake, then we can interpret it as representative of the state of sleep in which many of us live our lives. In other words, Gilgamesh is *insufficiently conscious* to meet the requirements of Utnapishtim's test. This correlation of sleep with a state of relative unconsciousness, or of lapses in consciousness, can be recognized in other literatures. Homer thematizes the state of sleep as being a condition of dangerous vulnerability. The Gospels repeatedly instruct us: "Awake"; "Sleep not"; "Be on watch." Christ's disciples, we are told, "fell asleep" as he prayed for the last time. Among the sayings of the prophet Mohammed is: "Sleep is the brother of death."[10] And the same theme is central to the teaching of Sufism. "Humanity is asleep, concerned only with what is useless, living in a wrong world,"[11] wrote the Sufi master Hakim Sanai, as his analysis of the human condition. Gurdjieff's body of thought, connected as it is with Sufism, is built upon the premise that the majority of humanity remains asleep in a state of unfulfillment. "Man's possibilities are very great," he wrote; "But nothing can be attained in sleep."[12]

When interpreted allegorically, all of the above references to sleep imply a relatively low level of consciousness on the part of those who cannot remain awake. To wake up, to become more conscious, requires tremendous effort, and to remain awake demands a constant struggle against the forces of inertia that would keep us asleep. For the Sufis and Gurdjieff, this struggle toward wakefulness is the price of immortality. Jelaluddin Rumi wrote in his *Mathnavi*: "Man is in the world to accomplish a mission. This mission is his true goal; if he does not accomplish it, he has done nothing."[13] The mission to which Rumi refers involves moving forward along the path of conscious evolution, for the Sufis believe that the friction resulting from the requisite struggle can create in a human being something indestructible and capable of surviving death. Immortality, in other words, is conquered through effort. In the words of El-Ghazali, another Sufi master, "The purpose of the exercise of Sufism is to gain an eternally durable existence."[14] The possibility of gaining an eternally durable self is afforded when life's obstacles and the constant vigilance against sleep are recognized as the opportunities and means by which we can evolve and achieve permanence. In this respect, as Utnapishtim aptly observed, a state of sleep is literally equivalent to death. The person who does not manage to remain awake in life is at the mercy of the laws of inertia and entropy, whose mechanical downward flow toward states of increasing disorder is the way of devolution and extinction. Only those who evolve survive, and evolution—upward movement against the downward flowing forces—can occur only by applying a counterforce: conscious effort. Gilgamesh's failure to remain awake—to make adequate conscious efforts against sleep—is at the expense of his own imperishability.

Some 1,500 years after the journey of Gilgamesh, the extraordinary Lord Odysseus, King of Ithaca, was to begin the famous odyssey that would keep him away from his family and kingdom for twenty years. Leaving Ithaca as a young man to fight for his friend's honor in the war against Troy, Odysseus would spend the next nine years commanding troops as a Greek general until, by using his superior intelligence and abilities as a master strategist, he would win the war for the Greeks by offering the Trojans his notorious "gift"—the Trojan horse. The following ten years he would spend struggling to surmount the myriad obstacles that blocked the way of his return. During this ten-year interlude between Odysseus' departure from Troy and his arrival on Ithaca (a journey that should have taken a matter of weeks), Odysseus wanders over unknown seas and makes gargantuan efforts to fight against evil and temptation in their many forms. He must outwit the brutish, uncivilized Cyclops, battle against man-eating giants, and endure the scourge of Scylla and Charybdis—sheer evil that cannot be fought. He is tempted by the Lotus Eaters to forget about home, allured by the Sirens to live in the glory of his past deeds, and offered immortality by the goddess Calypso—but on her own terms. Odysseus prevails throughout and chooses life on his terms, lived with nobility and with the constant vigilance that the preservation of self-identity and integrity demands; and he chooses "home." Odysseus represents for Homer the distinct, authentic individual. He is the "lion" and the "eagle," set apart from the common throng of humanity (in this case the crewmen and the suitors), who in Homer's imagery are the "sheep," "cattle," "fish," "swine," and "bats"—those who follow one another according to herd instinct. Of particular interest here is Odysseus' categorical difference from others, his absolute individuality and constancy of self. Homer clearly goes out of his way to set Odysseus in bold relief against a backdrop of undifferentiated others, and in doing so emphasizes Odysseus' uniqueness as bound up with his identity as a traveler. Odysseus is the traveler *par excellence*; his notoriety consists of his being, concurrently, "twice as wise as any other mortal" and "the wanderer, harried for years on end."[15]

From the opening lines of the poem, we are confronted with contrast: the man skilled in every way, the courageous captain favored by the gods for his devotion, set in opposition to the foolish, greedy, gluttonous crewmen and the arrogant, squandering, gluttonous suitors. At once, an obvious parallel emerges between the two groups of men: their descriptions are interchangeable. Both the suitors and the crewmen are dominated by their lower instincts; both bring upon themselves their own destruction through gluttony, greed, and overall indifference toward the gods. Odysseus is their opposite in all respects.

The fundamental natures of the crewmen and the suitors, we could say, are the same; only in external circumstances do the situations of the men temporarily differ. The suitors, after all, never leave Ithaca; except for the few who scout for Telemachus, they never step foot off the island. Allegorically speaking, they never take the first step toward living life as an existential odyssey. On the contrary, they wile away their adulthood feasting on and drinking up the fruits of others' labors, never laboring themselves, never making the least attempt to transcend their animal natures. This "wolfpack of suitors" remains, from beginning to end, completely egocentric and static in nature.

In at least superficial contrast, the crewmen differ from the suitors in that they take the significant step away from the island and outside the epicenter of their own egos. They temporarily rise above the level of living for personal gratification when they fight for a cause higher than themselves—another person's honor. But they do this only as a group, only on the level of group consciousness. Individually, they prove themselves incapable of transcending the level of personal gain, for they are always in need of a commander, a superego, to furnish them with orders and to elicit from them their worthier impulses. The crewmen possess no commander within themselves, no inner master capable of controlling and passing judgment on their various impulses. Their lack of self-control and sense of discernment is apparent in that, whenever Odysseus is absent, the baser instincts of the men immediately surface and prevail, placing them on par with the suitors. Upon leaving Aiolia Island, for example, and after Odysseus has "worked the sheet" for nine days alone and then fallen asleep within sight of land, the crewmen at once succumb to suspicion and greed, unanimously agreeing to open the bag of winds in case Odysseus is hoarding gold: "But while I slept the crew began to parley: silver and gold, they guessed, were in that bag."[16] Likewise, on Circe's island, in the absence of their commander, or more "authentic self," the men are immediately transformed into swine: "bodies, voices, heads, and bristles, all swinish now."[17] And on the Island of the Sun, when forewarned by Odysseus not to slaughter Helios' cattle, the men give their solemn pledge; but no sooner does Odysseus leave the scene, having gone to pray to the gods, than the conscience of the men leaves with him (he being Self and Conscience for all). In a gluttonous frenzy, they slay the sacred cattle, bringing upon themselves their own doom.

Odysseus alone is presented as one who has "the gift of self-possession"[18] —an individual will and sense of judgment that enables him at all times to select and control his manner of being. He possesses what the others lack: the inner master; the single dominating "I." The Sufis have a poignant saying expressive of their world-view, a saying with which Gurdjieff concurred: "God alone has the right to say 'I.'" This means that Selfhood as a possession is not provided at birth; instead, it is a distant goal toward which we labor for a lifetime. We could perhaps say that Odysseus—in his years of laboring consciously for the welfare of others—has earned, on a human level, the right to say "I." He has acquired consciousness of Self. So, when his twelve ships approach the island of the Laestrygonians, eleven ships of crewmen lacking self-possession row thoughtlessly and lazily into an enclosed bay of calm waters, and all are slaughtered as easy prey. The "I" of Odysseus, in contrast, provides him with the presence of mind and foresight to choose more turbulent, but ultimately safer waters. Not tempted in any ordinary way as are the crewmen—by the land of the Lotus Eaters or by any other docile, ineffectual existence—he perceives the rugged demands of life as opportunities for growth. He risks the peril of listening to the Sirens' song (and many other perils), that he might go on a wiser man.

Allegorically speaking, then, the suitors remain throughout in their basest animal nature. At Odysseus' table they "wheezed and neighed as though with jaws no longer theirs, while blood defiled their meat, and blurring tears [of laughter] flooded their eyes."[19] And after the slaughter, they lie in a pile like a recent catch of fish poured from the net, "twitching their cold lives away."[20] Finally, once dead, their souls fleet away "all squeaking as bats will in a cavern's underworld."[21] They never took the significant step away from Ithaca in the direction of self-creation. The crewmen, on the other hand, began the journey that could have led to individual metamorphoses, but they failed to recognize the sojourn for what it was. As a result, they frittered away chance upon chance for self-growth by perceiving all obstacles as burdens rather than opportunities, and by wallowing in self-pity. Odysseus' last glance at them finds them bobbing "like petrals on the waves,"[22] a group of small, helpless birds ready to drown. Odysseus alone recognizes the intrinsic value of suffering—that it can lead to greater wisdom and deeper consciousness. He therefore neither shuns hardship not wastes time in self-pity. "The gods have tried me in a thousand ways,"[23] he tells Alkinoos; and to his wife he says, "Grief . . . heaven sent me—years of pain,"[24] but never with a tone of accusation toward the gods, or even, it seems, of remorse. Odysseus understands his place vis-à-vis the gods: "Body and birth, a most unlikely god am I, being all of earth and mortal nature."[25] Yet his hard-earned self-possession and "inward poise" make him godlike. As Constantine P. Cavafy sang, Odysseus recognized the journey as a goal in itself.

Dante Alighieri undergoes a voyage of a different nature in his visionary journey through Hell, Purgatory, and Paradise. On the evening of Good Friday, in the year 1300 A.D., Dante finds himself spiraling downward through the concentric layers of the Earth's surface toward its core—the abode of Satan. Along the way, he is educated in the hierarchical nature of sin and its consequences, and he witnesses the horrible sufferings of those who died unrepentant, in that they deliberately chose their own destructive patterns of behavior as their God. Dante speaks with many souls who are doomed for eternity (or at least until the Second Judgment) to endure a punishment that bears a reciprocal relation to the "sins" they committed. The lustful, for example, are blown turbulently about by the wind in symbolic fashion of the aimlessness of misdirected passion. The gluttons reside in their own debris, which they can eat and expel and of which they are a part; their hunger can never be satiated. The suicides are without bodies, for they cannot receive back what they have willfully destroyed. Finally, at the Earth's center, Dante looks upon the pathetic figure of Satan, his three heads—representing Ignorance, Hatred, and Impotence—an ugly parody of the Holy Trinity; and his enormous body—frozen in a lake of ice as a result of his own feverish efforts to escape it—a powerful symbol of absolute restriction and of futile, meaningless action: the nature of all self-limiting patterns of behavior.

Having internalized the nature of sin—which always has its source in Pride—Dante regains the Earth's surface in the region of Mount Purgatory, an island in the midst of an unknown sea. Now in a state of complete and necessary humility, he begins his climb up the mountain in the first rays of morning sun on Easter Sunday. In contrast to the dark, oppressive atmosphere of Hell, that of Purgatory is light and uplifting; it is the region of Hope. During his ascent up the terraces of the mountain to its peak, the Earthly Paradise, Dante witnesses the many penitent souls who are striving toward self-perfection. In Purgatory, the souls also suffer in a manner symbolic of their weaknesses—the proud are bowed down with heavy boulders; the gluttons, rather than indulging their appetites, are fasting from all food and drink—but all of the suffering undergone in Purgatory is self-imposed for purposes of purification. Dante's journey through this realm teaches him the redemptive value of voluntary suffering, which is the meaning of the law of Purgatory: "To be broken is to be whole." By the time he achieves Earthly Paradise at the top of the mountain, Dante has shed his own limiting characteristics—Pride and Envy—and is free to soar through the heavenly spheres to the Empyrean, the region of the Pure.

During this final segment of his sojourn, Dante speaks with the purified souls of Paradise, and from them he learns the most significant lessons of his fantastic journey: "In His Will is our peace" (*Paradiso*, III) and "Love [is the force] that moves the Sun and the other stars" (*Paradiso*, XXXIII). The souls confined to Hell made their own willful desire their God; the souls in Purgatory strive to align their individual wills with the Divine Will; the contentment that reigns in Paradise results from the presence of a single Will—the Divine Will—which manifests as Love, Justice, and Truth. Dante's illuminating visionary journey culminates with a blinding glimpse of the three-fold nature of God, symbolized by three overlapping circles that form one perfect circle in motion.

Dante's masterpiece, with its tripartite structure, is almost universally accepted as a symbol of medieval European Christianity. However, a groundbreaking work was published at the beginning of this century by a Spanish Catholic priest and Professor of Arabic, Miguel Asin Palacios—*Islam and the Divine Comedy*—which effectively proves that Dante's poem was actually fashioned after two famous works in Islamic religious literature: *Isra*, or *The Nocturnal Journey*, during which Mohammed visits the infernal regions; and *Miraj*, or *The Ascension*, in which Mohammed ascends from Jerusalem to the Throne of God. Specifically, Palacios makes clear that Dante's entire intellectual outlook was influenced by one of the greatest Sufi masters of medieval Spain: Ibn 'Arabi of Murcia, which in Arabic means "The Greatest Master." Gurdjieff's extensive studies in Sufism and esoteric Christianity would certainly have exposed him to these two great thinkers and their conceptions of Hell, Purgatory, and Paradise. In fact, the notion of Purgatory is literally central to Gurdjieff's body of thought; exactly midway through *Beelzebub's Tales* is the chapter "The Holy Planet Purgatory," which Gurdjieff claimed was the "heart" of his epic tale.

In Gurdjieff's chapter on Purgatory, he, like Dante, provides a detailed topography and physical description of Purgatory as a place (in this case a planet). He emphasizes its tremendous beauty, its lush, Edenic landscape, its refined atmosphere. He portrays it as a privileged place where all the souls are highly conscious. Yet, despite its paradisical qualities, it is also a place of tremendous suffering. The inhabitants of Purgatory suffer, Beelzebub tells us, because they fully comprehend what is required of them by God, but due to their own limited natures they are incapable of meeting these requirements. Their imperfections prevent them from assisting fully in the Divine plan. The suffering of the souls in Gurdjieff's Purgatory—as in Dante's—results from their labors to divest themselves of their inner slaves and to attain freedom from egocentric attachments so that they might function in accord with the Divine Will.

Whatever the notion of Purgatory may imply about a possible state of souls after death, my interest here lies in its allegorical significance—as a state of being that can be entered into in everyday life. If we consider the above pictures allegorically, then we come to recognize Purgatory, not as a "place," but as a state of conscious effort and voluntary suffering that can be entered into at will for purposes of conscious evolution. It is the state of tension created when Will struggles against inertia. It is the same state that Gilgamesh failed to enter into when put to the test by Utnapishtim.

When Dante traverses the realms of Hell, Purgatory, and Paradise, he does so by Divine intervention, and throughout two-thirds of the journey he remains a spectator and passerby, observing the situations of others. Only when he passes through Purgatory does he become an active participant. He cleanses his face from all traces of Hell (sin) and enters into a condition of humility before beginning his ascent; he receives seven "p's" (*peccato* = sin) on his forehead from Saint Peter when he enters the gates; and he labors his way up the seven terraces until all the "p's" have vanished from his forehead and he has achieved personal freedom in the Garden of Eden—or the state of earthly Perfection. Specifically, he enters *fully* into a condition of purgatory when he does penance for his dominating characteristics (or "chief features," as Gurdjieff would call them) of Pride and Envy. But what does this "condition of purgatory" mean (the fasting of the gluttons, the constant running of the slothful) other than the making of conscious efforts to turn around destructive behavioral patterns, the overcoming of whatever within ourselves restricts us from achieving our full potential as human beings. Whenever we enter into any self-correctional process and work toward achieving greater equilibrium as a human being or greater authenticity of character, the process demands of us all the identifying characteristics of Purgatory. We must possess sufficient humility to admit to ourselves our imperfections; we must make great efforts of will toward changing established habits (and this requires voluntary suffering); and furthermore, we must be sufficiently self-aware, or cognizant of self, to be able to identify our own limiting characteristics.

Both the Sufis and Gurdjieff propose conscious evolution as a way of life and perceive the obstacles afforded by everyday life as the "work material" to be used in the transformational process. All Sufi practices and disciplines are directed toward the goal of spiritual transformation, and all lesser goals are renounced toward this end. In fact, the Sufis call themselves "The Travelers," for in comparison to their accelerated development, everyone else is standing still. In this respect, we could say that they make of Purgatory a way of life, living every possible moment in the state of tension created by efforts of will. For the Sufis, the journey through Purgatory is commensurate with their travel along the path of life.

In the above three epic poems—*Gilgamesh, The Odyssey*, and the *Divine Comedy*—the authors use the educational odysseys of their heros as frameworks around which to build entire mythologies; and within the parameters of these mythologies, they present their overall conception of the human condition. All three heroes are singled out by the gods from the rest of humanity, in that they are granted privileges not allotted to ordinary mortals. Gilgamesh, Odysseus, and Dante gain access, while in life, to the region of the dead, what for others remains forever in life the "undiscovered country"; and in this experience, they break through that very boundary that has always defined the limitation of human possibility. Their resulting superior knowledge places them in an elite segment of humanity. Such figures in literature take their place among our idols and superheroes. They supply us with hope and inspiration, and give us faith in the significance of the human condition; they elevate our spirits and help us transcend the everydayness of life; they act out our own latent urges to break through and stride beyond what we perceive as our limited sphere of possibility. In these and many other respects, the epic hero's superior human status is invaluable. Also of value, however, though in a different way, are the literary heroes and heroines of more limited stature, who journey into the world (without divine intervention) and gain wisdom of a less comprehensive nature. They may not come to understand the meaning of human existence, but they may gain a single penetrating insight that is sufficiently profound to alter their previous world-view. Three examples are Don Quixote, Candide, and Hans Castorp.

Alonso Quijano el Bueno—Alonso the Good—the *"bon enfant"* of La Mancha, Spain, was "one of those gentlemen" (a common denominator) who always had meat for his evening meals, his stew prepared in a particular way, lentils on Friday, pigeon on Sunday, and so on. His eating habits consumed three-fourths of his income, the rest of which he spent on fine clothes—velvet stockings, slippers to match, suits of the finest homespun, and so on. Upon reaching middle age, however, Alonso the Good—beloved by neighbors and acquaintances—comes to sense the emptiness of his routine, ordinary, predictable existence and its accompanying values, and with a complete change of heart he sells the greatest portion of his possessions to finance a totally different lifestyle—to travel throughout the world as a wandering knight and fight evil and injustice on all levels. Alonso Quijano el Bueno assumes a new identity—Don Quixote de la Mancha—leaves behind his "friends" and neighbors, and begins his unforgettable perambulations throughout Spain.

Don Quixote's overall ambition is to battle against the values of his own hateful Iron Age—fraud, deceit, malice, and selfishness—and to reinstitute an Edenic Golden Age that stood for Truth and Justice. "All then was peace, all was concord and friendship," he muses to some shepherds, and "those who lived in that time did not know the meaning of the words 'thine' and 'mine,'"[26] for then all things were held in common. Don Quixote's fight to re-establish the values of the Golden Age is no less than a single-handed battle to bring back into the world the values of Christianity, which include the common ownership of property. His new life, in his estimation, is the life of a true Christian, not of one who pays lip service to Christianity. To the shepherd Vivaldo, Don Quixote defends the superiority of his own interpretation of the Christian life:

> the religious, in all peace and tranquillity, pray to heaven for earth's good, but we soldiers and knights put their prayers into execution by defending with the might of our good right arms and at the edge of the sword those things for which they pray; and we do this not under cover of a roof but under the open sky, beneath the insufferable rays of the summer sun and the biting cold of winter. Thus we become the ministers of God on earth, and our arms the means by which He executes His decrees. . . . it follows that those who have taken upon themselves such a profession must unquestionably labor harder than do those who in peace and tranquillity and at their ease pray to God to favor the ones who can do little in their own behalf.[27]

Underneath the humorous veneer of Don Quixote's lofty manner of speech lies the serious plight of the individual who attempts to live an authentic life in an inauthentic world. Nothing is inherently funny in the value system Don Quixote upholds—Love, Justice, and Truth—or in his defense of his lifestyle as expressing his interpretation of the role of a Christian. He is simply trying to put into effect James's admonition that "faith without works is dead" (James 2:26), and is pointing out the hardship and sacrifice that such a lifestyle requires. The hilarity that surfaces throughout Cervantes' novel has its source in the ludicrous contrast of the single authentic and visionary individual against the common uninspired majority, from whose perspective the Don Quixotes of the world appear insane or foolish, or at the very least a threat to their comfortable existence. Three times Don Quixote departs from La Mancha in an attempt to carry out his self-imposed mission, and three times he returns home at the insistence of others: the first time to "replenish supplies"; the second time to rest; and the third time to give up altogether his chivalric lifestyle. Don Quixote comes to understand in the course of his courageous wanderings that of all evils and injustices he single-handedly attempts to combat, the one that is beyond his scope and power are the "others" who, out of "concern for his welfare" will not allow him to live the strenuous existence of a crusader for Truth. Don Quixote's "friends" and neighbors—all those for whom he was before the *bon enfant* of La Mancha—prefer the routine, ordinary Alonso the Good, in his velvet slippers eating lentils on Friday. Finding himself in the *cul-de-sac* situation of being too conscious to resume his former unconscious lifestyle, and at the same time too overpowered by others to live the life of his choice, Don Quixote can find no other solution than to die gracefully, so as not to hurt others and not to sacrifice his own integrity as a human being.

The decisive battle that Don Quixote loses is against what Gurdjieff called "that scourge of humanity, the herd instinct."[28] When he sheds his identity as Alonso the Good, and as Don Quixote articulates his famous line, "I know who I am, and who I may be if I chose,"[29] he underestimates the power of "the herd" and its determination to oppose whatever is different from the *status quo*. He perhaps also fathoms, at the conclusion of his altruistic travels, that more than good will and sacrifice are required to make a change in society; also crucial is the requisite level of inner being. In *Beelzebub's Tales*, Gurdjieff makes an ambiguous passing reference to the plight of Don Quixote in the context of discussing the League of Nations and the impotent end to which he believed it would come. One reason the League of Nations would fail, Beelzebub prophesies to Hassein, was because its members overestimated their own power to evoke change. They should stop "as is said there on Earth 'playing at Don Quixote' by attempting to stop war at one stroke,"[30] and should occupy themselves with solving problems that are within their scope. They might begin, for example, by stopping the practice of adulating their war "heroes" by rewarding them with honor and decorations—an action more feasibly within their ability.

The fact that Beelzebub attributes the above saying to Earth beings, who always perceive reality upside down, may mean that he intends the criticism of Don Quixote ironically, so that no actual criticism is intended; Cervantes also uses common adages throughout his novel to represent the "rabble" mentality. At the same time, it is Beelzebub himself who is extrapolating on the point that the League of Nations, given the scope of its ambition and the level of being of its members, is doomed to failure. This ambiguity surrounding Beelzebub's statement, combined with the fact that Cervantes' novel throughout addresses the theme of reality as perceivable and interpretable on different levels, makes sifting through these many ambiguities to determine definitively what Gurdjieff intended by this statement impossible. I can only surmise, based on my overall understanding of Gurdjieff's thought, the meaning I believe he probably intended. This would be that Alonso el Bueno's renunciation of his old lifestyle and his willingness to make sacrifices in order to fight for objectively good values indicates an evolution of consciousness on the part of the hero. Alonso realizes the truth of the commandment that Gurdjieff took to heart: "The highest aim and sense of human life is the striving for the welfare of one's neighbor," and he understands that this is achievable only through self-sacrifice. By putting this philosophy into action, Don Quixote moves further along in the octave of transformation. But a complete metamorphosis of Alonso

Quijano into Don Quixote is impossible because Alonso failed to do the crucial preparatory inner work; the shift of identities is too abrupt. In Gurdjieff's parlance, Alonso "attempted to get into heaven wearing galoshes."[31] The "I" of Don Quixote is insufficiently crystallized to allow him to preserve his identity in the face of the "herd." Had his inner work kept pace with his outer transformation, I believe Gurdjieff would have said that Don Quixote should have prevailed.

In the eighteenth-century travel tale *Candide*, Voltaire creates a devastating picture of the violent, destructive manifestations of human nature that result when action is unconscious. By setting into motion the honest, simple-hearted Candide, naïve in the ways of the world, and by having us witness through his eyes, as if for the first time, the atrocities of mechanical human behavior, Voltaire achieves an effect similar to what Gurdjieff accomplishes by using Beelzebub, an alien, as narrator. Both are outsiders, shocked by and not responsible for the actions they witness. Consequently, we, too, feel detached, and this detachment allows us at first to respond with a confused, bewildered kind of laughter; upon reflection, however, when we realize that we are inside and a part of this human condition, we can feel only the most solemn melancholy. Both are employing the art of black comedy.

Candide begins his educational journey when he finds himself suddenly forced to leave the protective environment of the small provincial town of Westphalia, Germany, and to make his own way in the world. He journeys out in good faith, with belief in human kindness, selflessness, and generosity—that all is for the best. After having been lied to, impressed into military service, and beaten, Candide witnesses human corruption on a massive scale, namely, war (or as Gurdjieff more aptly call it, "reciprocal destruction"):

> First the cannons battered down about six thousand men on each side; then volleys of musket fire removed from the best of worlds about nine or ten thousand rascals who were cluttering up the surface. The bayonet was a sufficient reason for the demise of several thousand others. Total casualties might well amount to thirty thousand men or so. . . . Passing by mounds of the dead and dying, he came to a nearby village which had been burnt to the ground . . . in strict accordance with the laws of war. Here old men, stunned from beatings, watched the last agonies of their butchered wives, who still clutched their infants to their bleeding breasts . . . ; others, half-scourged in the flames, begged for their death stroke. Scattered brains and severed limbs littered the ground. Climbing over ruins and stumbling over corpses, Candide finally made his way out of the war area. . . .[32]

Events unfold and Candide continues his travels through Holland, Spain, Portugal, and Africa, finding more torture, thievery, deceit, and intrigue.

Midway in the tale, Candide finds himself miraculously transported to a world of an entirely different order and caliber from the one he has become accustomed to observing. Human existence here is transcendent, elevated to a much finer plane. Dignity, generosity, and honesty are the values of the inhabitants of this extraordinary land. This is El Dorado, the lost land of the Incas. In El Dorado, the beauty and richness of the landscape mirrors the inner wealth of the people, so gold and precious gems in abundance decorate and beautify the scenery. All the residents of this country are free, but they choose to spend their time studying and worshipping God. Each citizen has the rank of a priest, and together they begin each morning by singing psalms of thanksgiving. Therefore, as Candide is surprised to learn, they have no need of monks "to teach, argue, govern, intrigue, and burn at the stake everyone who disagrees with them."[33] In fact, in El Dorado no traces can be found of the egoism and selfishness that have governed the world Candide has traversed outside of this isolated esoteric domain. In this context, honest and good-hearted as Candide is, he still stands out in sharp relief against the backdrop of El Doradians as a less refined, less conscious, and inferior human being. While the people of El Dorado regard dispassionately the gems and gold that lie scattered over their landscape, Candide cannot help but translate these stones into personal wealth and power. He is dazzled, not by their beauty, not by the spiritual wealth of the people they reflect, but by the potential for gain they represent for him personally. Motivated in part by impulses of possessiveness and egoism, Candide's nature will not permit him to remain on this level of existence, where wealth is shared in common and a competitive spirit does not exist. He leaves El Dorado, transporting with him as many of the precious gems as he can possibly carry.

This newly whetted appetite in Candide now becomes his greatest source of suffering after leaving El Dorado. While before, he was primarily an observer of deceitful behavior, his new-found wealth makes him a center of attention and the target of labyrinthine scheming. And even though Candide has suffered hardships and miseries far more painful in the course of his travels, the baseness of human greed plunges him into his deepest state of melancholy, in which "the malice of men rose up before his spirit in all its ugliness, and his mind dwelt only on gloomy thoughts."[34] Toward the end of the tale, after all Candide's money has been either lost, swindled, or stolen, after he has experienced the entire gamut of human suffering—most of which has been imposed by human beings—Candide inquires of a fellow traveler whether human beings have "always been liars, traitors, ingrates, thieves, weaklings, sneaks, cowards, backbiters, gluttons, drunkards, misers, climbers, killers, calumniators, sensualists, fanatics, hypocrites, and fools."[35] Just as hawks have always devoured pigeons, he is assured, human beings have always behaved with the same depravity.

The emotional nadir that Candide reaches is the crucial point of his education. He leaves Westphalia an optimistic young man who believes in the reasonable ways of the world and the inherent goodness of human beings. His travels from one country to another affirm again and again Gurdjieff's observation that human existence, when lived on the level of ordinary life, is a prison whose inmates carry on in a state of slavery to instincts, impulses, and outside forces. Candide's comprehension of this truth plunges him into a state of dejection; but this emotional low point also marks the death of his attachment to ordinary life. Only after he has internalized the fact that life lived unconsciously is completely meaningless, and even "evil," is he able to recognize the necessity of approaching life on a different level.

With further experience of the world superfluous, Candide ends his travels and settles in Turkey, where, together with some fellow travelers and sufferers, he plants and cultivates a garden. From his experience of the mechanical nature of human beings and the suffering that results from unconscious behavior, Candide concludes by focusing on the value of work—which keeps at bay the three evils of boredom, vice, and poverty. He creates a micro-society based on a philosophy of labor, in which each individual gains personally from his or her work while contributing to the welfare of others. Voltaire's metaphor—"we must cultivate our garden"—is rich with possible interpretations, but whatever else he may have been implying by this conclusion to his philosophical tale, it also seems clear, given the esoteric experience of El Dorado, that one level of work Candide must perform is inner work. He must raise his own spiritual awareness to a level corresponding to that of El Dorado. When there he still believed that money could buy happiness. By the end of the tale, he understands, as he says, that "the riches of this world are fleeting," and that what happiness can be found can come only from work on oneself. He understands that we must cultivate our inner gardens, refine our inner landscapes; and, as with physical labor, we and all of those around us will reap the fruits of our inner labors. Inner cultivation, he discovers, is the only real source of happiness.

As a final example of an edifying journey undergone by a literary hero, consider the uncanny trip of Hans Castorp, who travels from his native city of Hamburg, Germany, up a mountain in the Swiss Alps and back in Thomas Mann's masterpiece *The Magic Mountain*. Hans Castorp, age twenty-three, during the interim between graduating from college and entering into an apprenticeship with the reputable shipping company Thunder and Wilms, decides to spend his three-week interlude visiting his tubercular cousin at the International Sanatorium Berghof. The sanatorium is a mere three-day trek from the flatlands of Hamburg, but is situated a significant 5,000 feet higher in the atmosphere, "above the zone of shade trees and of songbirds,"[36] where the well-bred but ordinary Hans finds himself "out of his depth." A visit initially undertaken in a light-hearted vacation spirit extends into a stay of seven years' duration and results in an alchemical transformation of Castorp's being.

The family name Castorp has for generations been associated with culture and good breeding by the citizens of Hamburg. The family has money. It moves among influential circles and carries political weight. Hans has consequently been raised in an environment that condones the values considered appropriate to his status in society: he cultivates fine tastes in food and clothing, carries himself with an air of refinement, and observes with precision the rules of conduct prescribed by others. In short, "in his blonde correctness," Hans is "the fruit of inherited unconscious self-esteem."[37] And when the time came for him to choose a line of studies at the university, he leaned toward the technical side—toward the tangible and the solid. He chose to work as an engineer for a shipping firm. His intention in going to visit his cousin, then, is to pass twenty-one mid-summer days pleasantly before entering into his apprenticeship, not to take the journey too seriously—which would hamper its relaxation value—and then to return to the city and resume his life precisely where he had left it. In this environment and station Hans feels most comfortable—in his native Hamburg, "just a few feet above sea level."

On the train ride up the mountain, just two days' distance from Hamburg, Hans already begins to experience the dizzying, disconcerting sensations of altitude, the alien nature of the world high above sea level, where it snows even in August. And he begins to absorb the refined impressions that accompany an elevated space. In the region of the Alps where his train comes to a stop—5,000 feet above sea level—Hans confronts a foreign landscape, a white wilderness of eternal snow, a terrain that calls for reflection and beckons for answers. With the greeting of his cousin Joachim at the train station, Hans's alien status in this lofty region is confirmed. A quick perusal and a handshake are enough to reveal to him the changes wrought by Joachim's residency in this remote place. And as time passes, Hans comes to understand that not only the elevation is responsible for the alterations in his cousin's nature—not only the physical remoteness of the world below—although this is a significant factor. More important is the phenomenological distance, the remoteness of being that the inhabitants of this area have from those in the ordinary world. All the residents here—at the International Sanatorium Berghof—live their daily lives with cognizance of their own imminent deaths. All are tubercular patients in various stages of infection, fully aware of the remote possibility for cure.

To live life with full consciousness of one's own impending death, and of the impending death of everyone with whom one associates, as is the case with the tubercular patients at the sanatorium, is fundamentally different from living life in the denial of death, as do those at the bottom of the mountain. The internalization of the basic truth of our own finitude evokes the most radical change of being possible. Leo Tolstoy recognized this fact; it is his message in *The Death of Ivan Ilych*, the most important message he tried to convey. Martin Heidegger, in *Being and Time*, constructed a philosophy around the contrast of the authentic being who lives life in the face of death and the inauthentic being who flees from it. Gurdjieff, at the end of *Beelzebub's Tales*, proposes cognizance of death as the one change in human nature that could save the human race. On top of the "magic" mountain, Hans Castorp finds himself in a milieu of human beings who have, for the most part, received death sentences and comprehended the fact of their own mortality. And he bears witness to the different quality and texture of life this recognition evokes.

One obvious difference in this sober environment on the mountaintop is that time possesses a subjective, existential dimension lacking in ordinary life. The time abiding here is not the objectively measured time by which those below calculate their affairs—rising to alarm clocks, showing up for appointments, or catching trains. Time for the dying is life itself; it is the present broken free from the past and the future—life lived qualitatively rather than quantitatively. And this ever-present now in which they live, the moment sustained and severed from past and future, carries with it an existential freedom unknown by those at the foot of the mountain—freedom from convention, from propriety, from etiquette, from pretense, from artificiality, from "others"—freedom from everything but death. On one occasion, Hans asks his cousin why a young couple at the sanatorium behaves so "cheekily." Joachim replies, "Good Lord!"; "They are so free—I mean . . . time is nothing to them, and then they may die—why should they make a long face?"[38] And we find many other signs—both subtle and blatant—of the existential freedom that accompanies living in a sustained, qualitative present: bold looks and bouts of laughter that would be frowned upon down below; expressions of honest emotion breaking through ordinary reserve; a "metaphorical shrug of the shoulders," which is a customary habit among the *"moribundi"*; the added dimension to, or altered emphasis on sex, which for the dying possesses "an accent, a value, a significance which [is] utterly novel."[39] "I am not prudish, not an outraged, middle-class housewife," one woman says to Hans in reference to her behavior. "No," he understands; "your illness gives you freedom."[40] Important, too, is the philosophical climate in general that reigns up on the mountain. Conversation is poetic and profound. "But what a stately and solemn way the people hereabout have of talking—almost like poetry,"[41] Hans observes. He finds himself attending a lecture on the connection of love to illness, when all of his courses "in the flatland" dealt with such subjects as gear transmission in ship building. The once pedantic, practical Hans, in this environment in the Swiss Alps, feels an impulse to address the ultimate questions, "to take stock of himself in reference to the rank and status of *Homo Dei*."[42]

As time passes, Castorp's nature begins to change. From his point of view on the mountain, he considers life as he lived it down below and finds it queer, artificial, and meaningless. He describes to a patient the life he left behind in Hamburg:

> If a man does not serve the best and dearest wines at his dinners people don't go. . . . That is what they are like. Lying here and looking at it from a distance, I find it pretty gross. . . . It is a cruel atmosphere down there, cruel and ruthless. . . . You see, a person has to have a rather thick skin to find it natural, the way they have of thinking and talking.[43]

Having participated in a more authentic way of being, Hans cannot go back and resume his old ways. He chooses to remain among the sober dying rather than return to ordinary life. He befriends many patients, tries to ease their suffering, falls in love with a dying woman, is told that he himself is infected, and watches one person after another die. He becomes familiar, almost intimate with death, confronting it daily, meditating upon it. He "takes stock" of himself and human existence in relation to death, and he comes to understand that life lived without consciousness of death is not life; it is something else, something inferior, but not life. Real life demands full comprehension of personal mortality. With the internalization of this fundamental truth comes authentic existence—love of humanity, compassion for others. When Hans returns to the foot of the mountain after seven years, at the age of thirty, he understands that he and all others—even those down below, although they are unaware of it—are "the *moribundi*"—the dying.

What Hans comes to understand is what Tolstoy, Heidegger, Gurdjieff, and others have understood and tried to convey—that when we look upon everyone, ourselves included, as carrying a death sentence, all the many manifestations of egoism, selfishness, and artificiality fall away, and we can feel only compassion. We are all equalized by death. Thus, at the end of *Beelzebub's Tales*, after Hassein (Beelzebub's grandson) has listened to hundreds of stories about the abnormal behavior of terrestrial beings, he, grief-stricken by all the suffering on the Earth, implores his grandfather to tell him what possibility exists of salvaging the people and the planet. And Beelzebub replies:

> The sole means now of saving the beings of the Earth would be . . . [if] everyone of these unfortunates, during the process of his existence, should constantly sense and be aware of the inevitability of his own death, as well as of the death of everyone upon whom his eyes, or attention, rests. Only such a sensation and such an awareness could destroy the egoism now so completely crystallized in them that it has swallowed up the whole of their essence, and at the same time uproot that tendency to hate others which flows from it . . . which [is] the chief cause of all their abnormalities, unbecoming to three-brained beings and maleficent for them and for the whole of the Universe.[44]

The above passage serves as the conclusion of Gurdjieff's long epic tale, and expresses part of the wisdom Beelzebub has acquired during his many years of active participation in the affairs of the Earth. Centuries earlier, we are informed at the beginning of the epic, Beelzebub had been banished from his home planet Karatas, near the Center of the Universe, for an act of rebellion against HIS ENDLESSNESS—an act he attributes to his once youthful nature and undeveloped reason. Having been forced to pass his exile in this remote corner of the universe, Beelzebub chose to spend his time studying the psyche and nature of human beings and observing their development through history. He has also, on a number of occasions spanning long periods of time, become actively involved in human affairs for purposes of preserving Universal harmony. Finally, at the end of the twentieth century, Beelzebub has won pardon from exile as a result of his conscious labors for the planet, and he has been granted permission by HIS ENDLESSNESS to return to the Center of the Universe. Through "listening to" Beelzebub's many illustrative tales to his grandson Hassein, we learn of his activities during exile, and of his contribution to the conscious evolution of the inhabitants of Earth.

Of the different travel tales discussed, Gurdjieff's epic *Beelzebub's Tales* is most comparable in scope and subject matter to Dante's *Divine Comedy*. As has been noted, the central section of both works involves a visit to Purgatory and a discussion of its conditions, and both heroes' travels culminate with a flight to the Center of the Universe—a return to the presence of God. However, rather than presenting Satan as a symbol of self-imposed restriction—as does Dante with his image of Satan frozen in Cocytus—Gurdjieff makes Beelzebub his central character and presents him as an active and necessary participant in the evolution of consciousness. This is in keeping with the Sufis' understanding of the role that opposition plays in the process of growth. In this context, Beelzebub represents adversity, antagonism. He is the Iblis of Sufism, whose *divinely appointed* role is "to stand in opposition to" so that the Travelers (the Sufis) might make their way Home (to the Source). Indeed, in many references to divine names in the Koran, "He-who-leads-astray" is mentioned in conjunction with "He-who-guides," such as "God leads astray whomsoever He will, and He guides whomsoever He will" (XIV). Iblis is the aspect of God that leads astray. A verse of Rumi's reads: "Then [Iblis] called out to God's Eternal Attribute of 'Leading Astray': 'Stir up dust from the depths of temptation's ocean.'"[45] Also, in biblical verses such as Isaiah 45: 5–7, affirmation and denial are recognizable as co-existing principles in Yahweh: "I am Yahweh, and there is none else. . . . I form the light, and create darkness: I make peace, and create evil: I Yahweh do all these things."[46] Beelzebub (Iblis) is the indispensable adversary in the process of spiritual evolution. As an instrument of conflict, he creates the conditions that allow for human beings to transcend themselves and to overcome.

This interpretation of Iblis's role is illustrated by the following Sufi teaching tale:

> A certain devout man, convinced that he was a sincere Seeker after Truth, embarked upon a long course of discipline and study. He had many experiences under various teachers, both in his inner and outer life, over a considerable period of time. One day he was meditating when he suddenly saw the Devil sitting beside him.
>
> "Away, demon!" he cried, "for you have no power to harm me; I am treading the Path of the Elect."

The apparition disappeared. A truly wise Sufi who was passing by addressed the man sadly: "Alas, my friend, you have arrived at your ultimate possible experience."

"How so?" the seeker asked.

"What you perceived as the Devil was really an angel," the Sufi responded; "Had you not sent him away but had confronted him, your experiences of reality could have been infinitely more refined."[47]

Thus, by making Beelzebub the hero of his epic, and by dramatizing Beelzebub's role in the conscious evolution of human beings, Gurdjieff attempts to illuminate the covert, seldom-considered dimension of opposition: the adversary as a creator of individual consciousness; the provoker as a provider of a valuable opportunity for growth. He is reminding us that only through struggle against antagonistic forces can we create something imperishable in ourselves (Gilgamesh); separate ourselves from the "herd" and establish an "I" (Odysseus); achieve Earthly Paradise on the top of Mount Purgatory (Dante); shed from ourselves traces of the inferior Iron Age and replace them with noble values of the Golden Age (Don Quixote); refine our inner landscapes to match the grandeur of El Dorado (Candide); and achieve authenticity of Self by internalizing the reality of death (Hans Castorp). When life is traveled with these objectives in mind—all of which have to do with the awakening of consciousness—then, as Rumi divined, "The Path Itself becomes the place of honor."[48]

Five

THE *TALES* THEMSELVES: AN OVERVIEW

> The secret must be kept from all non-people;
> the mystery must be hidden from all idiots.
>
> —Omar Khayyam (eleventh-century Sufi), "The Secret"

In his *Talks on Beelzebub's Tales*, John G. Bennett recalls one night spent in G. I. Gurdjieff's small Paris apartment shortly before Gurdjieff's death. In a typical gathering of students—among them English, Americans, French, and Greeks—more than fifty people assembled to have dinner with Gurdjieff and to listen to him speak. Gurdjieff offered a toast, which in its simplicity seemed forceful: "Everyone must have an aim. If you have not an aim, you are not a man. I will tell you a very simple aim, *to die an honorable death*. Everyone can take this aim without any philosophizing—*not to perish like a dog*."[1] "As always," Bennett recalls, "he suddenly turns the conversation to a joke and in a minute the room is shaken with laughter at some story about the peculiarities of the English. But the impression remains of the overwhelming seriousness of our human situation, of the choice which confronts us between life and death."[2]

What seems simple—not to perish like a dog—is for Gurdjieff the most difficult aim a person can have. And making us aware of the choice between life and death, or between kinds and qualities of death, is a main concern of *Beelzebub's Tales to His Grandson*. In the *Tales*, however, the choice is presented in far more complex terms: we can either live our lives and die our deaths passively and mechanically, for the sole purpose of unconsciously supplying the Cosmos with required energies, whereby upon death we sacrifice our individuality; or, we can live in such a way as to supply required cosmic energies consciously, and of sufficient quantity and quality, so that death carries the potential of amounting to more than a payment of transformed energy, and we gain the possibility of becoming "immortal within the limits of the Solar System."[3] The choice between life and death as expressed in these terms is related to Gurdjieff's Theory of Reciprocal Maintenance, which embodies his answer to the question, "What is the meaning and purpose of life on Earth, and in particular of human life?" Like all organic life on Earth, human beings are apparatuses for transforming energies that are required for some other purpose. As a more complicated type of transforming apparatus than plants or animals, however, human beings possess some choice regarding how to supply the energies required by their existence. They can transform energy consciously or unconsciously, in greater or lesser quantities, and of varying qualities, thereby influencing the purpose and outcome of their deaths. These are among the choices of which Gurdjieff wants to make us aware in his *Tales*.

Manuel Rainoird aptly likens Gurdjieff in his work to a train guard who, out of sheer kind-heartedness, jostles and rouses the passengers before their train reaches some frontier, so that they will be ready and things will go smoothly.[4] *Beelzebub's Tales* does serve this purpose, but the setting is more dramatic than the analogy leads us to believe. In the *Tales*, Gurdjieff is trying to rouse his readers from sleep so that they might get things in order before reaching their final destination: death. For Gurdjieff, preparing for an "honorable death" means acquiring all possible understanding about life and the role of human beings in it. To this end, *Beelzebub's Tales* is appropriately subtitled "All and Everything." Here, Gurdjieff presents us with all the fruits of his conscious labors, all the understanding about human existence that he acquired, through tremendous efforts, in the course of his lifetime. His hope is that we might share part of this understanding.

1. The Scenario

"Everything" unfolds through the story of Beelzebub, a wise old being from the planet Karatas, which belongs to a solar system distant from Earth's. Due to circumstances connected with Beelzebub's youth, however, he has spent the greatest part of his long existence in this part of the Universe, "in conditions not proper to his nature,"[5] traveling between Mars and Earth in an attempt to cure Earth beings from the afflictions that result from their wrong perception of reality.

Many years ago, we are told, in Beelzebub's splendid and fiery youth, he saw something in the functioning of the World which, to his then unformed reason and limited understanding, struck him as illogical. And because he had a strong and forceful nature, many other beings were persuaded by Beelzebub to rebel against HIS ENDLESSNESS to such a degree that the center of the Megalocosmos was nearly brought to a state of revolution. Then,

> [h]aving learned of this, HIS ENDLESSNESS, notwithstanding HIS all-lovingness and all-forgiveness, was constrained to banish Beelzebub with his comrades to one of the remote corners of the Universe, namely, to the solar system "Ors" . . . and to assign as the place of their existence one of the planets of that solar system, namely, Mars, with the privilege of existing on other planets also, though only of the same solar system.[6]

Among those banished to Mars were sympathizers with Beelzebub and others who served as their attendants. In this way, Mars came to be populated by three-centered beings from the Center of the Universe, and Beelzebub came to spend his life in a place foreign to him, taking in "perceptions unusual for his nature" and "experiences not proper to his essence,"[7] all of which left a mark on Beelzebub and contributed to his exceptional nature.

During Beelzebub's exile to Mars, he made several extended visits to Earth. His first descent to this planet took him to Atlantis shortly before its disappearance, and the last involved a three-hundred year stay that brought Beelzebub into the twentieth century. Altogether, he descended on six occasions to Earth, his visits spanning a period of several millennia and landing him in times and places as diverse as ancient Babylon, twentieth-century America, Afghanistan at the beginning of the seventeenth century, and Russia at the time of the Bolshevik Revolution. Beelzebub built a large observatory during his exile on Mars, and this enabled him to observe events taking place on Earth during his absence from the planet. As a result of these circumstances, Beelzebub was exposed in some fashion to human beings and situations for hundreds of years, and his long interaction with the planet provided him with much food for thought concerning Earth, its history, and the behavior and psyche of its people.

When Beelzebub's narrative begins, he is no longer in exile. Through the intervention of the holy Ashiata Shiemash, a messenger who had at one time been sent by HIS ENDLESSNESS to coordinate life on Earth with the general harmony of the World, Beelzebub has been pardoned for fulfilling needs connected with Earth. Because of Ashiata Shiemash's request, and "the modest and cognizant existence of Beelzebub himself,"[8] Beelzebub has been given permission by HIS ENDLESSNESS to return to his place of origin, the planet Karatas at the Center of the Universe.

In spite of his long absence from home, the influence and authority that Beelzebub possessed as a youth have even increased. As a result of his having lived in circumstances of unusual hardship and deprivation, "all those around him were clearly aware that, thanks to his prolonged existence in . . . unusual conditions, his knowledge and experience must have broadened and deepened."[9] Although Beelzebub is now aged and tired and has only recently returned to Karatas, at the opening of the *Tales* he is embarking on yet another interplanetary journey to attend a conference that concerns events of great cosmic importance, about which he might offer his wisdom and experience.

Traveling with Beelzebub on the spaceship Karnak are the ship's crew, the attendants of Beelzebub (including his long-time servant, Ahoon), and Beelzebub's grandson Hassein, son of his favorite son, Tooloof. Having only met Hassein for the first time upon his return to Karatas, Beelzebub found that his grandson was at the significant age when his reason needed to be guided and developed (about twelve or thirteen years of age by Earth calculation), and he decided to assume responsibility for Hassein's education. The education commences with Hassein accompanying his grandfather to the conference on the planet Revozvradendr.

As Beelzebub begins his narration about his many years in exile, he is seated with Hassein and Ahoon on the upper deck of the Karnak, where they are talking among themselves while gazing out at the "boundless space." Beelzebub is starting to relate stories about the solar system to which he was exiled, when the ship's captain interrupts them with an urgent message: the ship will be unable to travel to its destination by the most direct route, for passing through that same space will be the large comet Sakoor, which emits harmful gases. The original travel plans must be altered, and the captain recognizes two alternatives: the first is to make a long detour around the gases, and the second is to wait until the gases have dispersed. In either case, a long delay will result. The captain, out of respect, has consulted Beelzebub regarding what should be done.

In response to the captain's inquiry, Beelzebub recalls the wisdom of the Sufi sage Mullah Nassr Eddin, who for every possible occasion had "an apt and pithy saying."[10] Beelzebub muses about the Mullah in the presence of the captain:

> "As all his sayings were full of the sense of truth for existence there, I also used them there as a guide, in order to have a comfortable existence among the beings of that planet.
>
> "And in the given case, too, my dear Captain, I intend to profit by one of his wise sayings.
>
> "In such a situation as has befallen us, he would probably say: 'You cannot jump over your knees and it is absurd to try to kiss your own elbow.'
>
> "I now say the same to you, and I add: there is nothing to be done; when an event is impending which arises from forces immeasurably greater than our own, one must submit."[11]

The decision is to wait somewhere until the gases have dispersed so as not to cause unnecessary wear and tear to the ship, and to pass the time of the delay in a way that is productive for all—by Beelzebub narrating to the others his experiences in the solar system Ors, in particular on the planet Earth. The accounts of Beelzebub's experiences while in exile, related to Hassein and Ahoon during the time of the ship's delay and during travel time to and from Revozvradendr, make up the bulk of *Beelzebub's Tales*.

After this postponement, which provides opportunity for many stories, the ship reaches Revozradendr, where Beelzebub and the others remain for two months. The events of this time, however, are not disclosed to the reader. Not until the Karnak is returning to Karatas do the tales of Beelzebub resume. The return trip is then interrupted by a visit to The Holy Planet Purgatory, where Beelzebub wishes to give his regards to members of his family, including his other son, Tooilan, and to a teacher from his youth. This detour to Purgatory takes us to the heart of Gurdjieff's book. Apart from the visit to The Holy Planet, the ship is in transit from the beginning to the end of the *Tales*, and it serves as the only setting for the dialogues between Beelzebub and Hassein.

As the Karnak nears the outer spaces of Beelzebub's home planet, it is unexpectedly approached by a host of Cosmic beings, including several archangels, a multitude of angels, and some cherubim and seraphim. The entire procession enters the ship bearing branches of palm for Beelzebub and singing the "Hymn to HIS ENDLESSNESS." The purpose for their visit is to restore to Beelzebub what he was deprived of at the time of his exile: his horns. This is accomplished by the most venerable archangel's holding over Beelzebub's head a sacred rod, which gradually causes Beelzebub's long-lost horns to grow.

All present observe the ceremony with much anticipation, for they understand that the degree of Objective Reason obtained by a being of Beelzebub's nature is revealed by the number of forks that appear on his horns. In Beelzebub's case, "First one fork appeared, then another, and then a third, and as each fork made its appearance a clearly perceptible thrill of joy and unconcealed satisfaction proceeded among all those present."[12] As yet a fourth fork appears, tension reaches its height and all assume the ceremony to be at an end, for inconceivable to any being present is the possibility that Beelzebub could have exceeded this already sacred level of Reason. But before those assembled have time to recover from their excitement over Beelzebub's fourth fork,

> there suddenly and unexpectedly appeared on the horns of Beelzebub quite independently a fifth fork of a special form known to them all.
>
> Thereupon all without exception, even the venerable archangel himself, fell prostrate before Beelzebub, who had now risen to his feet and stood transfigured with a majestic appearance, owing to the truly majestic horns which had arisen on his head.[13]

The fifth fork signifies that Beelzebub has attained a level of Reason only four degrees removed from the Absolute Reason of HIS ENDLESSNESS, so that even the archangels are inferior in Reason to Beelzebub.

When all those present recover from this moving experience, the most venerable archangel gives a speech in honor of Beelzebub who, "although he first transgressed on account of his youth, yet afterwards was able by his conscious labors and intentional sufferings to become worthy with his essence to be one of the very rare Sacred individuals of the whole of our Great Universe."[14] Through his own efforts, Beelzebub has achieved the highest level of Reason that "in general any being can attain."[15]

At this point, all the angels and cherubim leave the Karnak and disappear into space, and the others resume their places as the ship moves toward its final destination. Beelzebub, "now with a transfigured appearance corresponding to His merits and visible to all,"[16] returns with Hassein and Ahoon to that part of the ship where their previous talks have taken place. As a result of the ceremony they have witnessed, Beelzebub's grandson and servant both feel remorse for their own low levels of being, and "by their movements and the translucency of their inner psyche, it was evident that there had been a marked change in their attitude toward the person of Beelzebub...."[17]

In this state of humility, Hassein is overcome with timidity in the presence of his grandfather. His humility also gives rise to feelings of deep love and compassion for the three-brained beings from Earth whom he has learned of through his grandfather's stories. Assured by Beelzebub that the tales about Earth will continue after they have returned home, Hassein is given permission to ask one final question of Beelzebub before the landing of the ship. Encouraged by the opportunity, he addresses his grandfather boldly to ask how Beelzebub would reply if HIS ENDLESSNESS HIMSELF were to summon Beelzebub before HIM and say,

"Beelzebub!!!!
"You, as one of the anticipated, accelerated results of all My actualizations, manifest briefly the sum of your long-centuried impartial observations and studies of the psyche of the three-brained beings arising on the planet Earth and state in words whether it is possible by some means or other to save them and to direct them into the becoming path?"[18]

Beelzebub answers Hassein with a twofold response. First, he says, the question is itself proof that Hassein's education is proceeding well and that Beelzebub's stories have achieved in him sought-for results. Then, after meditating on the question, Beelzebub responds in a penetrating tone:

The sole means now for the saving of the beings of the planet Earth would be . . . [if] every one of those unfortunates during the process of existence should constantly sense and be cognizant of the inevitability of his own death as well as of the death of everyone upon whom his eyes or attention rests.[19]

Only with death kept always in the forefront of their minds would human beings be able to overcome the egoism that has destroyed their Essences, caused all their abnormalities, and made them harmful, not only to themselves, but to the whole of the Universe.

2. The Commentaries

For several reasons, including the unique difficulties presented by Gurdjieff's writing style, little commentary has been written on *Beelzebub's Tales*. Bennett did extensive work on the *Tales*, giving lectures on them from the time of Gurdjieff's death in 1949 until his own death in 1974. A few of these lectures were recorded and published in book form as *Talks on Beelzebub's Tales*. The English critic Alfred Orage, a long-time student of Gurdjieff, played a leading role in editing the English-language drafts of *Beelzebub's Tales* between 1925 and 1931. Orage died in 1934, but C. S. Nott published close to a hundred pages of notes on Orage's numerous talks on *Beelzebub's Tales*. Although these notes were not reworked for publication and read like a series of random thoughts, they offer valuable insights into Gurdjieff's work.[20] A beautifully written and inspiring essay by French author Manuel Rainoird, entitled "Belzebuth, un coup de maître" ("Beelzebub: A Master's Stroke"), includes insightful commentary on the work.[21] Finally, *Gurdjieff: An Approach to His Ideas*, by Michel Waldberg, also French, contains a serious and thoughtful chapter on *Beelzebub's Tales*, including valuable excerpts from the private notes of Charles Duit, another French writer. Duit felt indebted to *Beelzebub's Tales* for the influence it had on his personal life and work, and he wished to repay this debt by recording his seasoned understanding of the *Tales*. Duit's notes, however, remain unpublished.[22] Aside from these works, commentary is fragmentary and often superficial.

Both Bennett and Orage had the advantage of being able to converse with Gurdjieff about his writings and to verify their understanding of his work. Bennett spoke with Gurdjieff for the last time one week before Gurdjieff's death, and their conversation addressed the topic of humankind's lost ability to make independent judgments. Gurdjieff felt that suggestibility to the written and spoken word or, as he also put it, the "readiness to believe any old tale,"[23] is one of the greatest tragedies of modern humanity. This type of inner slavery, he believed, makes obtaining Objective Reason impossible, and thereby destroys our possibility for a normal existence on Earth. In *Beelzebub's Tales*, this weakness is presented as a prime reason for the unhappy plight of humanity. Bennett uses Gurdjieff's views about inner slavery to suggestibility to explain the writing style of *Beelzebub's Tales*.

Bennett asserts that Gurdjieff's writing style is directly connected with his fundamental concepts of human nature and destiny. If we are to serve the high purpose for which we were created, we must free ourselves from any form of inner slavery. Above all, we must work toward attaining a capability for independent judgment, strive to acquire Objective Reason, and not live according to the ways that are delegated as right and proper by others. And, as Bennett observes, "suggestibility cannot be cured by suggestion."[24] He means that a different kind of writing is needed to counteract our tendency to act as passive receptors and believe whatever we are told. The style of *Beelzebub's Tales* makes passive response impossible. Without a determined decision on the part of the reader to make great efforts to understand these writings, without the reader's constant and conscious participation in the act of reading, little if any sense can be gotten from the *Tales*.

Recognizing this aspect of Gurdjieff's style, Bennett says, is the first secret to understanding his writing. As a defense against suggestibility, Gurdjieff piles obstacle upon obstacle to insure that progress can be made only by the reader's unwavering decision to overcome those obstacles. The point is, Bennett says, "When we have organized ideas put in front of us that our minds are able to accept, it is very hard to prevent this mind from being lazy. We say:

'Now I understand' and we do not feel the need to do any work."[25] Gurdjieff's intention is obviously to have the opposite effect on the reader:

> Gurdjieff's methods are directly opposed to all our comfortable habits. He was concerned to bring people to understand for themselves and with this aim always before him, he never made anything easy or tried to convince anyone of anything. On the contrary, he made the approach to his ideas difficult, both intellectually and emotionally. However hard in itself a theme might be to understand, he would always make it harder by incompleteness of exposition, by introducing inner contradictions and even absurdities, and by breaking off [explanation] as soon as comprehension had begun to dawn. . . .[26]

An important part of Gurdjieff's method of exposition is the use of obstacles to insure the willful participation of the reader as a prerequisite for achieving understanding.

When confronted with a work like the *Tales*, Bennett emphasizes, the uncommitted and "suggestible" reader is either forced away or forced to commit himself or herself to great efforts to make any progress in understanding. "The issue before the man who begins reading [*Beelzebub's Tales*] is not 'Shall I accept or not what is written here?' but 'Shall I even read it and in doing so try to understand something?'"[27] A conflict takes place in the reader, but it is not an intellectual conflict of whether to affirm or deny Gurdjieff's perceptions and points of view. Nor is the struggle one of whether to accept what is written on the basis of faith. Gurdjieff's writing prevents either of these responses. The casual reader, first confronted by the intimidating length of the work and then prevented from easily understanding it because of the difficult style and idiosyncratic terminology, is in no position either to agree or disagree, accept or reject what is written. The struggle that takes place in the reader of *Beelzebub's Tales* is with his or her inner nature: whether to take the easier path of giving way to the law of inertia, justifying the decision on the basis of the length and extreme difficulty of the work, or whether to make the effort of will required by the task of trying to fathom such a writing, even at the risk of gaining little or no understanding in the end for the invested effort.

If the decision is made to go forward and work through the labyrinth, which one writer describes as "a deliberate and rigorous obscurity . . . of confusing terms and tangential associations in interminable sentences,"[28] the reader is still forced to renew commitment repeatedly in the face of constant temptation to abandon the project. Gurdjieff's insistent style demands constant affirmation from the reader, and each affirmation results in a victory of will over inertia. In this way, Gurdjieff creates the possibility for the reader to strengthen will and create being. The ability of the work itself to act creatively on the reader is part of what led Bennett to evaluate *Beelzebub's Tales* so highly as a piece of literature:

In its complexities and obscurities like an alchemical text, in its humor and robustness like a Rabelaisian chronicle, in its breadth like a monumental work of historical analysis, in its passion like a sermon and in its compassion like something almost sacramental—*Beelzebub's Tales* surpasses all ordinary points of view. It belongs to a new kind of thought. . . . It is an expression of Objective Reason.[29]

Moving from concerns of style to those of substance, the socialist Orage considers Gurdjieff's conception of a normal human being. As we are, said Gurdjieff, we can be thought of as human beings only "in quotation marks"; at most we possess "a pleasing exterior and dubious interior."[30] But as Orage points out in his commentary,

> In *Beelzebub's Tales*, one of the implications is the conception of a normal human being. We cannot conceive of a normal human being by taking the average of individuals. This distinction between average and [normal] is very important. A normal man is defined in the book, but this needs to be pondered for a long time to be grasped.[31]

Certainly "normal man" for Gurdjieff is the antithesis of "average man," who is unconscious, imbalanced, and mechanical—qualities he considers completely abnormal. For Gurdjieff, normalcy is related to harmony. It implies a state of equilibrium brought about by the balance of intellectual, emotional, instinctive, and moving centers—a balance he finds lacking in most human beings.

Without the equilibrium that a balance of centers provides, a person cannot be thought of as normal, for that person's state is equivalent to being under the influence of a drug. Reminding a person of his or her normal condition if that person is under the influence of a strong emotion or is identified with a political ideal, for example, is impossible, as Orage reminds us. Both states are drunken states compared to the existence intended for three-centered beings. Even in such states of physical, emotional, or intellectual drunkenness, though, an average person may still have at times an intimation of a different kind of existence, a more coherent and connected way of being for which he or she longs. Gurdjieff calls this intimation of something better a state of "Organic Shame"; it is the condition of lower vibrations aspiring to share the experience of higher vibrations. Orage understands the state of Organic Shame as the beginning of normalcy.

Normal human beings try to understand the reason for existence so that they might fulfill their obligations in life. It is our objective inheritance, says Orage, that we should know why we are here and know it early enough in life to be able to act on the knowledge and carry out our cosmic function. Plants and animals, in their natural states, fulfill the purposes for which they exist. Only human beings behave unnaturally by living indifferently to their cosmic significance. Referring to Gurdjieff's Theory of Reciprocal Maintenance, Orage writes,

> Man exists for a purpose not his own. This includes all beings—animals, birds, insects and bacteria. Each species is designed for a certain cosmic use. The norm of man is the discharge of the design for which he was created—like a machine designed to do a bit of work.[32]

But we have become abnormal and fail to fulfill our design, and our unnatural living has become such a menace that nature has constantly to struggle to adapt so that existence on Earth can continue.

Our present abnormal manner of living has its roots in a system of education that lacks essential understanding of the purpose of human existence. Because of the emphasis given by formal education, says Orage, cognizance of the cosmos has disappeared from the psyche of human beings. Just as we are aware of the flora and fauna of nature and of the civilization in which we exist, "so three-centered beings should be aware of the function of the cosmos—the sun in relation to the planets, the Earth to the moon. . . . A normal three-centered being would understand cosmic phenomena and how he is affected by radiations, emanations and tensions."[33] Such an understanding of cosmic laws Gurdjieff calls "being-knowledge," which he believes should be the possession of every normal human being. If systems of education were to emphasize a knowledge of cosmic phenomena, believes Gurdjieff, we would find ourselves developing naturally in the direction of Objective Reason.

According to Orage, Beelzebub himself is the most significant clue to what Gurdjieff considers a respectable human existence. Although not human, Beelzebub deviates so slightly in appearance from Earth beings that he was able to exist undetected on this planet for hundreds of years. And although of a remotely distant solar system, Beelzebub's makeup is still that of a three-centered being; he therefore falls under the same laws and possesses the same limitations and possibilities as does every other three-centered being in the Universe. Orage is correct in emphasizing that Beelzebub's different origin is a technicality, and that we are free to make the transition from Beelzebub to human being, and to take Beelzebub as Gurdjieff's example of a worthy human being.

Beelzebub possesses all the basic attributes of normalcy that Orage finds highlighted in *Beelzebub's Tales*. He is balanced and is informed about the workings of the Cosmos. He has suffered and has learned to interpret suffering constructively, to recognize it as a cosmic necessity. He lives consciously and works unselfishly to lighten the burdens of HIS UNIQUE BURDEN-BEARING ENDLESSNESS; and through his efforts, he strives always to attain a greater degree of Objective Reason. Orage summarizes Beelzebub's commendable "human" properties as follows:

Beelzebub represents the ideal normal man. . . . He has the whole of human experience behind him. He has a critique of human nature. He is objective, impartial and unprejudiced. He is indignant, but capable of pity and benevolence. He has made use of his exile to lead a conscious existence, and has spared no effort to actualize his potentialities. He is what we might be. He is what we ought to be. In his talks he presents us with a method by which we may become what we ought to be.[34]

If human beings were to follow Beelzebub's example, the implication is, then existence on Earth might approximate its intended state. "Our planet, the earth," writes Orage, "is the shame of the solar system. It is the ugly duckling, the misshapen dwarf, the beast of the fairy tales. . . . The idea is that, if men could become normal, this planet might redeem the solar system."[35]

Returning again to stylistic matters, Rainoird comments on the narrative point of view of the *Tales*. Full of admiration for *Beelzebub's Tales* and for the "literary mastery" of its author, Rainoird describes his general response to the work:

> I feel the strong necessity, once having read *Beelzebub's Tales to His Grandson*—if I say "read" it is for want of a better word, for the work is much more than that suggests, like an infinitely testing trial, a substance both assimilable and unassimilable by every organ—to pronounce in the midst of my stunned astonishment the words "great" and "new." But as I also run my eye through the library of contemporary fiction, I realize that here there is no possible term of comparison, and that when it comes to "great" and "new" there is no book to approach it—what work of philosophy, science, legend or history? And yet it is our history which is in question, yours and mine, universal and personal.[36]

Rainoird continues his excited evaluation:

> What do we know of the meaning of our life on Earth? If G. I. Gurdjieff works within a literary form so that this question may some day occur to us, he does so like no one else. All commentaries past, present and future are mere pools compared with this ocean. We are actually dealing here with the disconcerting question: "Who are we, where are we going?", but strongly flavored according to an unfamiliar recipe, and with an accompaniment of cymbals and other sonorous and percussive instruments. In this recipe iced water and itching powder are also included.[37]

Rainoird makes interesting observations regarding the point of view from which the *Tales* are told. The remoteness of Beelzebub's home planet from Earth, Rainoird points out, is at the same time coupled with Beelzebub's similarity to Earth beings. Beelzebub is from a planet and solar system that lie at the center of our Universe and yet are unknown to Earth beings. His experiences include exposure to places and beings unthought of by human beings, yet, at the same time, he is quite like a human being. Beelzebub's physical appearance allows him to pass undetected on this planet for many years, and his three-centered nature is identical to ours. He can therefore be thought of as representing human nature taken toward its evolutionary conclusion. Yet, concurrently, Beelzebub views human nature from a remote perspective:

> This vision from a very great distance . . . this overview on the scale of our Great Universe engulfs any reader and bathes him in an extraordinarily clear light, so that far from blurring the details . . . it has the effect of revealing them all the more.

And this distance has a two-fold effect, Rainoird postulates:

> The greater the height to which Beelzebub goes, the more the confusion of our usual jumble of ideas is dispelled. What emerges is the opposite— we see in high relief what was previously screened and misunderstood. The high has illuminated the low. Infinite spaces have ceased to frighten us. . . . [Instead,] they become living transmitting matter . . . of which Beelzebub is a more and more conscious emanation, through his merits and efforts.[38]

We can accept Beelzebub as "a kind of standard or model"[39] because his makeup is so similar to ours; his identical three-fold nature gives him our same possibilities and limitations, thereby allowing us to take seriously his judgment and to listen attentively to his advice. Beelzebub gains our sympathy because his "sins" parallel ours; they had to do with his once having forgotten his place and function in the Universe. He has suffered, therefore, as we suffer, the unfortunate consequences of having forgotten who and what we are. Beelzebub, though, is distant from human beings in that he has far exceeded us in the process of retribution. While we remain ignorant of having even forgotten our place and function in the Universe, he has already more than rectified the wrong he did many centuries ago. He is therefore distant in an evolutionary as well as a cosmic sense. This twofold distance, combined with his likeness, is what makes Beelzebub as narrator so illuminating, according to Rainoird. Beelzebub's point of view is based on first-hand experience, yet expressed through an evolutionary and spatial distance so that, although what we recognize in his narrative is ourselves, we come to view ourselves as something familiar yet alien, understandable yet strange, observing ourselves from close up and from afar in one and the same glance. The overall effect of such narration, Rainoird concludes, is a disconcerting illumination about ourselves as a species. Our manner of existence comes to be seen as one possible way of being among others. The benefit is that we are forced to rethink ourselves as three-centered beings, recognizing Beelzebub as an example of our evolutionary potentiality.

Similar comments on the disorienting effect of Beelzebub as narrator are made by Duit in the excerpts from his unpublished manuscript contained in Waldberg's book on Gurdjieff. Duit points out that Beelzebub's long discourses about the planet Earth are all addressed to his grandson, a child for whom everything about the Earth is alien. Beelzebub is forced, therefore, to translate ordinary Earth terms into Hassein's native language and to simplify his talk to a level understandable by one whose reason is in the early stages of development. This process of translating ordinary Earth terms into the language of Karatas accounts in part for the elaborate terminology of *Beelzebub's Tales*, claims Duit, and contributes greatly to the disconcerting effect of the narrative. ("Telescope," for instance in Karatian is "teskooano"; "water" is "saliakooriapa"; "death" is "rascooarno," and so on.) Duit is correct that the distancing effect of the vocabulary is not the sole purpose behind Gurdjieff's involved terminology; but whatever Gurdjieff's objective, his use of "foreign" vocabulary contributes much toward forcing the reader to view everyday life from a fresh perspective. As Duit writes,

> [When] the reader quickly reaches the point of considering the earth words from the viewpoint of the inhabitants of Karatas . . . , [that reader] has begun to consider mankind from the outside, and from much further outside than when he slipped into the skin of Montesquieu's Persians or Voltaire's Ingenu. It is our whole language, and hence our whole world which loses its familiarity, and no longer just various manners, customs, laws and conventions. Like Montesquieu, and like Voltaire, Gurdjieff interposes a distance between the reader and mankind. But here the process is radicalized to the utmost. It is not our society which is made foreign, but the whole earth, its history and geography, the most common and ordinary things.[40]

Through his use of language, Gurdjieff "exotocizes" us so that our lives and everyday activities display their underlying structure. "Life could be different," Gurdjieff manages to say. "Things are not just 'as they are.'"[41]

Waldberg, too, is interested in Gurdjieff's disarming language and antagonistic style. In addition to his strong endorsement of Duit's insights about Gurdjieff's work, Waldberg's analysis of Gurdjieff's writing style emphasizes the connection of bewilderment to the phenomenon of awakening. "One of the unique virtues of Gurdjieff's books," says Waldberg, "is that they establish a distance between the real and all that is banal and ordinary, and show us that the banal and ordinary are actually deeply foreign to us."[42] Under the effect of Gurdjieff's prose, the reader cannot help but be bewildered.

Yet "to bewilder, baffle and disorientate are the paramount actions of the master,"[43] Waldberg reminds us, for disorientation is the beginning of awakening.

Waldberg quotes Gurdjieff in conversation with P. D. Ouspensky: "Awakening begins when a man realizes that he is going nowhere and does not know where to go."[44] When we find ourselves in a state of bewilderment or disorientation, we tend to be more open to new ideas and possibilities. At such opportune moments, some kind of action or intervention on the part of the master is needed so that we are not lulled back to sleep by everyday life. Waldberg asks, "How does the master go about creating a state of bewilderment in his student and then prolonging that bewilderment until illumination occurs?" The answer in the case of *Beelzebub's Tales* is "by means of paradoxes, contradictions, repetitions, exclamations, apparently indolent answers or even refusals to reply, and with many other unexpected means,"[45] all of which are used by Gurdjieff for the purpose of disabusing and then enlightening the readers about themselves and their existence.

3. Reflections

In the above summaries of the main commentaries on *Beelzebub's Tales*, we considered Bennett's and Waldberg's rationales for Gurdjieff's "antagonistic" style; Rainoird's observations on the relevance of Beelzebub's remoteness from Earth (coupled with his similarity as a three-brained being); Duit's remarks regarding Hassein's level of reason; and Orage's allusions to the theme of "normal human being" as embodied in the *Tales*. These writers offered a tremendous service by helping to break ground for our understanding of *Beelzebub's Tales* and to suggest fruitful avenues we might follow and explore in our own dealings with the text. As valuable and acute as their insights are, however, they only begin to unlock the riddles and unearth the riches of this profound and utterly unique literary and philosophical work. The task of continuing our exploration of *Beelzebub's Tales* requires a major individual and collaborative effort on the part of dedicated readers, particularly those who are well-seasoned in Gurdjieff's teaching.

We have yet to probe in depth the complex literary and religious issue of Beelzebub (Iblis in Sufism; Arch-traitor in exoteric Christianity) as Gurdjieff's choice of narrator. The highly significant choice of narrative point of view has remained essentially unexplored. So many facets of this enigmatic work invite extensive examination: Gurdjieff's use of symbol and figurative language; the significance of setting in the *Tales*; his style as a merging of Eastern and Western conceptions of art; and the relevance of Hassein as receptor of Beelzebub's teaching. And these are only a handful of the major unexamined issues in the *Tales*.

Those of us who have located our centers of gravity in Gurdjieff's teachings have on some level responded to and comprehended the grave existential significance of his metaphor of the river of humanity that divides into two streams: that which flows back toward its source, emptying into the vast ocean; and that which gradually filters down through the rocks at the bottom of the stream, seeping into the underground. The first stream represents the way of evolution; its individual drops of water, upon entering the ocean, retain the potential for evolving into higher forms or concentrations. Those drops making up the second stream bear no individual significance, but collectively serve nature by means of an involuntary process. As Gurdjieff has warned us, a crossing over from the involutionary to the evolutionary stream demands a "constant unquenchable impulse of desire for this crossing." In *Beelzebub's Tales*, Gurdjieff has passed on to us the methods for escape and survival. Unable to transfer to his followers his own "hanbledzoin" (personal magnetism created by being-efforts), Gurdjieff has left us with the character of Beelzebub to inspire us and to provide us with an exemplary lifestyle for a three-centered being. It is to Beelzebub we must look for guidance in our efforts to enter the evolutionary stream.

None of us, I expect, has been as fortunate in our upbringing as Hassein, who at the age of twelve, and with Beelzebub as his grandfather and personal mentor, is already deeply initiated into the workings of the fundamental laws of world-creation and world-maintenance, and is in the process of developing his Being-mentation. No doubt, we are given to understand, Hassein will reach adulthood having acquired his own "I," and with conscious labors and intentional suffering will enter the first stream, evolving toward the acquisition of Objective Reason. Most of us, more in character with Ahoon, are products of faulty educational systems that never taught us the meaning or significance of making conscious efforts or of undergoing voluntary suffering. As a result, we have stumbled through life under the Law of Accident, only occasionally, if ever, sensing the actual terror of our situation. But also like Ahoon, we may have lived for years in close proximity to the character of Beelzebub without having realized his full significance or the possible role he can play in our survival.

Only at the conclusion of *Beelzebub's Tales*, when Beelzebub receives the sacred and inevitable results of his supreme efforts toward maintaining cosmic harmony and achieving his own self-perfection, does Ahoon feel in his master's presence remorse of conscience for his own level of being. As Ahoon apologizes to Beelzebub for having allowed so many years of lost opportunity to elapse, Beelzebub looks upon Ahoon with "love mingled with grief and resignation to the inevitable." The "inevitable" is that Ahoon alone can transform his remorse and chagrin into an unflagging desire to avoid filtering through the bottom of the stream of involution into nothingness. He who, like a buffoon, has so frequently imitated the external gestures and mannerisms of Beelzebub, has failed to do the necessary work to develop his being as Beelzebub has developed his. Beelzebub's grief and resignation to the inevitable come from his understanding that he is powerless to make any efforts for Ahoon; Beelzebub can indicate the way for others only by means of his own worthy example.

Let us not repeat Ahoon's mistake—that is, let us not, like buffoons, imitate the external gestures of Beelzebub (Gurdjieff) while failing to do the inner (and outer) work needed to acquire ever finer levels of being and understanding. The greatest tribute we can pay Gurdjieff for his teaching and writings is to engage in our own lifelong struggle to understand, share, and apply his rich traditional and contemporary legacy, and not to treat *Beelzebub's Tales* like Holy Writ—final and fixed words, beyond the approach of sincere and sustained study.

Six

THE HOLY PLANET PURGATORY

The cure for pain is in the pain.

—Jelaluddin Rumi (thirteenth-century Sufi), "Ode 425"

As a transition from Dante Alighieri's *Inferno* to the *Purgatorio* section of the *Divine Comedy*, Dante and Virgil emerge from the bowels of the Earth in the last lines of the *Inferno* to relish and revel in the sensations of open spaces, the renewed tastes of freedom from the spatial and psychic restrictions that have marked the increasingly restrictive realms of Hell. Concluding the *Inferno*, Dante writes:

> He first, I second, without thought of rest
>   we climbed the dark until we reached the point
>   where a round opening brought in sight the blest
>   and beauteous shining of the Heavenly cars.
> And we walked out once more beneath the Stars![1]

The reader of the *Inferno* feels the same sense of abandonment, of utter relief and liberation, as that experienced by Dante and Virgil upon emerging from the realms of senseless pain and involuntary suffering that have marked Hell, experiencing once again the radiant beauty and mingled hues of the sky, looking once again at the stars. This sensation of escape from the meaninglessness of an existence in which all human potential has been fettered away in sacrifice to unworthy ends, and where suffering is necessarily endured with no inner gain, is akin in feeling to having received another chance at life—a chance we grasp as a convict might who has just escaped a life sentence. The subtle and not-so-subtle beauties of the Earth are no longer taken for granted; instead, all impressions are imbibed with hunger and through renewed vision. And we begin our reading of the *Purgatorio* in a state of profound gratitude for life and with a deep sense of inner conviction to respond to life as the sacred opportunity it is, resolved to live it as meaningfully and appreciatively as we can.

We find that we now linger thoughtfully over and savor the descriptions of the unparalleled beauty, grace, and fineness that we have to remind ourselves are but portraits in words of the everyday world, which in previous frames of mind we took so for granted as barely to notice; but now, having been deprived in our journey through Hell of all uplifting sense-impressions and of any sense of freedom of choice, we witness the same world through vision marked by love and reverence:

> Sweet azure of the sapphire of the east
>> was gathering on the serene horizon
>> its pure and perfect radiance—a feast
> To my glad eyes, reborn to their delight
>> as soon as I had passed from the dead air
>> which had oppressed my soul and dimmed my sight.
> The planet whose sweet influence strengthens love
>> was making all the east laugh with her rays,
>> veiling the Fishes, which she swam above.
> I turned then to my right and set my mind
>> on the other pole, and there I saw four stars
>> unseen by mortals since the first mankind.
> The heavens seemed to revel in their light.[2]

Dante and Virgil begin their ascent up the terraces of Mount Purgatory to witness and converse with "those whose suffering makes them clean."[3] Their movement is toward Earthly Paradise at the top of the mountain, a state of earthly perfection experienced by all who compensate for and overcome their sources of inner slavery: pride, envy, gluttony, lust, and all other forms of inner restriction. From that point, they can soar to Paradise and the Center of the Universe, to exist in the presence of a God defined by Love, Wisdom, and Power (the farthest point from the qualities of Hatred, Ignorance, and Impotence that identify Satan at the center of the Earth). Dante's Earthly Paradise is that place of liberation from slavery that Gurdjieff claims is achievable for those who can avail themselves of the properties of the "organ kundabuffer" and of all predispositions to its consequences.[4]

On the concluding page of *Beelzebub's Tales to His Grandson*, G. I. Gurdjieff confirms that the reasons for the second and third series of his writings was to fulfill a fundamental task he had set himself under "essence oath": to prove "that Hell and Paradise do indeed exist, only not 'in another world' but here beside us on Earth."[5] And the central chapter of *Beelzebub's Tales* is "The Holy Planet Purgatory," which Gurdjieff called the "heart" of his writing.

We can recognize some obvious parallels between Dante's description of Purgatory as a place (a mountain in the southern hemisphere) and Gurdjieff's planet, with the emphasis both writers give to external beauty and internal suffering. Beelzebub describes to Hassein the external conditions of Purgatory as "the best, richest, and most beautiful of all the planets of our Universe,"[6] from the surface of which the skies radiate a wonderful turquoise and the atmosphere possesses the clarity and fineness of crystal. The springs of pure water are unparalleled in the Universe, and the air resounds with the music of thousands of songbirds. Beelzebub's description, like Dante's, emphasizes the extraordinary natural beauty: radiant skies, an atmosphere of refinement, pure waters—in Dante's scenario constituting the rivers Lethe (forgetfulness) and

Eunoe (remembrance of good deeds), which wind through and around Earthly Paradise—and refined and elevating music, whether put forth by songbirds or angels. The external conditions of Purgatory are such that beauty and sustenance are available in rich abundance; but internally the residents exist, in Beelzebub's words, in the most "terrible inevitable state of inexpressible anguish."[7] Yet for both Gurdjieff and Dante, Purgatory is a privileged "place."

Dante's *Purgatorio* is called the Canticle of Hope, as opposed to the Canticles of Pain (*Inferno*) and Happiness (*Paradiso*). The law abiding there distinguishes the mechanical suffering undergone in Hell from the voluntary suffering of Purgatory. Whereas the law of Hell is "An eye for an eye," the more mysterious law of Purgatory espouses that "To be broken is to be whole." The souls in Purgatory understand the value and necessity of voluntary suffering as the means to a unique wholeness that includes a sense of selflessness. Virgil explains to souls on Dante's behalf that "he goes [through Purgatory] to win his freedom,"[8] that is, to win a freedom from baser qualities that limit his true human stature. The tone of hope for freedom permeating Purgatory accounts metaphorically for its physical beauty and the emotional sustenance provided through majestic song, as well as for the emphasis there on physical speed and freedom of movement. At the same time, its uplifting atmosphere is inseparably intermingled with anguish and remorse of conscience, states which must be undergone to achieve liberation from egoism. Entering the domain of Purgatory is predicated upon a soul's being in a state of penance and humility—penance associated with remorse for self-limiting tendencies; humility having been acquired through recognition of pride as the source of all restriction. The suffering that marks Purgatory, and upon which all hope depends, is consciously and voluntarily undertaken to correct tendencies toward misdirected or perverted love in an effort to move toward the state of perfection symbolized by Earthly Paradise. Thus, all suffering bears a reciprocal relation to the soul's "chief features": the proud bend under the weight of heavy boulders, wishing they could bear heavier loads; the slothful move without respite; the gluttonous fast from all food and drink—all voluntary efforts to achieve autonomy of self. Once Dante has moved through the terraces of Purgatory, participating in penitential suffering and attaining the level of Earthly Paradise, his most acute pain is experienced when he inadvertently catches a glimpse of his own face reflected in the pure waters of Lethe. The ultimate form and degree of suffering—the self's confrontation with the self, and with the ramifications of restricting patterns of behavior for the self and others—causes Dante an inner anguish so severe he loses consciousness. Only when he recovers and drinks from the waters of Lethe is Virgil able to announce to him: "Here your will is upright, free, and whole . . . Lord of thyself I crown and mitre you."[9] Dante has achieved inner freedom, dominion over self, by undergoing the intensive voluntary suffering requisite to synchronize his will with that of the Divine. He has voluntarily participated in the breaking down of his ego to achieve wholeness.

The Purgatory that Beelzebub expounds upon to Hassein is likewise a privileged place merited through conscious labor and suffering. Over the entrance to this Holy Planet is an edict that reads: "ONLY-HE-MAY-ENTER-HERE-WHO-PUTS-HIMSELF-IN-THE-POSITION-OF-THE-OTHER-RESULTS-OF-MY-LABORS."[10] The souls of Purgatory must have been "perfected to the required gradation of Sacred Reason"[11] to exist in a state of compassion and empathy for all forms of creation. They must have overcome, to a great degree, their sense of separateness from others to achieve entrance to the Holy Planet. And suffering is undergone on Gurdjieff's Purgatory because the souls there, although having achieved a level of understanding according to which they comprehend what is required of them by the Divine Will, are nevertheless incapable of fulfilling these requirements because of limitations in their natures. Their awareness of knowing what has to be done but of not being able to do it creates the state of tension in which they exist, a state which John G. Bennett characterizes in a lecture on this chapter of *Beelzebub's Tales*:

> To be able to have everything, but to know that one hasn't got the [necessary] deathlessness, the ultimate freedom, and to know that one cannot have it until one has ultimately wiped out one's separate existence and wiped out all attachments to worlds, because worlds necessarily pull—that is the state of tension and suffering that is described as Purgatory.[12]

Bennett's allusion to the "pull of worlds" places Gurdjieff's Purgatory within his Ray of Creation, a descending octave of worlds that accounts for the relative degrees of freedom and restriction under which we place ourselves, depending on the ways in which we choose to live our lives. The Ray of Creation is a scale of seven orders of worlds, each under a different realm of cosmic laws, ranging from the level of the Absolute to the level of the Moon, as follows:

World 1	Absolute	1 law
World 3	All Galaxies	3 laws
World 6	Milky Way	6 laws (3 + 3)
World 12	Sun	12 laws (3 + 6 + 3)
World 24	Planets	24 laws (3 + 6 + 12 + 3)
World 48	Earth	48 laws (3 + 6 + 12 + 24 + 3)
World 96	Moon	96 laws (3 + 6 + 12 + 24 + 48 + 3)

Each order is under its own set of laws plus the laws of the higher worlds. Thus, the Earth is under its own laws, plus those governing all planets of the solar system; it is dependent on the Sun for life and is under the laws that apply on the level of the Sun; it is part of the Milky Way and is therefore subjected to the laws governing our galaxy, which in turn is governed by the laws applying to all galaxies. With the descent of the octave, the laws become increasingly mechanical.

World 96, associated with the Moon and with "lunacy," is the world of ultimate restriction, comparable to the lower, most confining circles of Dante's Hell, symbolized by Dante by lack of motion, utter confinement, and dim-wittedness—epitomized in the qualities associated with Satan: impotence, hatred, and ignorance. We place ourselves under the excessive laws of World 96 when we give ourselves over to states of sleep and unconsciousness: forms of addictiveness, explosions of anger, and abandonment to the dominion of the appetites. Such manifestations of lunacy mark negation of all human potential.

The Earth is only once removed from the state of ultimate restriction represented by the Moon; and organic life, of which we are the most intelligent part, is designed in such a way that it resides under 48 orders of laws. For example, human beings require three kinds of sustenance in order to live: impressions, air, and food. Air and food are transformed automatically by our lungs and digestive systems, while impressions are not automatically transformed but require acts of Will, efforts at "Self-Remembering," to undergo transformation into more refined forms of energy. We live in ignorance and sleep and must make willful efforts to wake up. All of these are laws governing the Earth, working to keep us enslaved at a low sphere of existence.

At the same time that our lives on Earth are constructed in this way, with the Earth's laws and with the pull of the even more restrictive world of the Moon, we also have access to the influence of higher orders, which we can cultivate through efforts of Will. That is, laws exist from which we can free ourselves, as do restrictions from which we can become liberated, by placing ourselves under the different laws governing higher worlds. P. D. Ouspensky explains in simple terms:

> We do not know ourselves—this is a law. If we begin to know ourselves, we get rid of a law. All men live under the law of identification—this is another law. Those who begin to remember themselves begin to get rid of the law of identification.[13]

We live in states of subjection to many unnecessary laws from which we can escape by (1) overcoming our mechanical manifestations and cultivating consciousness, (2) denying the pull of lower worlds and responding to the influence of higher orders, and (3) extricating ourselves from the Law of Accident and placing ourselves under the Law of Will, a Law associated with World 12 and the Sun.

Jelaluddin Rumi asks rhetorically, How can I "break out of this prison for drunks?"[14] He is asking how to achieve liberation from lower worlds. To do so is the overall aim of Sufism and of the Gurdjieff Work, being, as Nicoll explains, the allegorical meaning of Purgatory:

> What is the way out of this prison? . . . to begin to escape from these 48 orders of laws governing this planetary prison called the Earth a man

must cease to see the final solution in changing external conditions and must see it in changing himself. He must begin to change his relationship to this world and in order to do so he must begin to observe himself and the world and work on his mechanical reactions to it. . . . Everything taught in this Work about negative emotions, identifying, internal considering, Self-Remembering, about vanity and pride, about making accounts, about imagination, about False Personality, has to do with coming under fewer laws—that is, under better influences.[15]

Spiritual evolution marks ascent up the octave of the Ray of Creation; Consciousness and Will carry us in the direction of higher worlds.

Understood in these terms, Purgatory can be thought of as the state of tension created by making conscious efforts against mechanical behavior and inertia. In its position in the Ray of Creation, it is a part of World 12, a domain which is under one-fourth the laws of the Earth (though still of the Earth, as are all worlds), the residence or abode of those who have established Individuality and are under the Law of Will. In the first sense, Gurdjieff's picture of Purgatory is akin to Dante's as a state of willful effort toward greater refinement of being. And in the second sense, as a "place of residence" of those who have created their own "I" through struggling against their denying principle, we can recall Virgil's words to Dante on the top of Mount Purgatory: "Here your *will* is upright, *free*, and *whole* . . . *Lord of thyself* I crown and mitre you."[16] The emphasis is on Will and Individuality. As Alfred Orage interprets, "When Will, Consciousness, Individuality are developed harmoniously and simultaneously, then, in the process, we are purged and may be released from Purgatory."[17] World 12 is midway between the lower worlds (24, 48, 96) and the higher worlds (6, 3, 1), so in Purgatory both understanding of the higher and pull from the lower exist, causing the tension described by Beelzebub and the anguish of not being free from the lower and fully able to engage in the higher. In this respect, Hell becomes the pull from below and Paradise the taste of above—appendage states to Purgatory, as Beelzebub indicates to Hassein:

> in the legomonisms about the Holy Planet Purgatory these two words express the following concepts: the word "paradise" referred to the magnificence and richness of that holy planet, and the word "hell" referred to that inner state experienced by the higher being bodies who dwell there—that is, a state of constant anguish, grief, and oppression.[18]

Once a soul has gotten through Purgatory, refining and purifying its being from the dross of the lower worlds, the same limitations to Will and Individuality, which inhibit acting in accord with a higher will, no longer exist. As Beelzebub soars further from the Earth (World 48) and from the Planets of Earth's solar system (World 24), as he visits and departs from the Holy Planet Purgatory (World 12), and makes his way to the Center of the Universe (Worlds 6 and above), he is visited by the host of angels and archangels who pay homage to his attainment, through years of conscious labor and suffering, of the higher Objective Reason that enables him freely to serve HIS ENDLESSNESS and to assist relatively uninhibited in the divine plan.

Dante's masterpiece, the *Divine Comedy*, written in thirteenth-century Italy, has for hundreds of years been recognized as one of the treasures of world literature. The *Norton Anthology of World Masterpieces* introduces the epic poem as "the supreme and the centrally representative expression of the medieval mind in imaginative literature," "an organic whole designed with the utmost symmetry."[19] As is well-known, Dante's emphasis on symmetry is connected with the importance he gave to numbers and their symbolic significance, in particular the numbers three, seven, nine, and ten. The *Divine Comedy* has three main divisions, with thirty-three cantos in each section, plus one introductory canto to the whole, yielding one hundred cantos (a multiple of ten, which is the number of divine perfection). Seven circles exist in Hell, with seven terraces in Purgatory, and seven spheres in Paradise, plus two of another type in each case to make nine (human perfection), plus one to make ten.

Dante's journey entails movement to a higher essence—the sugarcane to the sugar—and it is one that demands extensive understanding on the part of its participant. The outset of his educational travel is obstructed by the presence of three beasts, representing whatever characteristics within Dante prevent his moving toward the light of the Sun. Virgil, his guide, who represents Human Reason, underscores the theme of right reasoning as the proper guide through two-thirds of the spiritual path, after which, just outside of Earthly Paradise (a state of earthly perfection), Reason becomes superfluous and is superceded by divine illumination. The whole serves as an allegory that places high priority on correct and comprehensive understanding of the purpose of life as spiritual odyssey, and of the consequences of actions. "Getting into heaven wearing galoshes," as Gurdjieff claimed most people try to do or believe it is possible to do, is impossible for Dante. The only way to higher spheres is by traversing and gaining extensive understanding of the lower and of the whole. Dante cannot fully understand one realm without possessing knowledge of the other two, and the three taken together embody an entire cosmology. Understanding the role of voluntary suffering is enhanced by its contrast with involuntary suffering; the force of love and its association with freedom is better comprehended in contrast to the enslaving nature of hatred and of negative emotions in general. Opposites are reconciled in Purgatory.

The *Divine Comedy* exhibits several parallels with *Beelzebub's Tales*. Both have a tripartite structure with Purgatory at the center. The movement of the narrators, who in both cases are also participants and main characters, is from Earth (and nearby planets) to Purgatory, to the Center of the Universe. The fundamental nature of the cosmic laws involving triads and octaves is under-scored, as is their necessity in a cosmos that allows for growth, regeneration and self-renewal, and the overcoming of the consequences of Time. The physical descriptions of Purgatory bear resemblances, as does their connection to moral and temporary suffering. The role of Reason in spiritual evolution is developed as a central theme in both works. Of course, Dante's poem has long been interpreted as an epic rendition of the doctrine of the Catholic Church and of medieval Christianity, in which case depictions of Satan and notions of good and evil contrast sharply with Gurdjieff's attempt to break down dualistic thinking and to present Satan (Iblis, Beelzebub) as on the path and sacrificial in the role of antagonizer: ("Without Iblis, the world's work would wither away").[20] And Dante's emphasis on Love as the force that moves the world perhaps contrasts with Gurdjieff's emphasis on Consciousness (though knowledge and understanding are essential in Dante's scheme and lead us to where we are able to love consciously). Accounting for differences, when Dante's work is studied in a comprehensive and penetrating way, a number of apparent discrepancies fade.

What may seem a surprising realization—that significant parallels can be recognized between the epic poem of a twelfth-century Florentine poet, which we may fairly assume Gurdjieff never read, and a modern odyssey about space travel—is less surprising when we consider the impressive scholarship of Miguel Asin Palacios, a Catholic priest and Arabic scholar, who in the early part of the twentieth century wrote a work of catalytic importance about Dante and his *Divine Comedy*, even though Palacios is still unfamiliar to many Dante scholars. In effect, Palacios sets out to prove in painstaking detail that Dante's lauded epic poem, long hailed for its originality, is, in fact, a close imitation, at times a replication, of Islamic literary models fashioned around the theme of Mohammed's night journey, including his visit to the infernal regions (*Isra*), and his ascension from Jerusalem through the heavenly spheres to the throne of God (*Miraj*). In particular, Dante drew his inspiration, as well as his structure, a number of his ideas, and much of his imagery, mostly from one key source: the writings of the Andalusian Sufi, Ibn 'Arabi of Marcia, known as "The Greatest Master," who died twenty-five years before Dante was born. The "great epic of medieval Christianity" is, after all, fashioned after Islamic, and in particular Sufi models, borrowing heavily from 'Arabi's tale of his own spiritual journey in the footsteps of Mohammed, put forth in *The Book of the Nocturnal Journey towards the Majesty of the Most Magnanimous* and in *Meccan Revelations*.[21] While we may fairly assume that Gurdjieff did not read Dante, given his Sufi background and allusions to Sufism, Gurdjieff would almost certainly have studied the writings of Ibn 'Arabi, "one of the most profound metaphysical influences upon both the Moslem and Christian worlds."[22] Perhaps the parallels that surface between the *Divine Comedy* and *Beelzebub's Tales* have their common source in older Islamic literature, including the writings of Ibn 'Arabi.

Some have said of Ibn 'Arabi that when he spoke of human beings, he spoke only in terms of Perfection, not condescending to speak of them in lesser terms. As with his contemporary Rumi, he held that it was for the sake of a perfected human being that the Universe came into existence. Such creatures are the "Sought-after-Entities," the "Pillars of the Cosmos." Achieving this status, which 'Arabi called "servanthood," is not only the highest possible calling, but the "only properly human aspiration."[23] It is a position in which unique Individuality paradoxically marks effacement of separate existence—what would appear to be permanent residence in the higher worlds of Gurdjieff's Ray of Creation. The fundamental shortcoming preventing attainment of higher worlds for 'Arabi is "heedlessness of God," the opposite of remembering (*dhikr* in Sufism), and of Self-Remembering (Gurdjieff). 'Arabi chastised: "You have the preparedness to receive perfection, if you understand. That is why you have been admonished and notified by the whole world . . . . So blame only yourself if you do not receive that to which you have been called."[24] He claimed to have "inherited" the works, states, and sciences (knowledge and understanding) of Mohammed—in Islam the last of the 124,000 prophets sent to the world since the time of Adam—a visionary understanding which revealed to 'Arabi that no one after himself, except for Jesus at the end of time, "would receive this inheritance in its fullness."[25] Gurdjieff would have sought out and studied such a person.

Palacios's *Islam and the Divine Comedy* traces the evolution of the legendary journey of Mohammed from its original source in a brief passage in the Koran through its various elaborations in plot and episode, to its literary adaptations (including those of Sufi writers), to the story's finest Islamic artistic rendition by the thirteenth century in Ibn 'Arabi's nocturnal journey and ascension to the Throne of God in the footsteps of Mohammed. Throughout his treatise, Palacios methodically demonstrates the Islamic sources of Dante's epic, until we recognize that what remains of Dante in his work is essentially his artistic imprint: the words themselves (although, insofar as ideas, imagery, symbolism, and other details are borrowed, even the words are not always Dante's), the rhyme, and the inspired and rhythmic tercets. The rest derives from ninth- through thirteenth-century variations of Mohammed's journey, the most influential being 'Arabi's: "At every step of the journey into research of the Islamic models for the *Divine Comedy*, Ibn 'Arabi of Murcia was the key."[26]

The evolution of the Mohammed legends is divided by Palacios into three basic cycles, beginning with "simple, fragmentary types" and ending with "those in which Oriental fantasy reaches its climax."[27] The first and second cycles include stories that had been formed by the ninth century. The third cycle emerged later after a solidification of the earlier versions into a single story had been accepted as authentic by theologians. The brief Koranic passage from which these legends originated is the following:

> Praised be He who called upon his servant to travel by night from the sacred temple [Mecca] to the far off temple [Jerusalem] whose precinct We have blessed, in order to show him Our wonders.[28]

Around this plot, legends developed about the Prophet's nocturnal journey and ascent, and about what he saw and learned in the course of his visionary travel.

In a conglomeration of first cycle "simple, fragmentary" stories, Mohammed is awakened at night by a spiritual guide who shows him a mountain, which he is unable to climb alone; he witnesses six scenes of the torture of sinners, in each case the punishments being correlative to the wrongdoings; and he is then shown a contrasting scene in which people who died in faith sleep peacefully among trees. On the outskirts of Purgatory exists a garden which is "green with eternal spring,"[29] watered by rivers that are clearer than crystal. In later adaptations, the garden is graced by soft breezes, which waft the air with scents of flowers and the music of thousands of songbirds; it is lush with fruit-bearing and other verdant trees. Having journeyed through Purgatory, the Prophet raises his eyes to Heaven to see Abraham, Moses, and Jesus gathered around the Throne of God awaiting his arrival. Any reader familiar with Dante will recognize at once in these early legends the outline of the *Divine Comedy*, which includes the wild beasts that bar the pilgrim's way to the mountain.

The second cycle, also dating from the ninth century, includes variations of the aforementioned details: Mohammed narrates, and Gabriel and/or Michael serve as guides and advisors, but the accounts of Hell, Purgatory, and Paradise are more elaborate. For example, Hell is formed of seven floors marking seven tiers of pain. Mohammed, having traversed Purgatory, is purified by drinking from one of its crystal rivers, whereby he rises through the air holding Gabriel's hand ("Through space they fly")[30]—traversing the seven heavens, at each stage Mohammed speaking with one of the prophets—Adam, Jesus, John, Joseph, Enoch, Aaron, Moses, and Abraham—on issues of theological and philosophical import.

With the development of the third cycle, the legend had become crystallized into a single story and underwent only literary adaptations, gaining in embellished figurative language and imagery: the *Isra* and *Miraj* "become thematized in versified prose and even poems."[31] Palacios remarks that in this third cycle of legends, Sufi renderings of the story are noteworthy in that, while the Prophet had been the sole pilgrim and narrator in all previous versions of the tale, the Sufis replace him with themselves, or place themselves alongside him, an alteration considered heresy by orthodox Moslems, but justified by Sufis in that they recognize themselves as perfectible and on the path to perfection:

> To adapt the scenes of the [night journey] and ascension of Mahomet to a story of which the protagonist . . . is a man of flesh and blood was permissible (perhaps) to the Sufis who claimed to be able to attain spirituality to the dignity of prophets and whose aim in writing such adaptations was always a religious one.[32]

The Holy Planet Purgatory

This was an important variation borrowed from Sufism by Dante: placing himself as living man at the center of a spiritual journey that culminates in a vision of God. Again, Palacios remarks on the Sufi renditions of the legend:

> The Sufis or mystics were not long in arrogating to themselves the role of protagonist that had hitherto been reserved for Mahomet . . . . The Sufi, as a type of humanity capable of perfection by gradual purification . . . rises to such heights of contemplation that he enjoys a foretaste of eternal bliss in the Beatific Vision.[33]

One of Ibn 'Arabi's narrations of his own *Isra* and *Miraj*, which appears in *Meccan Revelations* (or *Futuhat*), is introduced with the following prologue: "I set out from the land of Alandalus (Spain) in the direction of Jerusalem, my steed the faith of Islam, with asceticism as my bed and abnegation as provision for the journey."[34] A young boy appears as a spiritual guide, and in his company 'Arabi embarks on the same journey undertaken by Mohammed. During the Ascension, the first guide is replaced by "the envoy of Divine Grace,"[35] who leads the Sufi to the presence of God. Palacios spends page upon page analyzing the intricacies of 'Arabi's description of the three Islamic realms and comparing points with Dante. For our purposes, a brief allusion to each will suffice.

'Arabi devotes chapters of his *Meccan Revelations* to descriptions of Hell, "represented in the traditional manner as a pit or abyss of fabulous depth," formed of seven steps, its ground plan "almost identical with Ibn 'Arabi's design."[36] The *Sirat*, or Moslem purgatory, is "the sole means of entering paradise," consisting of "seven enclosures beset with obstacles," where souls are "detained until they are purified."[37] Of 'Arabi's paradise, Palacios remarks, "it may be safely said that nobody succeeded like the Murcia, Ibn 'Arabi, in blending all previous conceptions into one harmonious whole."[38] Like Mohammed, 'Arabi, on his own journey, soars through the seven heavens discussing philosophical and theological issues with the prophets (the nature of miracles, the art of poetry, the creative influence of divine names, and many other themes that allow him a framework within which to work out his world-view). Finally, he reaches the divine throne, which he finds surrounded by nine rows of angels of different ranks, with cherubim closest to the center, all chanting "anthems in honor of the Lord and radiating streams of light."[39] Concluding his lengthy treatise on Islamic sources of Dante's *Divine Comedy*, Palacios says:

> Among all the Islamic thinkers, the Murcian Ibn 'Arabi stands out as the most likely to have furnished Dante with his model for the hereafter. The infernal regions, the astronomical heavens, the circles of the mystic rose, the choirs of angels around the focus of Divine light, the three circles symbolizing the Trinity—all are described by Dante exactly as Ibn 'Arabi described them. This similarity betrays a relation such as exists between copy and model. That it should be a mere coincidence is impossible. The

historical facts are these: in the thirteenth century, twenty-five years before the birth of the Florentine poet, Ibn 'Arabi introduced into his *Futuhat* plans of the hereafter, all of which were circular or spherical in design. Eighty years after, Dante produces a marvelous poetical description of the after-life, the topographical details of which are so precise that they enabled the poet's commentators in the twentieth century to represent them graphically by geometric plans; and these plans are essentially identical with those designed by Ibn 'Arabi seven centuries before. If imitation by Dante can be disproved, the manifest similarity is either an insolvable mystery or a miracle of originality.[40]

Palacios did remarkable work on Ibn 'Arabi and Dante. One important point he does not mention, however, is that, for all its elaborate intricacy of detail and design, 'Arabi concludes his own *Isra* and *Miraj* with the following: "So my journey had been only in myself."[41]

Gurdjieff adopted the overall framework of the Islamic *Isra/Miraj* legends as the literary structure for *Beelzebub's Tales*. On the ship Occasion, "its supreme command . . . entrusted to [him] from above,"[42] Beelzebub moves freely through the planetary world of the Earth's solar system (World 24). He descends six times to the lower (infernal) regions associated with Earth's laws and its lunar influences (Worlds 48 and 96)—descents undertaken for purposes of intervention, and for his own education regarding the psyches of the beings bound to lower worlds. While in these lower regions, Beelzebub studies the psychoses that manifest as revolutions, addictions, unworthy sacrifices, reciprocal destruction, and many other forms. When he gains pardon from exile in "that very remote solar system situated almost beyond reach of the direct emanations of the most Holy Sun Absolute,"[43] he travels in the direction of the Center ("Through space they fly"), visiting Purgatory (World 12), which is described in the same fashion as in the Moslem legendary tales: turquoise skies, air as fine as crystal, pure waters, thousands of songbirds, luscious fruits, uninhibited speed of movement, beauty external, and suffering internal, voluntary, temporary, redemptive, and purifying. As Beelzebub approaches closer to the Center, he finds himself in the presence of angels and archangels, seraphim and cherubim, who appear in a luminous pale blue light that illuminates "all the space of the Universe,"[44] singing songs of praise to the Creator.

After Beelzebub has witnessed the entire gamut of consequences of heedlessness and unconscious living, understood the fundamental cosmic laws and the necessity of voluntary suffering, and acquired through sacrifice a higher level of Objective Reason than the archangels—knowledge gained through his educational journey from the lower through the higher spheres—he is free to return to Karatas, as was Mohammed to Mecca and Dante to Florence, where the visions of each were (in some fashion) put into writing.

Whereas Mohammed was the traditional spiritual traveler in the first cycles of the *Isra* and *Miraj* legends, Ibn 'Arabi and other Sufis replaced him by putting themselves at the center. Gurdjieff, as might be expected, goes all the way by putting Beelzebub, or himself in the guise of Beelzebub, in the place of Mohammed; the sacrificial antagonizer of Sufism takes the place of the Prophet (though Mohammed and Beelzebub have a common grandson in Hassein/Husain). Gurdjieff's positioning of Beelzebub at the center of the narrative contrasts with Dante's and Ibn 'Arabi's placements of Satan and Iblis at the bottom of Hell, frozen in ice as punishment and as a symbol of impotence and restriction. Gurdjieff wants to highlight the role of antagonism in spiritual evolution and to annihilate dualistic thinking about good and evil as defined by traditional morality. These terms for him are relative to consciousness and only measurable by objective conscience: "Every deed of a man is good in the objective sense if it is done according to his conscience, and every deed is bad if from it he later experiences remorse."[45] Finally, Gurdjieff wants to ensure, perhaps above all, that we do not go away thinking of Hell and Paradise as places "out there"—a concept he ridicules through Beelzebub's narratives to Hassein about the Earth beings who associate these terms with either a place where existence is "roses, roses,"[46] or where "the whole atmosphere stinks like a skunk."[47] Heaven and Hell are appendage states to Purgatory—the pull of the lower and the taste of the higher, always here, right "beside us on earth."[48]

Seven

A SAMPLE OF TALES

A tale, fictitious or otherwise, illuminates Truth.

—Jelaluddin Rumi (thirteenth-century Sufi)[1]

As mentioned in connection with Sufi literature, the structure of *Beelzebub's Tales to His Grandson* is non-linear; its stories are most often scattered rather than relayed in single episodes, meandering in and out of one another like strains of Oriental music. As threads are picked up again and again, the tales acquire multiple layers and dimensions. This literary approach makes isolation of individual tales, with the exception of simpler ones, extremely difficult.

An overarching plot is present in the tale of the rebellious youth who was exiled from his solar system for upsetting the balance of functions there, and who must atone for his youthful errors through conscious labors. Within this overarching context are the stories of Beelzebub's six descents to Earth (the last spanning three hundred years), and these descents provide the source for many other tales of varying length and complexity. The small selection of extracted tales that follows is intended to illustrate G. I. Gurdjieff's use of stories as teaching tools—as vehicles for espousing fragments of his world-view and for expanding awareness by posing alternative "logics." The stories are summarized and paraphrased.

1. "The Transcaucasian Kurd"

A Transcaucasian Kurd (a nomadic Moslem living in Kurdistan) once set foot out of his village to do some business in a neighboring town. On the way, he noticed in the marketplace a fruiterer's shop displaying handsomely arranged fruit, among which was one "fruit," the color and form of which particularly took the Kurd's fancy. Although he had almost no money with him, upon inquiring about the price of the beautiful "fruit," he found that it was not at all expensive, and so he was able, with his last two cents, to buy a whole pound.

Later in the day, having concluded his business in the nearby town, and on his way home by foot at sunset, he sat down by the side of the road and took from his provision bag some bread and the attractive "fruit" and began to eat. "But . . . horror of horrors! . . . very soon everything inside him began to burn. But in spite of this he kept on eating. . . ."

In time, there came along the same road a fellow villager who, seeing that the face of the Kurd was aflame, that his eyes were streaming with tears, and that in spite of this he continued to eat what were in reality red pepper pods, the villager said to him: "What are you doing you Jericho jackass? You'll be burnt alive! Stop eating that extraordinary product, so unaccustomed for your nature." But the Kurd replied: "No, for nothing on Earth will I stop. Didn't I pay my last two cents for them? Even if my soul departs from my body I shall still go on eating!" Whereupon the resolute Kurd—"it must of course be assumed that he was such"—did not stop but continued eating his red pepper pods.[2]

The tale is explicitly used by Gurdjieff to warn would-be readers of *Beelzebub's Tales* not to follow the example of the Kurd by forcing ourselves to ingest Gurdjieff's book just because we happen to be in possession of it; for if the nature of the *Tales* is too contrary to our own, the consequences of forced ingestion could be harmful rather than beneficial. Of course, his drawing of a parallel between his literary work and red pepper pods highlights the provocative nature of his philosophy and writing style, underscoring that the book is not full of lulling reveries or for those with delicate constitutions; instead, it is palatable only to those who have an iron stomach for the truth. In those who read it, Gurdjieff warns, all of their "romantic images of their present lives or naïve dreams about the future"[3] will disappear. The tale reminds us that looks can be deceiving and that we cannot rightly judge the worth or appropriateness of something on the basis of appearance. We are also reminded by this story of a characteristic of human nature that Gurdjieff remarks upon elsewhere—the human tendency to value what we pay for over what has been freely given. The Kurd is determined to eat the pepper pods because he paid his last two cents for them, money he earned by his own labor. Even though the cost is so little, he is not willing just to throw the peppers away as he might have done if they had been given to him. Based on this human characteristic, Gurdjieff believed that knowledge—truth itself—must carry a price tag, whether in dollars or in labor and suffering. "I have good leather to sell for those who want to make shoes out of it,"[4] he said. The leather, the understanding, was for sale; some form of payment had to be made to purchase it, because we appreciate what we earn more than what we are given.

2. "The Results of Some Idle Fishermen"

The earliest ancestors of the beings of the community that was later called Greece were often obliged, on account of frequent storms at sea, which hindered them in their marine occupations, to seek refuge in sheltered places during rains and winds. Out of boredom on these occasions, they invented games, which they played for their distraction. Although their first games were simple, in time one fisherman invented a game called "pouring-from-the-empty-into-the-void," which came to be the sole entertainment with which they occupied themselves. This game consisted of one person formulating a question about some "fiddle-faddle" or other, about some deliberate piece of absurdity, and the one to whom the question had been addressed had to provide as plausible an answer as possible. Later, one of them discovered how to make parchment from the skin of fish, and afterwards some of these fellows began inscribing their lengthy explanations on fishskins and calling this form of entertainment "science." Hence,

> from then on, as the craze for "cooking up" these sciences passed from generation to generation, the beings of that group whose ancestors had been simple Asiatic fishermen became "specialists" in inventing all kinds of sciences . . . And hence it is that almost half of the Reason of the contemporary beings of that ill-fated planet is in general formed from the "truths" invented there by those bored fishermen and their subsequent generations.[5]

Though a simple tale, "The Results of Some Idle Fishermen" touches upon at least three important themes that Gurdjieff discusses at length elsewhere in his writings and in other sections of *Beelzebub's Tales*. The game of the Greek fishermen, "The-pouring-of-the-empty-into-the-void," is titled by an expression that Gurdjieff uses frequently to refer to any discussion, dialogue, exchange, or activity that is a waste of sacred time in that it is passive and unconscious. In contrast to idle chatter, or a "pouring-from-the-empty-into-the-void," the example at the beginning of *Beelzebub's Tales* shows us how to use time appropriately; that is, for the furthering of our education and the education of others. When Beelzebub is informed by the captain of the Karnak that the ship's passage through space will be unavoidably delayed due to the path of a giant comet, Beelzebub says that they will all pass the time in meaningful conversation that is productive and useful for all. What follows in the interim are all of Beelzebub's tales, beginning with Beelzebub's invitation to the captain to explain to them the evolution of space travel and the modern refined sources of energy for locomotion. The captain's discourse on the matter evokes in Hassein a sense of sadness, in that he had never recognized before listening to the captain that things have not always been as they are, but that "in the past certain beings laboured hard and suffered much . . . and endured a great deal that perhaps they could have spared themselves . . . solely that we might have these advantages today and use them for our welfare."[6] Because time is used to further understanding rather than to "pour-from-the-empty-into-the-void," Hassein early on comes to comprehend through the captain's instructive discourse that we are all under an obligation to pay for our existence.

The fact that the game in the tale of the fishermen is said to result in the formation of the sciences is, in this case, a comment on what Gurdjieff considered to be the inadequacy and danger of the modern scientific mentality, which functions on the faulty presupposition that if it can gather enough information about the world, it will ultimately be able to understand and then control the world, or aspects of it. But as Gurdjieff purports in the "Purgatory" chapter, the world does not function like a machine; it contains within itself the element of hazard, so that renewal and recreation are possible. No valid ground exists for making absolute predictions on the basis of strict cause-and-effect relationships; at most, we can make relative predictions, because processes can always change and take unexpected directions. As the tale of the fishermen concludes, our reason is influenced by the faulty assumptions lying at the foundation of science. Gurdjieff wants to say that we are better off relying on intuition and instinct than believing in our ability to predict outcomes and control results.

The tale's reference to the evolution of the fishermen's game over generations to the point where many of the fishermen began to commit their lengthy discourses to parchment, reminds us of Gurdjieff's comments in the first chapter of the *Tales* and elsewhere about the "extraordinary disease" that has afflicted modern humanity. This consists of "all those persons . . . who sleep with half-open eyes," and who, if "somewhat literate" and with their rent paid for three months in advance, "inevitably [start] writing some 'instructive article,' if not a whole book."[7]

In all of these messages, we see Gurdjieff stressing a regard for the sacredness of life and of knowledge and right understanding. Time is life, and it should not be squandered in idleness. Every occasion provides an opportunity for learning, and every opportunity should be seized to further our understanding and that of others. And we are all responsible for the validity of what we say and write. Persons with single-minded views of the world and the way it functions should not be in a hurry to display their fragments of knowledge, but should strive always to broaden their pictures of reality and of the connectedness of one area of knowledge to another.

3. "The Results of an Unwise Wager"

Once a young member of Beelzebub's tribe became mixed up in "a very stupid affair." He had come to be on friendly terms with King Appolis from the city of Samlios in the country of Atlantis. This young tribesman would often visit the king to discuss various topics with him.

The community over which the king presided, and the city of Samlios in which he lived, were among the wealthiest places on Earth. For the upkeep of their grandeur, however, the king had to require a good deal of money and labor from his citizens. And it was in the nature of the ordinary people of this community that they would never voluntarily carry out their required duties, but would do so only out of "fear and apprehension of threats and menaces." On the other hand, the king was conscientious about his duties and contributed the labor and wealth that he required of his subjects. But because of the nature of his citizens, he had always to spend time and energy devising new methods of extracting the money and labor that were their obligation. His methods were always reasonable, though, and for this the king's subjects respected him.

Beelzebub's tribesman was superior in Reason to King Appolis, but he lacked practical experience, and he began to feel critical of the king's methods of running his community, believing that the king was unjust to coerce his citizens into fulfilling duties against their will. When the countryman could no longer refrain from accusing the king, he expressed his indignation at Appolis's "unconscionable conduct" toward his subjects. After the two discussed the situation at length, the king calmly providing explanations for his "severity," their discussion resulted in a wager: for the obtaining of all that was necessary from his subjects, the king would be obliged to employ only those measures and means dictated by the countryman. If the subjects should fail to contribute all that was required, Beelzebub's countryman would make up the treasury's deficit.

Because of the wager, not only did the subjects of Samlios stop paying into the treasury, but they started stealing from it. When the situation became catastrophic, with no end in sight, Beelzebub had to be called in to intervene in the affair. When he arrived in Samlios and understood what had happened, he and his council decided that the only recourse was to reinstitute the former order in such a way that King Appolis would appear blameless. This was achieved through much propaganda and by placing the entire blame for the situation on the king's administration. And to spare the real administration from harm, they had to be replaced temporarily, under various pretexts, by Beelzebub's countrymen. Only after much rioting, the destruction of much property, and several deaths, was King Appolis able to resume leadership of his community and to restore the old order that had prevailed prior to the wager. Beelzebub's countryman, out of remorse and chagrin, left the Earth forever.[8]

One dimension of the story has to do with the limitations of the rational mind when not developed in conjunction with other faculties and with practical experience. Beelzebub's kinsman is superior in Reason to the king, but his theories remain untested by real-life situations; nor does he understand the nature of the people of Samlios. The king represents the outcome of a more harmonious development of faculties. His Reason may be inferior, but it is in keeping with the level of development of the other aspects of his self: physically, he does the labor he requires of others; instinctively, he remains attuned to the level of being of his citizens; emotionally, he is good-willed and holds their best interests at heart; and holistically, he combines knowledge, feelings, instinct, and experience to make the wisest and fairest decisions he can, given his own level of development, in his attempt to provide the best life and opportunities for the people. The contrast of the two characters—the one who has developed in a harmonious manner and the other who has not—provides a statement on the necessity for a balanced development of the physical, emotional, intellectual, and instinctive faculties in combination with applied experience.

Another of the story's themes is presented through the attitude of the citizens, who will only fulfill their duties out of fear. All human beings have what Gurdjieff calls "being-duties," or obligations to the Earth and to the future, which should be carried out as a matter of course and as payment for life itself, not on the basis of desire for reward or fear of punishment. Two lines from a Rumi poem read:

Out beyond ideas of wrongdoing and rightdoing,
there is a field. I'll meet you there.[9]

I understand this field beyond good and evil to be the place of consciousness, a place where efforts are made out of the understanding that they should be made, and because an existence constituted by conscious efforts is more worthy for a human being than one in which action is based on fear or expectation, a point also proclaimed in a story about the famous woman Sufi Rabi'a of Basra (d. 801), recorded in Farid-Ud-Din Attar's *Memorial of the Friends of God*:

> One day some friends-of-God saw Rabi'a running along with fire in one hand and water in the other.
> "Lady of the next world, where are you going and what does this mean?"
> Rabi'a replied: "I'm going to burn paradise and douse hell-fire, so that both veils may be lifted from those on the quest and they will become sincere of purpose. God's servants will learn to see him without hope for reward and fear of punishment. As it is now, if you took away hope for reward and fear of punishment, no one would worship or obey.[10]

The same attribute on the part of King Appolis's citizens is criticized by Gurdjieff as unworthy through the dynamics of his story.

Additionally, "The Results of an Unwise Wager" shows that the most direct approach to achieving a particular end is not always the wisest approach. People with inferior understanding, like the citizens of King Appolis's community, have to be appealed to on their own level. Appolis, a wise and benevolent ruler, has to achieve his desired ends for the benefit of all, not by relying on the goodwill or conscience of his citizens, but by behaving in a manner that their level of reason allows them to understand. When Beelzebub arrives in Samlios to study the situation, he makes use of the same indirect methods to help re-establish order. He does not gather the citizens together, explain the situation, and rely on their sympathy and understanding. Instead, he and his council make use of propaganda and pretense and achieve their ends through a long-term, indirect approach. Gurdjieff once remarked that to speak the truth directly to all people in all situations is pathological. Clearly, if Beelzebub had approached the people and dictated to them in a straightforward way what had transpired, the catastrophe would have been greatly exacerbated, and any possibility for restoring order would have been destroyed.

Gurdjieff's choice of means and method for preserving his teaching evinces a method of indirection to achieve results. He left us with a vast network of interwoven tales to be unfolded, decoded, contemplated in juxtaposition to one another, read aloud and silently, and discussed again and again, instead of leaving us with a philosophical treatise that distinguished and elaborated upon the various points in his system of thought. The contrast between a direct and indirect disclosure of reality is one basic distinction between philosophy and poetry, an indirect conveyance of truth being the general way of literature, as Emily Dickinson implies through her poetic lines in "Poem 1129":

> Tell all the Truth but tell it slant
> Success in Circuit lies[11]

Equating Poetry with Truth in a number of pieces, she underscores how Truth blinds the Truth Seeker if approached directly.

4. "A Partial Tale about the Causes of War"

A central theme in *Beelzebub's Tales*, which, as Hassein remarks to Beelzebub, "runs like a crimson thread through all"[12] his stories, is the subject of "Man's periodical destruction of each other's existence," or war. An entire chapter is devoted to this subject, but it is also a theme addressed in other tales. War is referred to as "the arch-phenomenal process,"[13] "the most terrible of all the horrors which can possibly exist in the whole of the Universe,"[14] an unimaginable horror . . . and hideousness,"[15] a "terrifying terrestrial question."[16] For the very purpose of understanding this unspeakable phenomenon, Beelzebub decides to make his sixth and last descent to Earth.

Having for hundreds of years observed processes taking place on Earth from his laboratory on Mars, Beelzebub noticed, around the beginning of Earth's seventeenth century, the development of more sophisticated weaponry, with the result that reciprocal destruction on the planet was greatly facilitated. This fact strengthened in him the need to make clear to himself the causes for this phenomenally strange process, which was exclusive to this planet, as he explains to Hassein:

> As I had nothing particular to do at this time on the planet Mars, I decided to wind up without delay my current affairs and personally to descend to [this] planet, and there, on the spot, at any cost, to elucidate this question which had always troubled me, in order that having solved it I might no longer think about these phenomena of our Great Universe.[17]

Several Martian days later, Beelzebub landed in Afghanistan for the purpose of studying war. This last visit of his to Earth spans three hundred years and takes Beelzebub just into the twentieth century. Much transpires during this time, and since war is the main reason for his stay on the planet, it determines many of Beelzebub's decisions about where to go and when in the course of three centuries.

On one occasion during his tales to Hassein about Russia, Beelzebub relates his observations on Bolshevism, in doing so revealing his conclusions, formed over nearly three hundred years, about the reason for which he made his sixth descent:

> "I was . . . many times . . . in the same community Russia, where during that period of the flow of time their great process there of reciprocal-destruction took place and the destruction of everything already attained by them, which this time . . . was called 'Bolshevism.'
>
> "You remember I promised to relate to you about the fundamental real causes of this arch-phenomenal process.
>
> "Well . . . this grievous phenomenon arises there thanks to two independent factors, the first of which is the cosmic law Solioonensius, and the second is always the same abnormal conditions of ordinary being-existence established by them themselves.
>
> "In order that you should the better understand about both these factors, I will explain to you about each of them separately, and will begin with the cosmic law Solioonensius."[18]

Beelzebub expounds that three-brained beings everywhere in the Universe await the manifestation of the law Solioonensius with impatience and joy, just as human beings await holidays. But while Earth beings await holidays (holy days) with impatience so that they can be more jolly and "booze freely," beings on other planets wait anxiously for these times so that, thanks to the action of Solioonensius, their desire for evolving and acquiring Objective Reason increases of its own accord.

The causes for the action of this law, Beelzebub explains, are different for every planet, but they are always related to the "common cosmic Harmonious Movement." On Earth, the cause for the action of this law has to do with a periodic tension induced by a neighboring solar system influencing and pulling on the Earth's sun. When the Sun strains itself in order not to change its path, it "in turn provokes . . . tension in all the concentrations of its own system, among which is . . . the planet Earth."[19]

The tension produced in all the planets of the solar system by the Sun, Beelzebub continues, in turn acts upon the beings of those planets, engendering in them, "besides desires and intentions of which they are not aware, the feeling . . . of religiousness,"[20] or the desire for greater self-perfection. However, when the tension reaches Earth and the sacred feeling is invoked in the inhabitants there, rather than striving for greater self-perfection, they interpret the feeling as a case of nerves and respond with what has become one of their predominant features: the need to calm themselves down, the desire "to-attain-to-a-complete-absence-of-the-need-for-being-effort-and-for-any-essence-anxiety . . . -whatever."[21] That is, they strive to eliminate the anxiety that could be used for their evolution. One outlet for this accumulated tension is war, although what is at bottom a desire to relieve their nerves and to avoid making inner efforts can assume such grand interpretations as a "desire for political freedom."

Even though these beings respond in such an unnatural way to the actions of the law of Solioonensius, Beelzebub continues, the terrifying process of war could still not take place were it not for a second factor, namely, that the objective conscience of Earth inhabitants, although not atrophied in their subconscious, in their waking state is almost non-functioning. Only because our conscience has degenerated to such a degree that it generally does not take part in our ordinary waking decisions are the tensions caused by the law of Solioonensius able to take such "abnormal and pitiable forms."[22] Beelzebub concludes his explanation of war to Hassein by saying that Earth beings could never begin to imagine that they themselves are not the initiators of wars, but that these processes proceed through a combination of their lack of objective conscience with a cosmic law that is entirely independent of them.

Outside the context of *Beelzebub's Tales*, we have records of remarks by Gurdjieff about war as recorded by P. D. Ouspensky and by Olga and Thomas de Hartmann—commentaries that reveal a similar analysis of war to that provided by Beelzebub to Hassein, but with Gurdjieff as direct commentator. That is, Gurdjieff attributes war to cosmic tensions, human slavery and mechanical behavior, and to the "Law of Reciprocal Maintenance of Everything that Exists." Gurdjieff replied with the following in response to a direct question by Ouspensky, "Can war be stopped?":

> Yes, it can. But the whole thing is how? It is necessary to know a great deal in order to understand that.
>
> What is war? It is the result of planetary influences. Somewhere up there two or three planets have approached too near to each other; tension results. Have you noticed how, if a man passes quite close to you on a narrow pavement, you become all tense? The same tension takes place between planets. For them it lasts, perhaps, a second or two. But here, on the earth, people begin to slaughter one another, and they go on slaughtering for maybe several years. It seems to them at the time that they hate one another; or perhaps that they have to slaughter each other for some exalted purpose; or that they must defend somebody or something and that it is a very noble thing to do. . . .[23]

Still, in spite of cosmic influences, if we were human in the true sense of the word, we would have the inner strength to resist even these powerful outside forces. In our present state, however, we are at the mercy of all outside impressions. All of our "deeds, actions, words, thoughts, feelings, convictions, opinions, and habits are the results of external influences."[24] In response to the question of another man—"How to stop war?"—Gurdjieff gave weight to this contributing factor of lack of consciousness:

> There is a war going on at the present moment. What does it signify? It signifies that several millions of sleeping people are trying to destroy several millions of other sleeping people. They would not do this, of course, if they were to wake up....
>
> How many times have I been asked whether wars can be stopped? Certainly they can. For this it is only necessary that people should awaken. It seems a small thing. It is, however, the most difficult thing there can be because this sleep is induced and maintained by the whole of surrounding life, by all surrounding conditions.[25]

The question of how to break out of this sleep and wake up is the most vital we can pose about human existence and is the one at the core of Gurdjieff's teaching.

In the lengthy chapter on war in *Beelzebub's Tales*, Beelzebub further explains to his grandson the critical link between the Law of Reciprocal Maintenance and the phenomenon of war. According to this law, discussed at length in Gurdjieff's "Purgatory" chapter, "there exists in the World [a] law of the reciprocal maintenance of everything existing."[26] Included in that "everything," is human existence. As part of organic life on Earth, human life serves a purpose beyond the scope of individual or collective goals. Organic life—plants, animals, and human beings—does not exist for its own sake, but for the sake of supplying the cosmos with specific energies. These energies on the part of human beings can be served in one of two ways: through death, at which time life force is released into the cosmos; or through conscious labors and sufferings, a qualitatively superior and more refined form of life force than that released by death. Insofar as humanity remains in a state of sleep, the required cosmic energies must be met through death, and war contributes to the Earth's meeting of its cosmic quota. But to the extent that we could supply energies through consciousness and intentional suffering, the number of deaths resulting from war could be greatly reduced.

Gurdjieff is pessimistic about the eventuality of our reforming ourselves as a race and bringing an end to the process of reciprocal destruction. Ouspensky records him as saying:

> Those who dislike war have been trying to [stop it] almost since the creation of the world, and yet there has never been such a war as the present. Wars are not decreasing; they are increasing and war cannot be stopped by ordinary means.[27]

Beelzebub also relates to Hassein a number of attempts over the course of human history when people came together to form organizations for the purpose of ending war, the most recent of these at the time of Gurdjieff's writing *Beelzebub's Tales* having been the League of Nations. As Beelzebub rightly predicts to Hassein, this organization would fail like all the others because such societies always comprise the rich and famous—beings in whom conscience has atrophied—and never those who have acquired Objective Reason and Conscience. Another factor is that those who serve on organizations such as the League of Nations are not aware of their limitations as human beings and "are interested solely in resolving questions that are incomparably higher than their Reason."[28] Beelzebub formulates his conclusion to Hassein regarding the possibility of halting wars on Earth as follows:

> For the moment, we can only say that if this property [reciprocal destruction] of the terrestrial beings is to disappear from that unfortunate planet, it will be through Time alone, either under the guidance of a Being with very high Reason or thanks to certain exceptional cosmic events.[29]

Gurdjieff experienced his share of the ramifications of war. His father was killed during a Turkish invasion of Alexandropol. He lived through the Russian Revolution and two world wars. Because of political conditions, he was forced to move his Institute for the Harmonious Development of Man from Essentuki to Tiflis to Tashkent to Berlin to London to Paris during the years 1917 to 1922. His response to this form of human psychosis says everything about what life can be as opposed to what it is, in its contrast of human nature at its most subversive and mechanical (the reciprocal destruction of human beings) and human existence at its most noble (the quest for truth and spiritual evolution). Gurdjieff paid no heed to political conditions, other than to remain aware of them so as best to utilize them to aid himself and his followers in their common quest. The ways in which he managed to do this demonstrate his incredible ingeniousness, resourcefulness, common sense, wisdom, and dedication to harmonious development. Ouspensky tells of a journalist's interview with Gurdjieff, which took place on a train out of St. Petersburg in 1917, and was later published in an article titled "On the Road." The journalist, on the basis of appearances, took Gurdjieff to be a rich oil baron, and asked him if he planned to make profits from the war. Gurdjieff responded, of course unbeknownst to the journalist referring to his life as dedicated to spiritual evolution: "We always profit. It [the war] does not refer to us. War or no war it is all the same to us. We always make a profit."[30] Ouspensky recalls of this nightmarish time how Gurdjieff's system of ideas provided a Noah's Ark during a flood of dark chaos and insanity. And Thomas de Hartmann recalls Gurdjieff drawing the analogy between the quiet areas on the ocean, which exist in the midst of extreme turbulence during great storms, and the calm "places," in which people can live during the psychosis of war.

In 1918 in the Caucasas of Russia, Gurdjieff created such a calm in the midst of the Revolution by leading an expedition of followers into the mountains and escaping conditions that would surely have resulted in the deaths of a number of his aristocratic students. Gurdjieff's wife was among the group; she had served prior to their marriage as a lady-in-waiting in the palace of the tsar. De Hartmann had performed as a musician before Tsar Nicholas II, and the tsar had intervened on his behalf at one point to reduce his military duties so that he could devote himself to music. Olga de Hartmann was an opera singer. And yet Gurdjieff managed to get these and a number of other students Bolshevik passports, identifying them as gardeners, teachers, workers, and retirees (while they were still in possession of their official "White Russian" papers, identifying them as musicians, doctors, engineers, and guard officers). Gurdjieff taught these people practically useful mannerisms that later saved their lives when they encountered Bolshevik revolutionaries, namely, to dirty their fingernails; to chew and spit pumpkin seeds like peasants; and to blow their noses into their hands.

At the same time, he applied to the Bolshevik authorities to request permission and funding for leading a "scientific expedition" into the mountains in search of gold and dolmens. Amazingly at this juncture in Russian history, permission was granted and the group in quest of consciousness found at its disposal all of the necessary papers to satisfy authorities on both sides of the civil war, plus all kinds of supplies for their trip: tents, donkeys, horses, hatchets, guns, and even alcohol (which they claimed they needed to wash the gold, but which was filtered through hot bread and potatoes so that it could be drunk, then put into bottles and labeled as medication). With this ingenious plan, Gurdjieff and his students were able to live calmly for a period of the Russian Revolution, undeterred and even assisted by the epidemic of human psychosis. And this occurred at the time when Anna Akhmatova was committing to memory poetry that gave expression to suffering so severe it resulted in split consciousness on the part of sufferers—poetry she did not dare commit to paper, under threat of death by the Bolshevik censors of literature, and which could not be published in Russian until after the fall of the Soviet Union. As Gurdjieff, his wife, the de Hartmanns, and others, made their way through the mountains in search of their "gold," Akhmatova composed "Requiem" for the physically and spiritually dead and dying:

> In those years only the dead smiled,
> Glad to be at rest:
> And Leningrad city swayed like
> A needless appendix to its prisons.
> It was then that the railway-yards
> Were asylums of the mad;
> Short were the locomotive's
> Farewell songs.
> Stars of death stood
> Above us, and innocent Russia
> Writhed under bloodstained boots. . . .

No, it is not I, it is someone else who is suffering.
I could not have borne it. And this thing which has happened,
Let them cover it over with black cloths,
And take away the lanterns . . . Night.[31]

What else to do with such poverty of life as reciprocal destruction but to convert otherwise dissolute, unhallowed times into spirit or art, to step out of history into being?

The longer and more complex of the tales, like this one on war, which constitutes an entire chapter, while meandering in and out of other chapters and tales, yields understanding relative to the reader's efforts, as do all the themes and tales which, in their interconnectedness, shed light on one another until what gradually begins to emerge is an entire world-view. Other major themes threading through the tales include our faulty understanding of good and evil, which keeps us locked in binary vision; the reason for humanity's division into masters and slaves; the catastrophic and multifarious consequences of our atrophied conscience; and the depravity of what we currently call "education" in contrast to what true education should be. As our understanding of one thread increases, others take on new meanings and dimensions.

In 1950, Gorham Munson, an American literary critic, wrote a review of *Beelzebub's Tales* in which he predicted that the book would "not make much of a stir . . . but I believe that it will endure, attract more and more readers and prove a rich source for future writers."[32] Gurdjieff himself said that he had supplied material in *Beelzebub's Tales* from which future poets would write epics. The *Tales* have served as a rich source for writers such as Jean Toomer, René Daumal, and John Fowles. The recent book edited by Jacob Needleman and George Baker, *Gurdjieff: Essays and Reflections on the Man and His Teaching*—a superb collection of writings by physicists, musicians, art historians, psychologists, and others—testifies that Gurdjieff's teaching continues to evolve and serve as a source of inspiration and illumination, helping to work against myopic vision and to break down the artificial barriers that separate one discipline and area of knowledge from another. Hopefully, this present book has provided sufficiently convincing evidence that *Beelzebub's Tales*, for all its difficulty, contains riches worth seeking out. Keeping in mind the place of this work in the Gurdjieff teaching is especially important.

In 1933, Gurdjieff published a small book called *The Herald of Coming Good*, in which he revealed his plan for making available his forthcoming writings, referred to as the First Series (*Beelzebub's Tales to His Grandson*), the Second Series (*Meetings with Remarkable Men*), and the Third Series (*Life Is Real Only Then, When "I Am"*). He specifies in this booklet that of these three projected publications, only *Beelzebub's Tales* would be made available to the general public. His plans regarding his other books were that the Second Series would be made available only to those who had acquired a thorough knowledge of *Beelzebub's Tales*; exposure to the Third Series would depend on a thorough understanding of his previous writings. He makes the following request of his readers:

> I . . . address a sincere appeal to all readers of my books to help me to the best of their ability in every way to carry out this decision, so that no one interested in my writings should ever attempt to read them in any other than the indicated order; in other words, he should never read anything written by me before he is already well-acquainted with the earlier works. . . .[33]

Gurdjieff insisted that his writings be approached in the proper sequence because reading them out of order could harm rather than aid our possibilities of self-perfection. Although Gurdjieff later withdrew *Herald of Coming Good* from circulation, his reasons for doing so could not have had to do with this appeal to his readers, for he includes a similarly worded request in the Preface to his last book, *Life Is Real*.

In spite of the importance Gurdjieff attached to approaching his writings in a specified order, his injunction has been largely ignored. After Gurdjieff's death, the decision by some of his followers to publish and make generally available his later works caused factions to form among "Gurdjieffians." John G. Bennett writes in *Witness* of how he was among those opposed to the publication of *Meetings with Remarkable Men* and *Life Is Real* because of Gurdjieff's straightforward instructions on the matter. Nevertheless, Bennett's group was outnumbered by another, and the sequence was broken by publication of Gurdjieff's later works. *Meetings with Remarkable Men* has since been translated into many more languages than has *Beelzebub's Tales*.

One result of this decision is that Gurdjieff's last two books, because they are incomparably easier to approach than *Beelzebub's Tales*, have taken the place of the *Tales* as introductions to Gurdjieff's thought. And even these two books are, more often than not, preceded by exposure to Ouspensky's orderly systemization of Gurdjieff's teaching in *In Search of the Miraculous* and *The Fourth Way*, as demonstrated by the fact that, in the literature on Gurdjieff, *Beelzebub's Tales* is referred to infrequently, while Ouspensky's books are cited repeatedly. *Meetings with Remarkable Men* is the most popular of Gurdjieff's books, having even served as the source for a Peter Brook film on Gurdjieff's life.

Studying *Beelzebub's Tales* requires real commitment and effort. Passive reading is impossible, and the writing style is often frustrating and antagonistic, raising our ire and prompting us to question whether the same results could not have been achieved in an aesthetically more appealing way. Consider Gurdjieff's statement in *Meetings with Remarkable Men* that he regretted too late in life that he had not given "the legends of antiquity the immense significance that I now understand they really have."[34] This is a strong statement on his part, and I cannot help but wonder, had Gurdjieff been able to manage in his already incredibly rich and remarkable life to study more of the legends of antiquity, whether *Beelzebub's Tales* might have been written in a different style, and if so, whether its purpose would have been better or worse served. An appropriate response to this question—one that Gurdjieff would no doubt have approved—is a story that happens to include his favorite Nasrudin:

> Nasrudin sometimes took people for trips in his boat. One day a fussy pedagogue hired him to ferry him across a very wide river. As soon as they were afloat the scholar asked whether the waters were going to be rough.
> "Don't ask me nothing about it," said Nasrudin.
> "Have you never studied grammar?" the scholar asked.
> "No," said the Mullah.
> "In that case, half your life has been wasted."
> The Mullah said nothing.
> Soon a terrible storm blew up. The Mullah's crazy cockleshell was filling with water. He leaned over to his companion and asked, "Have you ever learnt to swim?"
> "No," said the pedant.
> "In that case, schoolmaster, all of your life has been wasted. We are sinking."[35]

Beelzebub's Tales is certainly not "bon ton literature," but it does provide a lifeboat, a Noah's Ark, as Ouspensky said of the teaching.

Eight

WHAT HAPPENS WHEN A MASTER DIES? A REVIEW OF THE RECENT LITERATURE

> Poles apart, I'm the color of dying,
>   you're the color of being born.
> Unless we breathe in each other,
>   there can be no garden.
>
>   —Jelaluddin Rumi (thirteenth-century Sufi), "Quatrain 921"

A common array of sentiments tends to thread through and mark the accounts of those who have attempted to articulate their initial encounters with the teachings of G. I. Gurdjieff. Although the words and manners of expression naturally vary, such sentiments include: the sudden and unexpected shock, experienced in the regions of the heart and solar plexus, upon having made contact with the real, the unadulterated, the uncompromisingly honest; the feeling of astonishment at encountering for once, having come no longer to expect it, formulations unscathed by mixed motives, inadvertent distortions, or half truths; the sensation of emerging, ever so perceptibly, from the stupor of sleep, and, with the passing away of the ether, a clearing of the mind, a gaining of lucidity, a coming to consciousness, or to a state sufficiently marked by consciousness to assure of the possibility of awakening; and the resonance of echoes deep within, of truths somehow once known and then forgotten—echoes that murmur of the sacredness of human existence and that trigger deep longings to remember more fully and then to act upon that sacredness. And intermingled with these sentiments is the unspeakable gratitude for having made the connection, experienced the contact, and located the beginnings of a way to a more coherent and authentic way of being.

    According to the Law of Accident, that the sophisticated and powerful volume of essays, interviews, and personal reminiscences edited by Jacob Needleman and George Baker, *Gurdjieff: Essays and Reflections on the Man and His Teaching*, became available to us during the last years of the twentieth century (in French in 1992; in English in 1995; and in Greek in 2001) appears to be no coincidence. If Lord Pentland, longtime president of the Gurdjieff Foundation in New York, was correct in his observation, a segment of around twenty-five years marks a turning point in the transmission of a teaching, bringing it to a crossroads at which the life of the teaching either passes away, comes to its death (just as any living organism reaches its point of expiration), or is resuscitated, re-inspired with life "in accordance with the appearance of new pressures and forces in the environment."[1] The beginning of the twenty-first century, then, signals the end of the second such interval and the beginning of the third, in the transmission of the Gurdjieff canon, marking a little over half a century since its emissary's death in October 1949.

The significance of this timing, the questions it raises and responsibilities it carries, is addressed by the majority of the volume's contributors. We have arrived at an interlude for taking stock, a theme giving unity to the collection and evinced by the multitude of questions put forth. Some contributors address the matter of a crossroads head on, as does Lord Pentland in the above-quoted interview. Likewise, French sculptor François Stahly acknowledges: "Perhaps the time has come to take a long cool look . . . there may be a moment in the development of a teaching when it needs to be redefined. To be presented as something which perhaps will end and perhaps be continued."[2] And Polish film director Jerzy Grotowski exclaims with passion, "The burning question is, who is going to assure the continuity of *the research*?"[3] Others grapple with related issues: "How to struggle against dilution?"; "How to benefit from Gurdjieff's teaching today?"; "What happens when a master dies?"

A basic concern, founded upon an important component of Gurdjieff's teaching, links a number of questions regarding how to preserve the Gurdjieff canon from possible death or from dilution or distortion, while at the same time making it available to a wider populace and invigorating it with forces and in directions appropriate to the times. Gurdjieff frequently emphasized that no living organism, such as a teaching is, remains in a state of stasis; all organic systems are perpetually in flux, either decaying or evolving, degenerating or regenerating; but nothing living remains of its own accord in a stable state over time. And only devolution occurs mechanically according to the natural laws of entropy. "Each teaching is subject to the ravages of time unless great care is taken in maintaining the original vibration,"[4] Ravi Ravindra, physicist and comparative religion professor, reminds us. And the only countervector that can be posited against the mechanical forces of nature is consciousness. The "great care" mentioned by Ravindra can result only from individual conscious efforts, the matter requiring great delicacy, attentiveness, and foresight in this case being how to infuse the original vibration of the teaching with new forces and energies appropriate to the present era without distorting the vibration.

Philosophy professor David Appelbaum, in his article "Time and Initiative," discusses at length the significance of appropriate "timing" in relation to acts of conscious intervention to counteract entropic forces. Elaborating on Gurdjieff's interpretation of time (which lies at the center of Gurdjieff's cosmology), Appelbaum explains that, given the reality that all living organisms exist in states of perpetual flux, what presents itself as an opportunity for regulating the continual fluxion is what he calls "time's new dimension, originary time, 'timing.'"[5] "Timing is the essence of any line of development";[6] it is the means through which we can ensure the continued life of an organism. This is so because acts of human initiative that coincide with correct timing allow for the creation of forces that are able to neutralize or reverse the "destructive, destabilizing effects of anarchical time,"[7] resulting in states of homeostasis or anti-entropy. Conventional theories of time (constancy, cyclicity, cataclysm, and evolution) deprive human beings of the dimension of initiative, according to Appelbaum, placing "all human endeavors . . . *in* time the way that water is in a glass,"[8] thereby relegating human beings and their endeavors to a "time" of craving and appetite, decay and decomposition. Gurdjieff's understanding, however, allows for human beings, through a conscious mastery of timing, to become "co-authors" of the cosmic laws governing the results of time's flow: "Human beings can be more than unknowing subjects of universal law. They can, on occasion, be agents of prime law itself."[9] Appelbaum equates the rightful attunement to timing on which this realization depends with a state of "poise," the "attentive pause during which one's powers of attention are gathered prior to entry into the fray."[10] Through the struggle to achieve poise— the "lived understanding of timely action"[11]—we can manage to regulate organic processes, regain the dimension of human initiative, and realize our higher human nature. "In timing lies a special opportunity for humanity."[12]

The possible alternative fates of the Gurdjieff teaching, then, would appear to be few. Left to its own devices and apart from the benefit of careful intervention, it will naturally and lawfully proceed in the direction of decomposition, eventually expiring. To the extent that preserving the teaching in its original form is possible (which is different from preserving its original vibration, in Ravindra's terminology), that is, to the degree that we could "freeze the thing" or "put it in the refrigerator,"[13] as Grotowski refers to such attempts, it runs the risks of losing touch with the times, diminishing in relevance for a changing world, and "breeding people who are like farmed trout as far as flavor is concerned,"[14] an apt analogy offered by Michel Legris. The only viable option, then, for those who would preserve this extraordinary body of lived wisdom and keep it flowing along the lines of its original vibration, is continually and consciously to rethink, regauge, regroup, and reapply it; or, in the words of Lord Pentland: "It means organizing it; and re-organizing it; and re-organizing it, in accordance with the appearance of new pressures and forces in the environment, both from very high up and from the general environment."[15]

Pentland urges, regarding the possible transmission of the teaching, its reliance on those who possess the qualities of what he calls being "good caretakers" in the world, in combination with an intense inner motivation in their personal search—a combination not frequently existent in the same person. "Sometimes the ones who are most sincere in their inner search are rather invisible to . . . the public, because they sometimes avoid positions of outer responsibility,"[16] Pentland observes. On the other hand, "Sometimes the people who are best at organizing . . . sensible ones, are not those most serious in their inner search."[17] Much depends, in his estimation, upon the hope of locating or fostering impassioned good caretakers—those with the ability and willingness to function in positions of authority while pursuing with urgency their interior struggle toward transformation. "As one watches over 25 years, you'll see that doesn't happen by itself."[18]

Further direction is offered by Ravindra, who alerts us regarding the "twin forces of sentimentality and scholasticism,"[19] which tend to deplete spiritual traditions of their lifeforce: "It is almost inevitable that in any tradition the words accompanying the sightings from the mountaintop will sooner or later be reproduced in . . . textbooks and be read, argued about, debated . . . without the accompanying practice."[20] While scholasticism, "making big fat books about the ideas,"[21] is certainly a force to be on guard against, and one that has worked to fossilize and calcify the messages of other great teachings, allowing their adherents to maintain a safe and comfortable distance from a once active spirit, this force is probably the lesser of the two threats to the Gurdjieff work at the present juncture in its transmission, given the teaching's nature and relative freshness, and the manner in which Gurdjieff couched it in his writings and in the movements and music. Indeed, to imagine a "typical" scholar poring over *Beelzebub's Tales* and struggling to decode its obscurities is difficult, and even comical. On the other hand, it is obvious that those who have been attracted to the Gurdjieff work and have also pursued avenues leading them to, or through, academia and years of scholarship, are "underground" (a term used by Michel Camus),[22] meaning they are anomalies, atypical, out-of-the-ordinary people in their lines of work in the world.

Theoretical physicist Basarab Nicolescu, for example, underscores the absence of any meaning or value system guiding technoscience as "the characteristic trait of our epoch,"[23] and credits this dismal fact to the absence of genuine scientists practicing in the world today. By "genuine," Nicolescu simply means those for whom science does not automatically translate into progress and power, and who are aware of the seriousness of maintaining in themselves an equilibrium of knowledge and being. Those few who meet these criteria tend to be among the biologists, Nicolescu remarks; but they are "practically absent among physicists."[24] Nicolescu, the exception, works to link the world of theoretical physics to a larger value system provided in part by Gurdjieff's philosophy of nature.

And psychologist and pioneer family therapist Robin Skynner acknowledges having twice denied P. D. Ouspensky's account of the Gurdjieff teaching presented in *In Search of the Miraculous* even a cursory reading because he was put off by cosmological ideas. Only after undergoing a scientifically supervised LSD experiment—which resulted in a life-altering experience of a profound and fundamental truth (a "sense of the universe as being ordered and comprised of many levels" and a realization that "everything is exactly like it is, only more so"), as well as in heightened perceptions over a period of two weeks ("the flint-embedded walls of a local church appearing encrusted with sparkling jewels")[25]—did Skynner take up Ouspensky's book a third time with the intention of reading it seriously. Now years later, he works to sort through and flesh out modern psychological theories with the help of Gurdjieff's understanding.

And we could hardly regard as "typical," internist and heart specialist William J. Welch, who has served as president of the New York Gurdjieff Foundation since the death of Lord Pentland. Welch describes how he was wrested from what he came to perceive as the tedious world of Madison Avenue, as well as from his own skepticism that "nothing really made sense and there was no place to turn,"[26] and from a milieu of people who thought of consciousness as something "you lost when you took ether or were hit on the head."[27] He found a new understanding of the meaning of the "examined life," which he acquired through his contact with its living exemplar, Alfred Orage. Welch witnessed Orage's self-abnegating lifestyle, adopted voluntarily after giving up a prestigious and influential position at the center of London's literati for the purpose of furthering the teaching and working to support its continuation at Gurdjieff's Institute in France. Welch records that the conviction and devotion of the extraordinary Orage, "bearing down with such precision and clarity on the meaning and aim of existence . . . was to defeat my natural skepticism."[28] Welch responded to the sincerity at the heart of this teaching, which insisted that he verify or disprove for himself everything it claimed. Later on, he entered medical school and pursued the life of an internist (including serving as president of the New York Heart Association), while Gurdjieff remained "a light over my shoulder . . . throwing into focus the noise and fury of an upside down world."[29] When Gurdjieff makes his way into alcoves carved out in combination with scholastic endeavors, the people, and often the circumstances, tend to be unusual and worthy of stories to be told.

On the other hand, the force of sentimentality does pose a significant threat to the quality of actualization and transmission of this body of knowledge, at this juncture in time as well as at any other; especially if we consider as among its manifestations states of "identification" and "imagination." These two terms and concepts—"identifying" and "imagining"—require serious long-term study in order to be grasped and understood as Gurdjieff used them, being part of his unique vocabulary and carrying different senses and meanings in his context than in their everyday use. Succinctly put, states of identification are the chief obstacles to Self-Remembering, and we can and do identify with virtually anything under the sun: with our roles vis-à-vis others, for example, such as that of spouse or parent; with a position held in the work world; or with a religion, a philosophy, or a country. And most critical, because most difficult to recognize, is our identification with ourselves, with the self-images that come to mind when we refer to ourselves as "I." A passage from Farid-Ud-Din Attar's Sufi tale *Conference of the Birds*, quoted in this collection by Jean-Claude Carriere, offers a helpful illustration of what Gurdjieff meant by identifying: Attar said to the birds, "when they were impatient to soar across the seven valleys, 'Everything that stops you becomes your idol.'"[30] All of our temporary idols are those things in life with which we identify.

Imagination, another state that keeps us from authenticity and inner freedom, likewise assumes myriad forms, but basically manifests as the fanciful opinions we have of our own abilities to do, to be, to evoke change; the glorified notions we hold of the "progress" we are making or are capable of making in our efforts at transformation. "In general, we live in a fantasy world of our own making,"[31] Ravindra writes. He is describing imagination. Identification keeps us from developing an authentic self, in that we substitute in its place so many false impersonators; imagination keeps us from that self to the extent that we think we already possess it, or are well on our way to possessing it.

The Gurdjieff Work demands years of self-observation and self-study, with the objective of creating something real in the place of many phantoms, fantasies, and illusions. René Zuber, speaking with genuine gratitude toward Gurdjieff, was able to record in his notebook, after what must have been some years of effort and inner struggle: "What did Gurdjieff cure me of? Of imagination. He cured me of imagining my own life instead of living it."[32] Expressions of gratitude to Gurdjieff frequently take such form: He helped me to recognize the illusory so I could begin to recognize the real. The possible threat to the quality of manifestation and transmission of this teaching, which falls under the category of "sentimentality," is ironically in the temptation to substitute Gurdjieff in place of the other sources of identification we have managed to recognize in ourselves and eradicate. It lies in identifying with the man himself and defining ourselves in relation to his teaching. This is a hazard against which Gurdjieff warned: "He did not want you to identify with him,"[33] Michel Conge recalls, and those attracted to his teaching must guard against this eventuality (just as we must guard against identifying with anything whatsoever). "Only when an individual is ready to give up his most intimate attachment, Needleman writes, "is he free to receive something indescribably glorious."[34] That glorious "something" is the germination of a self—defined by nothing from the outside and identified with no one. In a worthy tribute to Gurdjieff, Michel Camus writes: "Here and there, in the underground, a man identified himself with nothing. Gurdjieff was one such."[35]

To identify with Gurdjieff, then, to deify him and sanctify his teaching, is to betray everything this "remarkable man" (in his sense of those words) lived and stood for. And above all, we should avoid committing this form of treason,

Conge warns: "It would be wrong of us . . . to betray him by making a god out of him. We must not make his teaching into a new religion."[36] The ways to avoid betrayal are two. First, to remember always that the teaching is founded upon critical thinking, the necessity of calling everything into question, verifying everything for ourselves. And that includes calling Gurdjieff into question: "Do not believe. Do not believe what I tell you. Find out for yourself,"[37] Dorothea Dooling recalls him saying. This insistence gives the teaching its integrity, and whenever we fail to remember and apply his injunction, we lapse into states of bad faith. The second essential point that must be kept vigilantly in mind is that Gurdjieff and the knowledge he brought are a "bridge" to the quality of existence we seek and not the end of the search. "He is . . . a bridge thrown down between ourselves and the world of objective reality," says Conge.[38] If we can internalize this fact—that he is not the destination—so that we do not allow him to become the "idol" that stops us in our journey across the seven valleys; and if we can combine this understanding with the other—that everything along the way must be verified, including this teaching—then the spirit of Gurdjieff and his work can continue to live through us and our endeavors. Grotowski perceives Gurdjieff's work in this sense of its open-endedness: "In a certain way, he was doing a scientific work in order to understand"; "His experience . . . established a foundation in which there were still many holes, things not resolved, things to uncover, to understand on many levels."[39] With the above qualifications as our credentials—that we recognize the work as one of continuous creation, and that we do not identify with Gurdjieff and become fixated along the way of the journey—we can enter into the excavating work as fellow archaeologists, fellow researchers in the field of objective science.

Where does all this leave us after more than a fifty-year juncture in the transmission of the teaching since the death of Gurdjieff? What, after all, does happen when a master dies? How are we to respond to such questions as that addressed to Michel Legris: "But can his teaching—if there is a teaching—survive him?"[40] Or to that posed by François Stahly: "Can he respond to the problems of today? Or is this just a historical phenomenon of the beginning of the century?"[41] For most of those who have devoted years of their lives to the study of this work, a recognition comes over time, which at some point crystallizes into a recognizable fact: the death of a great man is not tantamount to the death of the life force set in motion by his presence and actions in life; Gurdjieff's physical death does not preclude our knowing him. The majority of writers presented in this volume never met Gurdjieff in the flesh; yet they came to know him in a profound sense. Jean-Claude Carriere writes: "It seems to me . . . that the Gurdjieff I never knew can, if I so wish, accompany me in many ways."[42] Jacques LaCarriere lightly distinguishes in passing: "Meeting you, or rather meeting your shadow . . . I came strongly under the influence of your teaching."⁴³ And Arnaud Desjardins straightforwardly affirms: "Gurdjieff is always present in my life."⁴⁴ Clearly, we can come to know a "living" Gurdjieff in a real sense, and he can continue to exert his influence as master—along the lines of the example offered by Michel Random, of Nobel Prize winner Abdas Salam, who attributed his reception of the distinguished award to his Master, Jelaluddin Rumi.⁴⁵

NOTES

Chapter One

1. G. I. Gurdjieff, *Meetings with Remarkable Men* (New York: Dutton, 1969), p. 57.
2. *Ibid.*
3. *Ibid.*, p. 42.
4. *Ibid.*, p. 39.
5. *Ibid.*, p. 31.
6. G. I. Gurdjieff, *Life Is Real, Only Then, When "I Am"* (New York: Triangle Editions, 1975), p. 18.
7. John G. Bennett, *Gurdjieff: Making a New World* (New York: Harper & Row, 1973), pp. 49–50.
8. G. I. Gurdjieff, quoted in Bennett, *Gurdjieff: Making a New World*, p. 270.
9. *Ibid.*
10. G. I. Gurdjieff, *Views from the Real World: Early Talks of Gurdjieff in Moscow* (New York: Dutton, 1973), p. 194.
11. *Ibid.*, p. 273.
12. C. S. Nott, *Teachings of Gurdjieff: The Journal of a Pupil* (York Beach, Maine: Samuel Weiser, 1962), p. 82.
13. G. I. Gurdjieff, quoted in Bennett, *Gurdjieff: Making a New World*, p. 165.
14. James Webb, *The Harmonious Circle: The Lives and Work of G. I. Gurdjieff, P. D. Ouspensky, and Their Followers* (New York: G. P. Putnam's Sons, 1980), p. 557.
15. James Moore, *Gurdjieff and Mansfield* (London: Routledge & Kegan Paul, 1980), p. 222.
16. G. I. Gurdjieff, quoted in Bennett, *Gurdjieff: Making a New World*, p. 169.
17. Webb, *The Harmonious Circle*, p. 196.
18. *Ibid.*, p. 369.
19. John G. Bennett, *Witness: The Story of a Search* (Charlestown, West Virginia: Claymont Communications, 1983), p. 253.
20. Moore, *Gurdjieff and Mansfield*, p. 191.
21. John G. Bennett and Elizabeth Bennett, *Idiots in Paris: Diaries of J. G. Bennett and Elizabeth Bennett* (Gloucestershire, England: Coombe Springs Press, 1980), p. ix.
22. *Ibid.*, p. 86.
23. Interview with Jerzy Grotowski, in Moore, *Gurdjieff and Mansfield*, p. 95.
24. Kathleen Riordan Speeth, *The Gurdjieff Work* (Berkeley: And/Or Press, 1976), p. 100.
25. Michel Waldberg, *Gurdjieff: An Approach to His Ideas*, trans. Steve Cox (London: Routledge & Kegan Paul, 1981), p. ix.
26. G. I. Gurdjieff, quoted in Bennett, *Witness*, p. 380.

Chapter Two

1. G. I. Gurdjieff, *Meetings with Remarkable Men* (New York: Dutton, 1969), p. vii.
2. John G. Bennett, *Gurdjieff: Making a New World* (New York: Harper & Row, 1973), p. 85.

3. *Ibid.*, p. 278.
4. G. I. Gurdjieff, *The Herald of Coming Good: First Appeal to Contemporary Humanity* (New York: Weiser, 1971), p. 13.
5. Bennett, *Gurdjieff: Making a New World*, p. 93.
6. G. I. Gurdjieff, *Views from the Real World: Early Talks of Gurdjieff in Moscow* (New York: Dutton, 1973), p. 275.
7. Bennett, *Gurdjieff: Making a New World*, p. 135.
8. G. I. Gurdjieff, *Beelzebub's Tales to His Grandson* (New York: Dutton, 1973), pp. 306–307.
9. Translated by Bennett, *Gurdjieff: Making a New World*, p. 181.
10. Eva de Vitray-Meyerovitch, *Rumi and Sufism*, trans. Simone Fattal (Post-Apollo Press: Sausalito, California, 1987), p. 43.
11. *Ibid.*, p. 44.
12. *Ibid.*, p. 49.
13. *Ibid.*, p. 52.
14. P. D. Ouspensky, *In Search of the Miraculous* (New York: Harcourt, Brace, & World, 1949), pp. 382–383.
15. Thomas de Hartmann and Olga de Hartmann, *Our Life with Mr. Gurdjieff* (New York: Harper & Row, 1983), p. 102.
16. De Vitray-Meyerovitch, *Rumi and Sufism*, pp. 44–46.
17. De Hartmann and de Hartmann, *Our Life with Mr. Gurdjieff*, p. vi.
18. *Ibid.*, p. 101.
19. Ouspensky, *In Search of the Miraculous*, p. 385.
20. G. I. Gurdjieff, quoted in Bennett, *Gurdjieff: Making a New World*, p. 155.
21. Martin Lings, *What Is Sufism?* (Berkeley: University of California Press, 1977), p. 15.
22. Martin Lings, *A Sufi Saint in the Twentieth Century: Shaikh Ahmad al-Alawi, His Spititual Heritage and Legacy* (Los Angeles: University of California Press, 1973), p. 39.
23. Idries Shah, *The Way of the Sufi* (New York: Dutton, 1970), p. 190.
24. *Ibid.*, p. 125.
25. Frithjof Schuon, *Sufism: Veil and Quintessence*, trans. William Stoddart (London: Allen and Unwin, 1963), p. 47.
26. Javad Nurbakhsh, *Jesus in the Eyes of the Sufis*, trans. Terry Graham, Leonard Lewisohn, and Hamid Mashkuri (London: Khaniqahi-Nimatullahi Publications, 1992), p. 7.
27. *Ibid.*, pp. 34–35.
28. Rumi, "Quatrain 91," in *Open Secret: Versions of Rumi*, trans. John Moyne and Coleman Barks (Putney, Vermont: Threshold Books, 1984), p. 7.
29. De Vitray-Meyerovitch, *Rumi and Sufism*, p. 117.
30. Lings, *A Sufi Saint in the Twentieth Century*, p. 35.
31. Rumi, "Quatrain 91," in *Open Secret*, p. 7.
32. Gurdjieff, *Meetings with Remarkable Men*, p. 135.
33. *Ibid.*, p. 227.
34. *Ibid.*
35. Bennett, *Gurdjieff: Making a New World*, p. 27.
36. Shah, *The Way of the Sufi*, p. 40.
37. John G. Bennett, *Witness: The Story of a Search* (Charlestown, West Virginia: Claymont Communications, 1983), pp. 355–363.

38. Gurdjieff, *Meetings with Remarkable Men*, p. 46.
39. Idries Shah, *The Exploits of the Incomparable Mulla Nasrudin* (New York: Dutton, 1971), p. 9.
40. Gurdjieff, *Beelzebub's Tales*, p. 57.
41. *Ibid.*, p. 23.
42. *Ibid.*, p. 57.
43. Michel Waldberg, *Gurdjieff: An Approach to His Ideas*, trans. Steve Cox (London: Routledge & Kegan Paul, 1981), p. 12.
44. Adapted from Shah, *The Exploits*, pp. 26, 28.
45. Idries Shah, *Special Illumination: The Sufi Use of Humour* (London: Octagon, 1977), p. 7.
46. André Breton, quoted in Waldberg, *Gurdjieff*, p. 8.
47. Waldberg, *Gurdjieff*, p. 9.
48. Idries Shah, "The Teaching Story: Observations on the Folklore of our 'Modern' Thought," in *The Elephant in the Dark and Other Writings on the Diffusion of Sufi Ideas in the West*, ed. Leonard Lewin (New York: Dutton, 1976), p. 65.
49. *Ibid.*, pp. 64–65.
50. Alfred Orage, "Commentary on *Beelzebub's Tales*," in C. S. Nott, *Teachings of Gurdjieff: The Journal of a Pupil* (York Beach, Maine: Samuel Weiser, 1962), p. 195.
51. Waldberg, *Gurdjieff*, pp. 38–39.
52. Rumi, in Idries Shah, *The Sufis* (New York: Doubleday, 1971), p. 14.
53. Gurdjieff, *Beelzebub's Tales*, p. 6.
54. Rumi, in Shah, *The Way of the Sufi*, p. 37.
55. El-Ghazali, in Idries Shah, *Thinkers of the East* (London: Jonathan Cape, 1971), p. 178.
56. Rumi, "Learning Signs of the Zodiac," in *Open Secret*, p. 8.
57. Bennett, *Gurdjieff: Making a New World*, p. 211.
58. Hakim Sanai, *The Walled Garden of Truth*, trans. David Pendlebury (New York: Dutton, 1976), p. 34.
59. Gurdjieff, *Beelzebub's Tales*, p. 424.
60. Dante Alighieri, *Purgatorio*, Canto XXVII, trans. John Ciardi, in *The Norton Anthology of World Masterpieces*, ed. Maynard Mack, vol. 1 (New York: Norton, 1992), p. 1439.
61. Mevlevi, "The Sufi Quest," in Shah, *Thinkers of the East*, p. 198.
62. Kathryn Mansfield to her husband, 3 December 1922, in *The Letters of Kathryn Mansfield*, ed. J. Middleton Murry, vol. 2 (New York: Knopf, 1951), p. 512.
63. Shah, *Thinkers of the East*, p. 137.
64. Rumi, in Shah, *The Way of the Sufi*, p. 37.

Chapter Three

1. P. D. Ouspensky, *In Search of the Miraculous* (New York: Harcourt, Brace, & World, 1949), p. 26.
2. *Ibid.*, p. 296.
3. *Ibid.*, p. 297.
4. *Ibid.*, p. 296.
5. *Ibid.*, p. 26.
6. *Ibid.*, p. 65.
7. *Ibid.*

8. *Ibid.* p. 66.
9. G. I. Gurdjieff, *Views from the Real World: Early Talks of Gurdjieff in Moscow* (New York: Dutton, 1973), p. 69.
10. Ouspensky, *In Search of the Miraculous*, p. 70.
11. C. S. Nott, *Teachings of Gurdjieff: The Journal of a Pupil* (York Beach, Maine: Samuel Weiser, 1962), p. 223.
12. Gurdjieff, *Views from the Real World*, p. 183.
13. G. I. Gurdjieff, *Meetings with Remarkable Men* (New York: Dutton, 1969), p. 14.
14. *Ibid.*, p. 15.
15. *Ibid.*, p. 16.
16. *Ibid.*, p. 18.
17. James Webb, *The Harmonious Circle: The Lives and Work of G. I. Gurdjieff, P. D. Ouspensky, and Their Followers* (New York: G. P. Putnam's Sons, 1980), p. 275.
18. *Ibid.*, p. 274.
19. Gorham Munson, "The Significance of Jean Toomer," in *Destinations: A Canvass of American Literature since 1900* (New York: J. H. Sears & Co., 1928), p. 184.
20. *Ibid.*
21. *Ibid.*, p. 185.
22. *Ibid.*
23. See Rudolph Paul Byrd, "Jean Toomer: Portrait of an Artist, the Years with Gurdjieff"(Ph.D. diss., Yale University, 1985); Michael J. Krasny, "Jean Toomer and the Quest for Consciousness" (Ph.D. diss., University of Wisconsin, 1972).
24. Kathryn Mansfield to her husband, Boxing Day, 1922, in *The Letters of Kathryn Mansfield*, ed. J. Middleton Murry, vol. 2 (New York: Knopf, 1951), p. 46.
25. Nott, *Teachings of Gurdjieff*, p. 47.
26. Ouspensky, *In Search of the Miraculous*, p. 386.
27. *Ibid.*
28. Kathryn Mansfield to her husband, 23 October 1922, in Murry, *The Letters of Kathryn Mansfield*, vol. 2, p. 510.
29. Kathryn Mansfield to a friend, 16 December 1922, *ibid.*, p. 514.
30. Alfred Orage, "Talks with Kathryn Mansfield," in *Selected Essays and Critical Writings*, ed. Herbert Read and Denis Saurat (New York: Books for Libraries Press, 1935), p. 125.
31. Kathryn Mansfield, 27 October 1922, in Murry, *The Letters of Kathryn Mansfield*, vol. 2, p. 512.
32. Kathryn Mansfield, quoted in Orage, *Selected Essays and Critical Writings*, p. 130.
33. *Ibid.*
34. *Ibid.*, p. 127.
35. *Ibid.*, p. 129.
36. *Ibid.*
37. *Ibid.*, p. 131.
38. Michel Waldberg, *Gurdjieff: An Approach to His Ideas*, trans. Steve Cox (London: Routledge & Kegan Paul, 1981), p. 9.
39. Frank Lloyd Wright, quoted in James Moore, *Gurdjieff and Mansfield* (London: Routledge & Kegan Paul, 1980), p. 208.
40. Moore, *Gurdjieff and Mansfield*, p. 193.
41. *Ibid.*

Chapter Four

1. See N. K. Sanders, introduction to *The Epic of Gilgamesh*, trans. N. K. Sanders (London: Penguin, 1973).
2. Sanders, *Gilgamesh*, p. 61.
3. *Ibid.*, p. 102.
4. *Ibid.*, p. 105.
5. *Ibid.*, p. 107.
6. *Ibid.*
7. *Ibid.*, p. 108.
8. *Ibid.*, p. 114.
9. *Ibid.*, p. 107.
10. Idries Shah, *Caravan of Dreams* (Baltimore: Penguin, 1974), p. 16.
11. Hakim Sanai, *The Walled Garden of Truth*, trans. David Pendlebury (New York: Dutton, 1976), p. 34.
12. P. D. Ouspensky, *In Search of the Miraculous* (New York: Harcourt, Brace, & World, 1949). p. 145.
13. Idries Shah, *The Sufis* (New York: Doubleday, 1971), p. 148.
14. Idries Shah, *Thinkers of the East* (London: Jonathan Cape, 1971), p. 178.
15. *The Odyssey*, trans. Robert Fitzgerald, in *The Norton Anthology of World Masterpieces*, ed. Maynard Mack (New York: Norton, 1992), p. 208.
16. *Ibid.*, p. 326.
17. *Ibid.*, p. 331.
18. *Ibid.*, p. 277.
19. *Ibid.*, p. 488.
20. *Ibid.*, p. 512.
21. *Ibid.*, p. 525.
22. *Ibid.*, p. 371.
23. *Ibid.*, p. 311.
24. *Ibid.*, p. 466.
25. *Ibid.*, p. 291.
26. Miguel de Cervantes, *Don Quixote*, trans. Samuel Putnam, in *The Norton Anthology of World Masterpieces*, ed. Maynard Mack (New York: Norton, 1992), p. 1872.
27. *Ibid.*
28. G. I. Gurdjieff, *Meetings with Remarkable Men* (New York: Dutton, 1969), p. 49.
29. Cervantes, *Don Quixote*, p. 1843.
30. G. I. Gurdjieff, *Beelzebub's Tales to His Grandson* (New York: Dutton, 1973), p. 161.
31. *Ibid.*, p. 43.
32. Voltaire, *Candide*, trans. Robert M. Adams, in *The Norton Anthology of World Masterpieces*, ed. Maynard Mack (New York: Norton, 1992), p. 340.
33. *Ibid.*, p. 368.
34. *Ibid.*, p. 373.
35. *Ibid.*, p. 376.
36. Thomas Mann, *The Magic Mountain*, trans. H. T. Lowe-Porter (New York: Knopf, 1927), p. 5.
37. *Ibid.*, p. 38.

38. *Ibid.*, p. 68.
39. *Ibid.*, p. 301.
40. *Ibid.*, p. 750.
41. *Ibid.*, p. 240.
42. *Ibid.*, p. 602.
43. *Ibid.*, p. 253.
44. Gurdjieff, *Beelzebub's Tales*, p. 1083.
45. William C. Chittick, *The Sufi Path of Love: The Spiritual Teachings of Rumi* (Albany: State University of New York Press, 1983), p. 287.
46. *Cf.* Rivkah Scharf Kluger, *Satan in the Old Testament*, trans. Hildegard Nagel (Evanston, Illinois: Northwestern University Press, 1967).
47. Adapted from Shah, *Caravan of Dreams*, p. 178.
48. Eva de Vitray-Meyerovitch, *Rumi and Sufism*, trans. Simone Fattal (Post-Apollo Press: Sausalito, California, 1987), p. 59.

Chapter Five

1. John G. Bennett, *Talks on Beelzebub's Tales* (York Beach, Maine: Samuel Weiser, 1988), p. vii.
2. *Ibid.*
3. G. I. Gurdjieff, in P. D. Ouspensky, *In Search of the Miraculous* (New York: Harcourt, Brace, & World, 1949), p. 94.
4. Manuel Rainoird, quoted in Michel Waldberg, *Gurdjieff: An Approach to His Ideas*, trans. Steve Cox (London: Routledge & Kegan Paul, 1981), p. 28.
5. G. I. Gurdjieff, *Beelzebub's Tales to His Grandson* (New York: Dutton, 1973), p. 52.
6. *Ibid.*
7. *Ibid.*, p. 51.
8. *Ibid.*, p. 54.
9. *Ibid.*
10. *Ibid.*
11. *Ibid.*, p. 57.
12. *Ibid.*, p. 366.
13. *Ibid.*, p. 367.
14. *Ibid.*, p. 368.
15. *Ibid.*, p. 367.
16. *Ibid.*, p. 368.
17. *Ibid.*, p. 371.
18. *Ibid.*, p. 372.
19. *Ibid.*, p. 373.
20. See C. S. Nott, *Teachings of Gurdjieff: The Journal of a Pupil* (York Beach, Maine: Samuel Weiser, 1962), pp. 125–215.
21. Manuel Rainoird, "Belzebuth, un coup de maître," *Monde Nouveau*, 104 (1956), pp. 54–63.
22. See Waldberg, *Gurdjieff*.
23. Bennett, *Talks on Beelzebub's Tales*, p. 11.
24. *Ibid.*
25. *Ibid.*, p. 8.
26. *Ibid.*, p. 9.

27. *Ibid.*, p. 11.
28. J. Walter Driscoll, *Gurdjieff: An Annotated Bibliography* (New York: Garland, 1985), p. viii.
29. Bennett, *Talks on Beelzebub's Tales*, pp. 4–5.
30. Gurdjieff, quoted in Nott, *Teachings of Gurdjieff*, p. 168.
31. Alfred Orage, quoted in Nott, *Teachings of Gurdjieff*, p. 167.
32. *Ibid.*, p. 194.
33. *Ibid.*, p. 141.
34. *Ibid.*
35. *Ibid.*, p. 142.
36. Rainoird, quoted in Waldberg, *Gurdjieff*, p. 26.
37. *Ibid.*, p. 27.
38. *Ibid.*, p. 28.
39. *Ibid.*, p. 29.
40. *Ibid.*, pp. 22–23.
41. *Ibid.*, p. 23.
42. Waldberg, *Gurdjieff*, p. 9.
43. *Ibid.*
44. *Ibid.*, p. 10.
45. *Ibid.*, p. 11.

Chapter Six

1. Dante Alighieri, *Inferno*, trans. John Ciardi, in *The Norton Anthology of World Masterpieces*, ed. Maynard Mack, vol. 1 (New York: Norton, 1992), p. 1423.
2. Dante Alighieri, *Purgatorio*, trans. John Ciardi, in Mack, *The Norton Anthology of World Masterpieces*, vol. 1, p. 1424.
3. *Ibid.*, p. 1425.
4. G. I. Gurdjieff, *Beelzebub's Tales to His Grandson* (New York: Dutton, 1973), p. 1118.
5. *Ibid.*, p. 1135.
6. *Ibid.*, p. 338.
7. *Ibid.*, p. 337.
8. *Ibid.*, p. 1426.
9. Dante, *Purgatorio*, p. 1439.
10. Gurdjieff, *Beelzebub's Tales*, p. 316.
11. *Ibid.*
12. John G. Bennett, "Commentaries on *Beelzebub's Tales*," audiotape of lecture presented in Gloucestershire, England, 4 December 1974.
13. P. D. Ouspensky, *The Fourth Way: A Record of Talks and Answers to Questions Based on the Teaching of G. I. Gurdjieff* (New York: Knopf, 1957), p. 202.
14. Rumi, "Quatrain 81," in *Open Secret: Versions of Rumi*, trans. John Moyne and Coleman Barks (Putney, Vermont: Threshold Books, 1984), p. 37.
15. Maurice Nicoll, *Psychological Commentaries on the Teachings of G. I. Gurdjieff and P. D. Ouspensky*, vol. 2. (London: Watkins, 1980), p. 763.
16. Dante, *Purgatorio*, p. 1439 (emphasis added).
17. Alfred Orage, quoted in C. S. Nott, *Teachings of Gurdjieff: The Journal of a Pupil* (York Beach, Maine: Samuel Weiser, 1962), p. 173.
18. Gurdjieff, *Beelzebub's Tales*, p. 737.

19. Mack, *The Norton Anthology of World Masterpieces*, p. 1273.
20. Javad Nurbakhsh, *Jesus in the Eyes of the Sufis*, trans. Terry Graham, Leonard Lewisohn, and Hamid Mashkuri (London: Khaniqahi-Nimatullahi Publications, 1992), p. 111.
21. Miguel Asin Palacios, *Islam and the Divine Comedy*, trans. Harold Sutherland (London: Frank Cass & Co., 1968), pp. 45, 47.
22. Idries Shah, *The Sufis* (New York: Doubleday, 1971), p. 155.
23. William Chittick, *Imaginal Worlds: Ibn al-Arabi and the Problem of Religious Diversity* (New York: State University of New York Press, 1994), p. 37.
24. *Ibid.*, p. 38.
25. *Ibid.*, p. 8.
26. Palacios, *Islam and the Divine Comedy*, pp. 276–277.
27. *Ibid.*, p. 4.
28. *Ibid.*, p. 3.
29. *Ibid.*, p. 7.
30. *Ibid.*, p. 12.
31. *Ibid.*, p. 38.
32. *Ibid.*, p. 54.
33. *Ibid.*, p. 45.
34. *Ibid.*, p. 46.
35. *Ibid.*
36. *Ibid.*, p. 92.
37. *Ibid.*, p. 115.
38. *Ibid.*, p. 150.
39. *Ibid.*, p. 32.
40. *Ibid.*, p. 172.
41. Ibn 'Arabi, quoted in Chittick, *Imaginal Worlds*, p. 63.
42. Gurdjieff, *Beelzebub's Tales*, p. 105.
43. *Ibid.*, p. 479.
44. *Ibid.*, p. 1074.
45. *Ibid.*, p. 313.
46. *Ibid.*, p. 201.
47. *Ibid.*, p. 202.
48. *Ibid.*, p. 1135.

Chapter Seven

1. Quoted by Idries Shah in *The Sufis* (New York: Doubleday, 1971), p. 14.
2. G. I. Gurdjieff, *Beelzebub's Tales to His Grandson* (New York: Dutton, 1973), pp. 19–21.
3. *Ibid.*, p. 5.
4. G. I. Gurdjieff, quoted in Michel Waldberg, *Gurdjieff: An Approach to His Ideas*, trans. Steve Cox (London: Routledge & Kegan Paul, 1981), p. ix.
5. Gurdjieff, *Beelzebub's Tales*, pp. 7–9.
6. *Ibid.*, p. 72.
7. *Ibid.*, p. 7.
8. *Ibid.*, pp. 109–120.
9. Rumi, "Quatrain 158" in *Open Secret: Versions of Rumi*, trans. John Moyne and Coleman Barks (Putney, Vermont: Threshold Books, 1984), p. 8.

10. Michael A. Sells, ed., trans., *Early Islamic Mysticism: Sufi, Quran, Miraj, Poetic, and Theological Writings* (New York: Paulist Press, 1966), p. 151.
11. Emily Dickinson, "Poem 1129," in *The American Tradition in Literature*, ed. George Perkins and Barbara Perkins, vol. 2. (New York: McGraw-Hill, 1994), p. 141.
12. Gurdjieff, *Beelzebub's Tales*, p. 246.
13. *Ibid.*, p. 213.
14. *Ibid.*, p. 246.
15. *Ibid.*, p. 247.
16. *Ibid.*, p. 251.
17. *Ibid.*, p. 118.
18. *Ibid.*, pp. 213–214.
19. *Ibid.*, p. 215.
20. *Ibid.*
21. *Ibid.*, p. 280.
22. *Ibid.*, p. 217.
23. G. I. Gurdjieff, in P. D. Ouspensky, *In Search of the Miraculous* (New York: Harcourt, Brace, & World, 1949), pp. 23–24.
24. *Ibid.*, p. 21.
25. *Ibid.*, p. 143.
26. Gurdjieff, *Beelzebub's Tales*, p. 342.
27. Gurdjieff, in Ouspensky, *In Search of the Miraculous*, p. 103.
28. Gurdjieff, *Beelzebub's Tales*, p. 982.
29. *Ibid.*, p. 1022.
30. Gurdjieff, in Ouspensky, *In Search of the Miraculous*, p. 326.
31. Anna Akhmatova, "Requiem," in *Selected Poems*, trans. D. M. Thomas (New York: Penguin, 1988), pp. 89–90.
32. Gorham Munson, quoted in Louis Pauwels, *Monsieur Gurdjieff* (Paris: Editions du Seuil, 1954), p. 122.
33. G. I. Gurdjieff, *The Herald of Coming Good: First Appeal to Contemporary Humanity* (New York: Samuel Weiser, 1971), p. 57.
34. G. I. Gurdjieff, *Meetings with Remarkable Men* (New York: Dutton, 1969), p. 36.
35. Idries Shah, *The Exploits of the Incomparable Mulla Nasrudin* (New York: Dutton, 1971), p. 18.

Chapter Eight

1. Lord Pentland, "Transmission: An Interview with Lord Pentland" in *Gurdjieff: Essays and Reflections on the Man and His Teaching*, ed. Jacob Needleman and George Baker (New York: Continuum, 1996), p. 389.
2. François Stahley, "An Exacting Way: An Interview with François Stahley," in Needleman and Baker, *Gurdjieff: Essays and Reflections*, p. 415.
3. Jerzy Grotowski, "A Kind of Volcano: An Interview with Jerzy Grotowski," in Needleman and Baker, *Gurdjieff: Essays and Reflections*, p. 101.
4. Ravi Ravindra, "Gurdjieff Work and the Teaching of Krishna," in Needleman and Baker, *Gurdjieff: Essays and Reflections*, p. 215.
5. David Appelbaum, "Time and Initiative," in Needleman and Baker, *Gurdjieff: Essays and Reflections*, p. 112.
6. *Ibid.*

7. *Ibid.*
8. *Ibid.*, p. 108.
9. *Ibid.*, pp. 114–115.
10. *Ibid.*, p. 114.
11. *Ibid.*, p. 115.
12. *Ibid.*, p. 112.
13. Grotowski, "A Kind of Volcano," p. 101.
14. Michel Legris, "Tell Me in Five Minutes," in Needleman and Baker, *Gurdjieff: Essays and Reflections*, p. 177.
15. Lord Pentland, "Transmission," p. 389.
16. *Ibid.*, p. 385.
17. *Ibid.*
18. *Ibid.*
19. Ravindra, "Gurdjieff Work," p. 215.
20. *Ibid.*
21. Grotowski, "A Kind of Volcano," p. 102.
22. Michel Camus, "From Consciousness of the Body to 'The Body of Consciousness,'" in Needleman and Baker, *Gurdjieff: Essays and Reflections*, p. 263.
23. Basarab Nicolescu, "Gurdjieff's Philosophy of Nature," in Needleman and Baker, *Gurdjieff: Essays and Reflections*, p. 38.
24. *Ibid.*, p. 63.
25. Robin Skynner, "Gurdjieff and Modern Psychology," in Needleman and Baker, *Gurdjieff: Essays and Reflections*, p. 131.
26. William J. Welch, "Recollections," in Needleman and Baker, *Gurdjieff: Essays and Reflections*, p. 371.
27. *Ibid.*, p. 370.
28. *Ibid.*
29. *Ibid.*, p. 373.
30. Jean-Claude Carriere, "An Inner Journey: The Actor as Companion," in Needleman and Baker, *Gurdjieff: Essays and Reflections*, p. 150.
31. Ravindra, "Gurdjieff Work," p. 216.
32. René Zuber, "Notebooks," in Needleman and Baker, *Gurdjieff: Essays and Reflections*, p. 353.
33. Michel Conge, "Facing Mr. Gurdjieff," in Needleman and Baker, *Gurdjieff: Essays and Reflections*, p. 361.
34. Jacob Needleman, "Gurdjieff, or the Metaphysics of Energy," in Needleman and Baker, *Gurdjieff: Essays and Reflections*, p. 83.
35. Camus, "From Consciousness of the Body to 'The Body of Consciousness,'" p. 263.
36. Conge, "Facing Mr. Gurdjieff," p. 354.
37. Dorothea Dooling, "The Ladder of Evolution," in Needleman and Baker, *Gurdjieff: Essays and Reflections*, p. 195.
38. Conge, "Facing Mr. Gurdjieff," p. 354.
39. Grotowski, "A Kind of Volcano," p. 98.
40. Legris, "Tell Me in Five Minutes," p. 176.
41. Stahly, "An Exacting Way," p. 409.
42. Carriere, "An Inner Journey," p. 154.
43. Jacques LaCarriere, "Letter to a Contemporary Gnostic," in Needleman and Baker, *Gurdjieff: Essays and Reflections*, p. 157.

44. Arnaud Desjardins, "Homage to Gurdjieff," in Needleman and Baker, *Gurdjieff: Essays and Reflections*, p. 233.

45. Michel Random, "The Men of Blame and the Fourth Way," in Needleman and Baker, *Gurdjieff: Essays and Reflections*, pp. 230–231.

BIBLIOGRAPHY

Akhmatova, Anna. "Requiem." In *Selected Poems*. Translated by D. M. Thomas. New York: Penguin, 1988.

Alighieri, Dante. "Inferno." Translated by John Ciardi. In *The Norton Anthology of World Masterpieces*. Edited by Maynard Mack. New York: Norton, 1992.

———. *Purgatorio*. Translated by John Ciardi. In *The Norton Anthology of World Masterpieces*. Edited by Maynard Mack. New York: Norton, 1992.

Appelbaum, David. "Time and Initiative." In *Gurdjieff: Essays and Reflections on the Man and His Teaching*. Edited by Jacob Needleman and George Baker. New York: Continuum, 1996.

Bennett, John G. "Commentaries on *Beelzebub's Tales*." Audiotape of lecture presented in Gloucestershire, England, 4 December 1974.

———. *Gurdjieff: Making a New World*. New York: Harper & Row, 1973.

———. *Talks on Beelzebub's Tales*. York Beach, Maine: Samuel Weiser, 1988.

———. *Witness: The Story of a Search*. Charlestown, West Virginia: Claymont Communications, 1983.

———, and Elizabeth Bennett. *Idiots in Paris: Diaries of J. G. Bennett and Elizabeth Bennett*. Gloucestershire, England: Coombe Springs Press, 1980.

Byrd, Rudolph Paul. "Jean Toomer: Portrait of an Artist, the Years with Gurdjieff." Ph.D. diss. Yale University, 1985.

Camus, Michel. "From Consciousness of the Body to 'The Body of Consciousness.'" In *Gurdjieff: Essays and Reflections on the Man and His Teaching*. Edited by Jacob Needleman and George Baker. New York: Continuum, 1996.

Carriere, Jean-Claude. "An Inner Journey: The Actor as Companion." In *Gurdjieff: Essays and Reflections on the Man and His Teaching*. Edited by Jacob Needleman and George Baker. New York: Continuum, 1996.

Cervantes, Miguel de. *Don Quixote*. Translated by Samuel Putnam. In *The Norton Anthology of World Masterpieces*. Edited by Maynard Mack. 2 vols. New York: Norton, 1992.

Chittick, William. *Imaginal Worlds: Ibn al-Arabi and the Problem of Religious Diversity*. New York: State University of New York Press, 1994.

———. *The Sufi Path of Love: The Spiritual Teachings of Rumi*. Albany: State University of New York Press, 1983.

Conge, Michel. "Facing Mr. Gurdjieff." In *Gurdjieff: Essays and Reflections on the Man and His Teaching*. Edited by Jacob Needleman and George Baker. New York: Continuum, 1996.

De Hartmann, Thomas, and Olga de Hartmann. *Our Life with Mr. Gurdjieff.* New York: Harper & Row, 1983.

Desjardins, Arnaud. "Homage to Gurdjieff." In *Gurdjieff: Essays and Reflections on the Man and His Teaching*. Edited by Jacob Needleman and George Baker. New York: Continuum, 1996.

De Vitray-Meyerovitch, Eva. *Rumi and Sufism*. Translated by Simone Fattal. Post-Apollo Press: Sausalito, California, 1987.

Dickinson, Emily. "Poem 1129." In *The American Tradition in Literature*. Edited by George Perkins and Barbara Perkins. Vol. 2. New York: McGraw-Hill, 1994.

Dooling, Dorothea. "The Ladder of Evolution." In *Gurdjieff: Essays and Reflections on the Man and His Teaching*. Edited by Jacob Needleman and George Baker. New York: Continuum, 1996.

Driscoll, J. Walter. *Gurdjieff: An Annotated Bibliography*. New York: Garland, 1985.

Grotowski, Jerzy. "A Kind of Volcano: An Interview with Jerzy Grotowski." In *Gurdjieff: Essays and Reflections on the Man and His Teaching*. Edited by Jacob Needleman and George Baker. New York: Continuum, 1996.

Gurdjieff, G. I. *Beelzebub's Tales to His Grandson*. New York: Dutton, 1973.

———. *The Herald of Coming Good: First Appeal to Contemporary Humanity*. New York: Samuel Weiser, 1971.

———. *Life Is Real, Only Then, When "I Am."* New York: Triangle Editions, 1975.

———. *Meetings with Remarkable Men*. New York: Dutton, 1969.

———. *Views from the Real World: Early Talks of Gurdjieff in Moscow*. New York: Dutton, 1973.

Homer. *The Odyssey*. Translated by Robert Fitzgerald. In *The Norton Anthology of World Masterpieces*. Edited by Maynard Mack. 2 vols. New York: Norton, 1992.

Kluger, Rivkah Scharf. *Satan in the Old Testament*. Translated by Hildegard Nagel. Evanston, Illinois: Northwestern University Press, 1967.

Krasny, Michael J. "Jean Toomer and the Quest for Consciousness." Ph.D. diss. University of Wisconsin, 1972.

LaCarriere, Jacques. "Letter to a Contemporary Gnostic." In *Gurdjieff: Essays and Reflections on the Man and His Teaching*. Edited by Jacob Needleman and George Baker. New York: Continuum, 1996.

Legris, Michel. "Tell Me in Five Minutes." In *Gurdjieff: Essays and Reflections on the Man and His Teaching*. Edited by Jacob Needleman and George Baker. New York: Continuum, 1996.

Lewin, Leonard, ed. *The Elephant in the Dark and Other Writings on the Diffusion of Sufi Ideas in the West*. New York: Dutton, 1976.

Lings, Martin. *A Sufi Saint in the Twentieth Century: Shaikh Ahmad al-Alawi, His Spititual Heritage and Legacy*. Los Angeles: University of California Press, 1973.

———. *What Is Sufism?* Berkeley: University of California Press, 1977.

Mack, Maynard, ed. *The Norton Anthology of World Masterpieces*. 2 vols. New York: Norton, 1992.

Mann, Thomas. *The Magic Mountain*. Translated by H. T. Lowe-Porter. New York: Knopf, 1927.

Mevlevi. "The Sufi Quest." In Idries Shah. *Thinkers of the East*. London: Jonathan Cape, 1971.

Moore, James. *Gurdjieff and Mansfield*. London: Routledge & Kegan Paul, 1980.

Moyne, John, and Coleman Barks, trans. *Open Secret: Versions of Rumi*. Putney, Vermont: Threshold Books, 1984.

Munson, Gorham. "The Significance of Jean Toomer." In *Destinations: A Canvass of American Literature since 1900*. New York: J. H. Sears & Co., 1928.

Murry, J. Middleton, ed. *The Letters of Kathryn Mansfield*. 2 vols. New York: Knopf, 1951.

Needleman, Jacob. "Gurdjieff, or the Metaphysics of Energy." In *Gurdjieff: Essays and Reflections on the Man and His Teaching*. Edited by Jacob Needleman and George Baker. New York: Continuum, 1996.

———, and George Baker, eds. *Gurdjieff: Essays and Reflections on the Man and His Teaching*. New York: Continuum, 1996.

Nicolescu, Basarab. "Gurdjieff's Philosophy of Nature." In *Gurdjieff: Essays and Reflections on the Man and His Teaching*. Edited by Jacob Needleman and George Baker. New York: Continuum, 1996.

Nicoll, Maurice. *Psychological Commentaries on the Teachings of G. I. Gurdjieff and P. D. Ouspensky*. 5 vols. London: Watkins, 1980.

Nott, C. S. *Teachings of Gurdjieff: The Journal of a Pupil*. York Beach, Maine: Samuel Weiser, 1962.

Nurbakhsh, Javad. *Jesus in the Eyes of the Sufis*. Translated by Terry Graham, Leonard Lewisohn, and Hamid Mashkuri. London: Khaniqahi-Nimatullahi Publications, 1992.

Orage, Alfred. "Commentary on *Beelzebub's Tales*." In C. S. Nott. *Teachings of Gurdjieff: The Journal of a Pupil*. York Beach, Maine: Samuel Weiser, 1962.

———. "Talks with Kathryn Mansfield." In *Selected Essays and Critical Writings*. Edited by Herbert Read and Denis Saurat. New York: Books for Libraries Press, 1935.

Ouspensky, P. D. *The Fourth Way: A Record of Talks and Answers to Questions Based on the Teaching of G. I. Gurdjieff*. New York: Knopf, 1957.

———. *In Search of the Miraculous*. New York: Harcourt, Brace, & World, 1949.

Palacios, Miguel Asin. *Islam and the Divine Comedy*. Translated by Harold Sutherland. London: Frank Cass & Co., 1968.

Pauwels, Louis. *Monsieur Gurdjieff*. Paris: Editions du Seuil, 1954.

Pentland, Lord. "Transmission: An Interview with Lord Pentland." In *Gurdjieff: Essays and Reflections on the Man and His Teaching*. Edited by Jacob Needleman and George Baker. New York: Continuum, 1996.

Perkins, George, and Barbara Perkins, eds. *The American Tradition in Literature*. 2 vols. New York: McGraw-Hill, 1994.

Rainoird, Manuel. "Belzebuth, un coup de maître," *Monde Nouveau*, 104 (1956), pp. 54–63.

Random, Michel. "The Men of Blame and the Fourth Way." In *Gurdjieff: Essays and Reflections on the Man and His Teaching*. Edited by Jacob Needleman and George Baker. New York: Continuum, 1996.

Ravindra, Ravi. "Gurdjieff Work and the Teaching of Krishna." In *Gurdjieff: Essays and Reflections on the Man and His Teaching*. Edited by Jacob Needleman and George Baker. New York: Continuum, 1996.

Rumi. "Learning Signs of the Zodiac." In *Open Secret: Versions of Rumi*. Translated by John Moyne and Coleman Barks. Putney, Vermont: Threshold Books, 1984.

———. "Quatrain 81." In *Open Secret: Versions of Rumi*. Translated by John Moyne and Coleman Barks. Putney, Vermont: Threshold Books, 1984.

———. "Quatrain 91." In *Open Secret: Versions of Rumi*. Translated by John Moyne and Coleman Barks. Putney, Vermont: Threshold Books, 1984.

———. "Quatrain 158." In *Open Secret: Versions of Rumi*. Translated by John Moyne and Coleman Barks. Putney, Vermont: Threshold Books, 1984.

Sanai, Hakim. *The Walled Garden of Truth*. Translated by David Pendlebury. New York: Dutton, 1976.

Sanders, N. K., trans. *The Epic of Gilgamesh*. London: Penguin, 1973.

Schuon, Frithjof. *Sufism: Veil and Quintessence*. Translated by William Stoddart. London: Allen and Unwin, 1963.

Sells, Michael A., ed., trans. *Early Islamic Mysticism: Sufi, Quran, Miraj, Poetic, and Theological Writings*. New York: Paulist Press, 1966.

Shah, Idries. *Caravan of Dreams*. Baltimore: Penguin, 1974.

———. *The Exploits of the Incomparable Mulla Nasrudin*. New York: Dutton, 1971.

———. *Special Illumination: The Sufi Use of Humour*. London: Octagon, 1977.

———. *The Sufis*. New York: Doubleday, 1971.

———. "The Teaching Story: Observations on the Folklore of our 'Modern' Thought." In *The Elephant in the Dark and Other Writings on the Diffusion of Sufi Ideas in the West*. Edited by Leonard Lewin. New York: Dutton, 1976.

———. *Thinkers of the East*. London: Jonathan Cape, 1971.

———. *The Way of the Sufi*. New York: Dutton, 1970.

Skynner, Robin. "Gurdjieff and Modern Psychology." In *Gurdjieff: Essays and Reflections on the Man and His Teaching*. Edited by Jacob Needleman and George Baker. New York: Continuum, 1996.

Speeth, Kathleen Riordan. *The Gurdjieff Work*. Berkeley: And/Or Press, 1976.

Stahley, François. "An Exacting Way: An Interview with François Stahley." In *Gurdjieff: Essays and Reflections on the Man and His Teaching*. Edited by Jacob Needleman and George Baker. New York: Continuum, 1996.

Voltaire. *Candide*. Translated by Robert M. Adams. In *The Norton Anthology of World Masterpieces*. Edited by Maynard Mack. 2 vols. New York: Norton, 1992.

Waldberg, Michel. *Gurdjieff: An Approach to His Ideas*. Translated by Steve Cox. London: Routledge & Kegan Paul, 1981.

Webb, James. *The Harmonious Circle: The Lives and Work of G. I. Gurdjieff, P. D. Ouspensky, and Their Followers*. New York: G. P. Putnam's Sons, 1980.

Welch, William J. "Recollections." In *Gurdjieff: Essays and Reflections on the Man and His Teaching*. Edited by Jacob Needleman and George Baker. New York: Continuum, 1996.

Zuber, René. "Notebooks." In *Gurdjieff: Essays and Reflections on the Man and His Teaching*. Edited by Jacob Needleman and George Baker. New York: Continuum, 1996.

ABOUT THE AUTHOR

Anna T. Challenger is Associate Professor of English and Chairperson of the English Department at the American College of Thessaloniki in Greece. She received her MA in Philosophy and her Ph.D. in English from Kent State University, Ohio. She has published articles on G. I. Gurdjieff in the *Journal of Liberal Arts* and in the *Gurdjieff Review*.

INDEX

Aaron, 92
Abraham, 18, 92
Accident, Law of, 81, 87, 113
Adam, 13, 91, 92
aesthetics, 31–45
Afghanistan, 69, 103
Ahoon, 69, 70, 71, 81–82
Akhmatova, Anna, 108–109
Alexandropol, Armenia, 1, 2
Alkinoos, 53
All and Everything (Gurdjieff), 5, 6
Allegory of the Cave, 7
America, 69
Anthology of Black Humor (Breton), 25
Appelbaum, David, 114–115
Appolis, King, 100, 102
'Arabi, Ibn, x, 11, 18, 19, 54, 90–91, 93, 94–95
art, xi, 31–45
 objective, 32–33, 44–45
 subjective, 31–33
Assyria, 12
Atlantis, 69
Attar, Farid-Ud-Din, 28, 102, 118

Babylonia, 12, 69
Baker, George, 109, 113
Bakr, Abdu, 1
Baudelaire, Charles, 25
Beatific Vision, 93
Beelzebub, xi, 5, 13, 22, 68–72, 76–79, 84, 90
Beelzebub's Tales to His Grandson (Gurdjieff), x, 5–6, 9–10, 13, 20, 23–28, 39, 58, 64, 67, 84, 109
 as art, 44–45
 commentaries on, 72–80
 structure of, 26–27, 97
 style of, 72–75
 and travel literature, 47–66
being, 34
Being and Time (Heidegger), 62
"Belzebuth, un coup de maître" (Rainoird), 73

Bennett, Elizabeth, 8
Bennett, John G., 2, 11, 20, 28, 67, 72–74, 80, 86, 110
"Bokharian Dervish Hadjii-Asvatz-Troov, The" (Gurdjieff), 13, 14–15
Book of the Nocturnal Journey of the Most Magnanimous, The ('Arabi), 90
Borsh, Father, 1–2
Breton, André, 25
Brook, Peter, 1, 110
Brothers Karamazov, The (Dostoyevski), 5
Buddha, 35
Buddhism, 12

Café de la Paix, 5
Café Henri IV, 5
Calypso, 51
Camus, Michel, 116, 118
Candide, 56, 59–61, 66
Candide (Voltaire), xi, 59–61
Cane (Toomer), 40
Carnegie Hall, 3, 13
Carriere, Jean-Claude, 118, 119
Castorp, Hans, 56, 61–64, 66
Catholic Church, 90
Cavafy, Constantine P., 53
Center of the Universe, 64–65, 68, 69, 84, 88, 89, 94
Cervantes, Miguel de, xi, 57, 58
Challenger, Anna T., x–xi
Chiromancy of the Stock Exchange, The (Gurdjieff), 4
Christianity, 12, 17, 18, 54, 57, 80, 90
Circe, 52
Cocainist, The (Gurdjieff), 4
Conference of the Birds (Attar), 28, 118
Conge, Michel, 118
conscious evolution, 34–36, 56
Consciousness, Objective, 22
"Conversation of Two Sparrows, The," 37

Creation, Ray of, 86, 88, 91
cummings, e. e., 5
Cyclops, 51

dance, xi, 3, 13–15
Dante Alighieri, x, xi, 28, 53–56, 65, 66, 83, 84, 87, 88, 89–90, 93–95
Darwin, Charles, 35
Daumal, René, 109
David, 18
da Vinci, Leonardo, 32
Death of Ivan Ilych, The (Tolstoy), 62
de Hartmann, Olga, 105, 108
de Hartmann, Thomas, 3, 6, 14, 15, 105, 107–108
de Saltzmann, Alexandre, 3
de Salzmann, Madame, 15
Desjardins, Arnaud, 120
Destinations (Munson), 38
Devil, 22
dhikr, 22, 91
Dickinson, Emily, 103
Divine Comedy (Dante), xi, 28, 53–56, 65, 83, 89–94
Don Quixote, 56, 57, 66
Don Quixote (Cervantes), ix, 56–59
Dooling, Dorothea, 119
Dostoyevski, Fyodor, 5
Dreyfus trial, 3
Duit, Charles, 73, 79, 80

Earthly Paradise, 54, 66, 84, 85, 89
Eddin, Mullah Nassr. *See* Nasrudin
Eden, Garden of, 55
El Dorado, 60, 61, 66
"Elephant in the Dark," 25–26
El-Ghazali, 27, 50
Eliot, T. S., 5
El-Zubeir, 1
Enoch, 92
Eunoe, 85
evolution, conscious, 35–36, 56

faqir, 21
Fourth Way, 21
Fourth Way, The (Ouspensky), 110
Fowles, John, 109
Futuhat. See Meccan Revelations

Georgiades, Georgios, 1, 2
Gilgamesh, 12, 48–50, 55, 56, 66
Gilgamesh, epic of, xi, 2, 48–50, 56
Gnosticism, 18
God, 7, 22, 26, 54, 65, 84
Grotowski, Jerzy, 9, 114, 115, 119
Gujdvani, Abdulhalik, 21
Gulliver's Travels (Swift), 41
Gurdjieff, G. I.,
 and aesthetics, 31–45
 All and Everything, 5, 6
 and art, xi, 31–45
 biography, 1–11
 birth of, 1
 "Bokharian Dervish Hadjii-Asvatz-Troov, The" 13, 15
 Chiromancy of the Stock Exchange, The, 4
 Cocainist, The, 4
 and dance, xi, 3, 12–14
 Herald of Coming Good, The, 5, 109–110
 and humor, 25–26
 and Jean Toomer, 39–41
 and Kathryn Mansfield, 39–44
 and languages, 1, 11
 Life Is Real Only Then, When "I Am," 5–6, 109–110
 and literature, 37–39
 Meetings with Remarkable Men, 2, 20, 32, 37, 47, 109, 110
 and music, xi, 6, 8, 13, 15–16
 "Sacred Reading from the Koran," 13
 "Sayyid No. 1," 13
 "Sayyid No. 7," 13
 "Sayyid No. 9," 13
 "Sayyid Song and Dance," 13
 "Song of the Dervish," 16
 Struggle of the Musicians, The, 5, 15, 16
 and Sufism, 7, 11–28
 Three Brothers, The, 5
 and travel literature, 47–66
 Unconscious Murder, The, 4
Gurdjieff: An Approach to His Ideas (Waldberg), 23, 73
Gurdjieff and Mansfield (Moore), 44

Gurdjieff: Essays and Reflections on the Man and His Teaching (Needleman and Baker), 109, 111–117
Gurdjieff Foundation, 113, 117

Hadjii-Asvatz-Troov, 15
Hanslick, Eduard, xi
Hardy, Thomas, 41
Hassein, 25, 26, 69, 70, 71–72, 79, 80, 84, 95, 103, 105
Heaven, xi
Hegel, G. W. F., ix
Heidegger, Martin, ix, 62, 64
Helios, 52
Hell, xi, 53, 54, 55, 83, 84, 85, 87, 89, 92, 93, 95
Herald of Coming Good, The, 5, 109–110
Hinduism, 12
HIS ENDLESSNESS, 65, 68, 69, 71, 72, 76
"Holy Planet Purgatory, The" (Gurdjieff), x, 54, 83–95
Homer, xi, 51
humor, 23–25

Iblis, 65, 80, 90, 95
Idiotism, Science of, 7, 9, 28
Inferno (Dante), 83, 85
In Search of the Miraculous (Ouspensky), 110, 116
Institute for the Harmonious Development of Man, 3–4, 6, 39, 40, 41, 42, 43, 107, 115
"Interpreter of Desires" ('Arabi), 11
Ishmael, 18
Islam, 12, 17, 18, 91
Islam and the Divine Comedy (Palacios), x, 54, 91–94
Isra, or *The Nocturnal Journey*, 54, 90, 92, 93, 94

Jesus Christ, 18, 35, 50, 92
John, 92
Jonaid, Shaikh, 18
Joseph, 92

Karatas, 64, 68, 69, 70, 79, 94
Karnak, 69, 70, 71, 99

Kars, Turkey, 1, 2
Kazantzakis, Nikos, xi
Khayyam, Omar, 67
Khwajagan Order, 2, 20–21
Kierkegaard, Søren, ix, x
Knopf, Alfred A., 6
knowledge, 34–35
Koran, 17, 19, 22, 26, 65, 91
Kubravi Order, 13

Laborie, Maitre, 3
LaCarriere, Jacques, 117
Law
  of Accident, 81, 87, 113
  of Will, 87, 88
League of Nations, 58, 106–107
Legris, Michel, 115, 119
Lethe, 84, 85
Life Is Real Only Then, When "I Am" (Gurdjieff), 5–6, 109–110
Lings, Martin, 17
literature, 37–39
  Armenian, 12
  contemporary, 38
  Islamic, 26, 55, 90
  travel, xi, 47–62
Lotus Eaters, 52
LSD, 116

Magic Mountain, The (Mann), xi, 61–64
Mahomet. See Mohammed
Making a New World (Bennett), 11
Mann, Thomas, xi, 61
Mansfield, Kathryn, 3, 5, 9, 29, 39–44
Mars, 68–69, 103
Mathnavi (Rumi), 47, 50
Meccan Revelations ('Arabi), 18, 90, 93, 94
Meetings with Remarkable Men (Brook), 1, 110
Meetings with Remarkable Men (Gurdjieff), 2, 5–6, 11, 20, 32, 37, 47, 109, 110
Melville, Herman, xi
Memorial of the Friends of God (Attar), 102
Mevlevi, 28–29
Mevlevi Order, 13, 14, 20

Miraj, or *The Ascension*, 54, 90, 92, 93, 94
Mohammed, 18, 19, 28, 50, 54, 90, 91–93, 94, 95
monk, 21
Montesquieu, Baron de, 79
Moore, James, 44
Moses, 1, 18, 92
Mother of Records, 38
Mount Purgatory, 54, 66, 84, 88
Munson, Gorham, 40–41, 109
music, xi, 6, 8, 13, 15–16

Naqshband, Khaja Bahaudin, 20
Naqshbandi Order, 13, 20–22
Nasrudin, 22–24, 70, 111
Needleman, Jacob, 109, 113, 118
Neo-Platonism, 18
neurophysiology, 12
New Age, The, 5–6, 42
Nicholas II, Tsar, 3, 15, 108
Nicolescu, Basarab, 116
Nicoll, Maurice, 87
Nietzsche, Friedrich, ix
Nijinsky, Vaslav, 15
Norton Anthology of World Masterpieces, 89
Nott, C. S., 4

Objective Consciousness, 22
Objective Reason, 71, 73, 75, 76, 81, 89, 104, 107
Occasion, 94
Odysseus, xi, 50–53, 56, 66
Odyssey, The (Homer), xi, 50–53, 56
Oedipus, 44, 45
Orage, Alfred, 3, 5–6, 26, 42–43, 72, 73, 75–77, 80, 88, 117
Organic Shame, 75
Ostrowska, Countess Julia, 3
Ouspensky, P. D., 13, 16, 22, 32, 41, 80, 87, 105, 106, 107, 110, 111, 116

Palacios, Miguel Asin, x, 54, 90–94
Paradise, 53, 54, 55, 84, 88, 92, 95
Paradiso (Dante), 54, 85
"Partial Tale about the Causes of War, A," 103–111
Pavlova, Anna, 15

Pentland, Lord, 113, 114, 115–116, 117
philosophy, Indian, 12
"Pink Flower, The" (de Hartmann), 14
Pistis Sophia, 18
Plato, ix, 7
Pound, Ezra, 5, 8
Prieuré des Basses Loges, 3–4, 6, 12, 22
Proteus, 1
psychology, 12
Purgatorio (Dante), x, 28, 83, 85
Purgatory, 53–55, 70, 83–95, 99
Pythagoras, 12

Qadiri Order, 13
Qalander Order, 13
"Quatrain 921" (Rumi), 113

Rabi'a of Basra, 102
Rainoird, Manuel, 68, 73, 77–79, 80
Random, Michel, 120
Ravindra, Ravi, 114, 115, 116, 118
Ray of Creation, 86, 88, 91
Reason, Objective, 71, 73, 75, 76, 81, 89, 104, 107
Reciprocal Maintenance, Theory of, 3, 67, 76, 105, 106
Rembrandt, 8
"Requiem" (Akhmatova), 108–109
"Results of an Unwise Wager, The," 100–103
"Results of Some Idle Fishermen, The," 98–100
Revozvradendr, 69, 70
"Riches" (El-Zubeir), 1
Rose Garden, The (Sa'di), 29
Rumi, Jelaluddin, 13, 15, 17, 19–20, 25, 27, 28, 45, 47, 50, 65, 66, 87, 90, 97, 101–102, 113, 120
Russia, 3, 69, 104
Russian Academy, 1
Russian Revolution, 69, 107–108

"Sacred Reading from the Koran" (Gurdjieff), 13
Sa'di, Muslih-uddin, 29
Saint Augustine, ix
Saint Basil the Great, 12
Saint Francis of Assisi, 17
Saint Peter, 55

Sakoor, 70
Salam, Abdas, 120
Sanai, Hakim, 17, 25, 28, 50
Sarmoun Brotherhood, 2
Satan, xi, 53, 65, 84, 87, 90
"Sayyid No. 1" (Gurdjieff), 13
"Sayyid No. 7" (Gurdjieff), 13
"Sayyid No. 9" (Gurdjieff), 13
"Sayyid Song and Dance" (Gurdjieff), 13
Schuon, Frithjof, 17
Science of Idiotism, 7, 9, 28
Scylla and Charybdis, 51
"Secret, The" (Khayyam), 67
Self-Remembering, 3, 22, 87, 88, 91, 117
Shah, Idries, 20, 22, 25–26
Shakespeare, William, 42
Shame, Organic, 75
Shams of Tabriz, 13
Shiemash, Ashiata, 69
"Significance of Jean Toomer, The" (Munson), 40
Sirat, 93
Sirens, 52
Skynner, Robin, 116
Socrates, ix, x
Solioonensius, 104–105
"Song of the Dervish" (Gurdjieff), 16
Soviet Union, 108
Sphinx, 44, 45
Stahly, François, 114, 119
Stop Exercise, 14
Strange Life of Ivan Osokin, The (Ouspensky), 22
Struggle of the Musicians, The (Gurdjieff), 5, 15, 16
"Sufi Quest, The" (Mevlevi), 28
Sufism, x, 7, 11–28, 29, 50, 52, 54, 56, 65–66, 80, 87, 89, 92–93, 94–95, 97
Swift, Jonathan, 41
Switzerland, 8

Taj Mahal, 32
Talks on Beelzebub's Tales (Bennett), 67
"Talks with Kathryn Mansfield" (Orage), 42
Tchelebi, Divan Mehmed, 13

Telemachus, 51
Théâtre des Champs-Elysées, 3, 13, 16
Theory of Reciprocal Maintenance, 3, 67, 76, 105, 106
Thomas, Dylan, 5
Thoreau, Henry David, 47
Thousand and One Nights, A, 2, 38–39
Three Brothers, The (Gurdjieff), 5
time, 114–115
"Time and Initiative" (Appelbaum), 114–115
Tolstoy, Leo, xi, 62, 64
Tooilan, 70
Tooloof, 69
Toomer, Jean, 3, 38–40, 109
"Transcaucasian Kurd, The," 97–98

Unconscious Murder, The (Gurdjieff), 4
Utnapishtim, 48–50, 55

Virgil, 28, 83, 84, 85, 88, 89
Voltaire, xi, 59, 61, 79

Waldberg, Michel, 23, 25, 27, 44, 73, 79–80
war, 103–111
Way of the Sufi (Shah), 20
Welch, William J., 117
Whirling Dervishes, 13–14, 22, 28
Will, Law of, 87, 88
Witness (Bennett), 110
Wright, Frank Lloyd, 9, 44

Yahweh, 65
yogi, 21

Zen, x
Zoroastrianism, 12
Zuber, René, 118

VIBS

The **Value Inquiry Book Series** is co-sponsored by:

Adler School of Professional Psychology
American Indian Philosophy Association
American Maritain Association
American Society for Value Inquiry
Association for Process Philosophy of Education
Canadian Society for Philosophical Practice
Center for Bioethics, University of Turku
Center for International Partnerships, Rochester Institute of Technology
Center for Professional and Applied Ethics, University of North Carolina at Charlotte
Center for Research in Cognitive Science, Autonomous University of Barcelona
Centre for Applied Ethics, Hong Kong Baptist University
Centre for Cultural Research, Aarhus University
Centre for Professional Ethics, University of Central Lancashire
Centre for the Study of Philosophy and Religion, College of Cape Breton
College of Education and Allied Professions, Bowling Green State University
Concerned Philosophers for Peace
Conference of Philosophical Societies
Department of Moral and Social Philosophy, University of Helsinki
Gannon University
Gilson Society
Ikeda University
Institute of Philosophy of the High Council of Scientific Research, Spain
International Academy of Philosophy of the Principality of Liechtenstein
International Center for the Arts, Humanities, and Value Inquiry
International Society for Universal Dialogue

Natural Law Society
Personalist Discussion Group
Philosophical Society of Finland
Philosophy Born of Struggle Association
Philosophy Seminar, University of Mainz
Pragmatism Archive
R.S. Hartman Institute for Formal and Applied Axiology
Research Institute, Lakeridge Health Corporation
Russian Philosophical Society
Society for Iberian and Latin-American Thought
Society for the Philosophic Study of Genocide and the Holocaust
Society for the Philosophy of Sex and Love
Yves R. Simon Institute.

Titles Published

1. Noel Balzer, *The Human Being as a Logical Thinker.*

2. Archie J. Bahm, *Axiology: The Science of Values.*

3. H. P. P. (Hennie) Lötter, *Justice for an Unjust Society.*

4. H. G. Callaway, *Context for Meaning and Analysis: A Critical Study in the Philosophy of Language.*

5. Benjamin S. Llamzon, *A Humane Case for Moral Intuition.*

6. James R. Watson, *Between Auschwitz and Tradition: Postmodern Reflections on the Task of Thinking.* A volume in **Holocaust and Genocide Studies.**

7. Robert S. Hartman, *Freedom to Live: The Robert Hartman Story,* edited by Arthur R. Ellis. A volume in **Hartman Institute Axiology Studies.**

8. Archie J. Bahm, *Ethics: The Science of Oughtness.*

9. George David Miller, *An Idiosyncratic Ethics; Or, the Lauramachean Ethics.*

10. Joseph P. DeMarco, *A Coherence Theory in Ethics.*

11. Frank G. Forrest, *Valuemetrics^N: The Science of Personal and Professional Ethics*. A volume in **Hartman Institute Axiology Studies.**

12. William Gerber, *The Meaning of Life: Insights of the World's Great Thinkers.*

13. Richard T. Hull, Editor, *A Quarter Century of Value Inquiry: Presidential Addresses of the American Society for Value Inquiry.* A volume in **Histories and Addresses of Philosophical Societies.**

14. William Gerber, *Nuggets of Wisdom from Great Jewish Thinkers: From Biblical Times to the Present.*

15. Sidney Axinn, *The Logic of Hope: Extensions of Kant's View of Religion.*

16. Messay Kebede, *Meaning and Development.*

17. Amihud Gilead, *The Platonic Odyssey: A Philosophical-Literary Inquiry into the* Phaedo.

18. Necip Fikri Alican, *Mill's Principle of Utility: A Defense of John Stuart Mill's Notorious Proof.* A volume in **Universal Justice.**

19. Michael H. Mitias, Editor, *Philosophy and Architecture.*

20. Roger T. Simonds, *Rational Individualism: The Perennial Philosophy of Legal Interpretation.* A volume in **Natural Law Studies.**

21. William Pencak, *The Conflict of Law and Justice in the Icelandic Sagas.*

22. Samuel M. Natale and Brian M. Rothschild, Editors, *Values, Work, Education: The Meanings of Work.*

23. N. Georgopoulos and Michael Heim, Editors, *Being Human in the Ultimate: Studies in the Thought of John M. Anderson.*

24. Robert Wesson and Patricia A. Williams, Editors, *Evolution and Human Values.*

25. Wim J. van der Steen, *Facts, Values, and Methodology: A New Approach to Ethics.*

26. Avi Sagi and Daniel Statman, *Religion and Morality*.

27. Albert William Levi, *The High Road of Humanity: The Seven Ethical Ages of Western Man*, edited by Donald Phillip Verene and Molly Black Verene.

28. Samuel M. Natale and Brian M. Rothschild, Editors, *Work Values: Education, Organization, and Religious Concerns*.

29. Laurence F. Bove and Laura Duhan Kaplan, Editors, *From the Eye of the Storm: Regional Conflicts and the Philosophy of Peace*. A volume in **Philosophy of Peace.**

30. Robin Attfield, *Value, Obligation, and Meta-Ethics*.

31. William Gerber, *The Deepest Questions You Can Ask About God: As Answered by the World's Great Thinkers*.

32. Daniel Statman, *Moral Dilemmas*.

33. Rem B. Edwards, Editor, *Formal Axiology and Its Critics*. A volume in **Hartman Institute Axiology Studies.**

34. George David Miller and Conrad P. Pritscher, *On Education and Values: In Praise of Pariahs and Nomads*. A volume in **Philosophy of Education.**

35. Paul S. Penner, *Altruistic Behavior: An Inquiry into Motivation*.

36. Corbin Fowler, *Morality for Moderns*.

37. Giambattista Vico, *The Art of Rhetoric* (*Institutiones Oratoriae*, 1711-1741), from the definitive Latin text and notes, Italian commentary and introduction by Giuliano Crifò, translated and edited by Giorgio A. Pinton and Arthur W. Shippee. A volume in **Values in Italian Philosophy.**

38. W. H. Werkmeister, *Martin Heidegger on the Way*, edited by Richard T. Hull. A volume in **Werkmeister Studies.**

39. Phillip Stambovsky, *Myth and the Limits of Reason*.

40. Samantha Brennan, Tracy Isaacs, and Michael Milde, Editors, *A Question of Values: New Canadian Perspectives in Ethics and Political Philosophy.*

41. Peter A. Redpath, *Cartesian Nightmare: An Introduction to Transcendental Sophistry.* A volume in **Studies in the History of Western Philosophy.**

42. Clark Butler, *History as the Story of Freedom: Philosophy in Intercultural Context,* with Responses by sixteen scholars.

43. Dennis Rohatyn, *Philosophy History Sophistry.*

44. Leon Shaskolsky Sheleff, *Social Cohesion and Legal Coercion: A Critique of Weber, Durkheim, and Marx.* Afterword by Virginia Black.

45. Alan Soble, Editor, *Sex, Love, and Friendship: Studies of the Society for the Philosophy of Sex and Love, 1977-1992.* A volume in **Histories and Addresses of Philosophical Societies.**

46. Peter A. Redpath, *Wisdom's Odyssey: From Philosophy to Transcendental Sophistry.* A volume in **Studies in the History of Western Philosophy.**

47. Albert A. Anderson, *Universal Justice: A Dialectical Approach.* A volume in **Universal Justice.**

48. Pio Colonnello, *The Philosophy of José Gaos.* Translated from Italian by Peter Cocozzella. Edited by Myra Moss. Introduction by Giovanni Gullace. A volume in **Values in Italian Philosophy.**

49. Laura Duhan Kaplan and Laurence F. Bove, Editors, *Philosophical Perspectives on Power and Domination: Theories and Practices.* A volume in **Philosophy of Peace.**

50. Gregory F. Mellema, *Collective Responsibility.*

51. Josef Seifert, *What Is Life? The Originality, Irreducibility, and Value of Life.* A volume in **Central-European Value Studies.**

52. William Gerber, *Anatomy of What We Value Most.*

53. Armando Molina, *Our Ways: Values and Character,* edited by Rem B. Edwards. A volume in **Hartman Institute Axiology Studies.**

54. Kathleen J. Wininger, *Nietzsche's Reclamation of Philosophy*. A volume in **Central-European Value Studies.**

55. Thomas Magnell, Editor, *Explorations of Value*.

56. HPP (Hennie) Lötter, *Injustice, Violence, and Peace: The Case of South Africa*. A volume in **Philosophy of Peace.**

57. Lennart Nordenfelt, *Talking About Health: A Philosophical Dialogue*. A volume in **Nordic Value Studies.**

58. Jon Mills and Janusz A. Polanowski, *The Ontology of Prejudice*. A volume in **Philosophy and Psychology.**

59. Leena Vilkka, *The Intrinsic Value of Nature*.

60. Palmer Talbutt, Jr., *Rough Dialectics: Sorokin's Philosophy of Value*, with Contributions by Lawrence T. Nichols and Pitirim A. Sorokin.

61. C. L. Sheng, *A Utilitarian General Theory of Value*.

62. George David Miller, *Negotiating Toward Truth: The Extinction of Teachers and Students*. Epilogue by Mark Roelof Eleveld. A volume in **Philosophy of Education.**

63. William Gerber, *Love, Poetry, and Immortality: Luminous Insights of the World's Great Thinkers*.

64. Dane R. Gordon, Editor, *Philosophy in Post-Communist Europe*. A volume in **Post-Communist European Thought.**

65. Dane R. Gordon and Józef Niznik, Editors, *Criticism and Defense of Rationality in Contemporary Philosophy*. A volume in **Post-Communist European Thought.**

66. John R. Shook, *Pragmatism: An Annotated Bibliography, 1898-1940*. With Contributions by E. Paul Colella, Lesley Friedman, Frank X. Ryan, and Ignas K. Skrupskelis.

67. Lansana Keita, *The Human Project and the Temptations of Science*.

68. Michael M. Kazanjian, *Phenomenology and Education: Cosmology, Co-Being, and Core Curriculum*. A volume in **Philosophy of Education.**

69. James W. Vice, *The Reopening of the American Mind: On Skepticism and Constitutionalism.*

70. Sarah Bishop Merrill, *Defining Personhood: Toward the Ethics of Quality in Clinical Care.*

71. Dane R. Gordon, *Philosophy and Vision.*

72. Alan Milchman and Alan Rosenberg, Editors, *Postmodernism and the Holocaust.* A volume in **Holocaust and Genocide Studies.**

73. Peter A. Redpath, *Masquerade of the Dream Walkers: Prophetic Theology from the Cartesians to Hegel.* A volume in **Studies in the History of Western Philosophy.**

74. Malcolm D. Evans, *Whitehead and Philosophy of Education: The Seamless Coat of Learning.* A volume in **Philosophy of Education.**

75. Warren E. Steinkraus, *Taking Religious Claims Seriously: A Philosophy of Religion,* edited by Michael H. Mitias. A volume in **Universal Justice.**

76. Thomas Magnell, Editor, *Values and Education.*

77. Kenneth A. Bryson, *Persons and Immortality.* A volume in **Natural Law Studies.**

78. Steven V. Hicks, *International Law and the Possibility of a Just World Order: An Essay on Hegel's Universalism.* A volume in **Universal Justice.**

79. E. F. Kaelin, *Texts on Texts and Textuality: A Phenomenology of Literary Art,* edited by Ellen J. Burns.

80. Amihud Gilead, *Saving Possibilities: A Study in Philosophical Psychology.* A volume in **Philosophy and Psychology.**

81. André Mineau, *The Making of the Holocaust: Ideology and Ethics in the Systems Perspective.* A volume in **Holocaust and Genocide Studies.**

82. Howard P. Kainz, *Politically Incorrect Dialogues: Topics Not Discussed in Polite Circles.*

83. Veikko Launis, Juhani Pietarinen, and Juha Räikkä, Editors, *Genes and Morality: New Essays*. A volume in **Nordic Value Studies.**

84. Steven Schroeder, *The Metaphysics of Cooperation: The Case of F. D. Maurice.*

85. Caroline Joan ("Kay") S. Picart, *Thomas Mann and Friedrich Nietzsche: Eroticism, Death, Music, and Laughter*. A volume in **Central-European Value Studies.**

86. G. John M. Abbarno, Editor, *The Ethics of Homelessness: Philosophical Perspectives.*

87. James Giles, Editor, *French Existentialism: Consciousness, Ethics, and Relations with Others*. A volume in **Nordic Value Studies.**

88. Deane Curtin and Robert Litke, Editors, *Institutional Violence*. A volume in **Philosophy of Peace.**

89. Yuval Lurie, *Cultural Beings: Reading the Philosophers of* Genesis.

90. Sandra A. Wawrytko, Editor, *The Problem of Evil: An Intercultural Exploration*. A volume in **Philosophy and Psychology.**

91. Gary J. Acquaviva, *Values, Violence, and Our Future*. A volume in **Hartman Institute Axiology Studies.**

92. Michael R. Rhodes, *Coercion: A Nonevaluative Approach.*

93. Jacques Kriel, *Matter, Mind, and Medicine: Transforming the Clinical Method.*

94. Haim Gordon, *Dwelling Poetically: Educational Challenges in Heidegger's Thinking on Poetry*. A volume in **Philosophy of Education.**

95. Ludwig Grünberg, *The Mystery of Values: Studies in Axiology,* edited by Cornelia Grünberg and Laura Grünberg.

96. Gerhold K. Becker, Editor, *The Moral Status of Persons: Perspectives on Bioethics*. A volume in **Studies in Applied Ethics.**

97. Roxanne Claire Farrar, *Sartrean Dialectics: A Method for Critical Discourse on Aesthetic Experience.*

98. Ugo Spirito, *Memoirs of the Twentieth Century.* Translated from Italian and edited by Anthony G. Costantini. A volume in **Values in Italian Philosophy.**

99. Steven Schroeder, *Between Freedom and Necessity: An Essay on the Place of Value.*

100. Foster N. Walker, *Enjoyment and the Activity of Mind: Dialogues on Whitehead and Education.* A volume in **Philosophy of Education.**

101. Avi Sagi, *Kierkegaard, Religion, and Existence: The Voyage of the Self.* Translated from Hebrew by Batya Stein.

102. Bennie R. Crockett, Jr., Editor, *Addresses of the Mississippi Philosophical Association.* A volume in **Histories and Addresses of Philosophical Societies.**

103. Paul van Dijk, *Anthropology in the Age of Technology: The Philosophical Contribution of Günther Anders.*

104. Giambattista Vico, *Universal Right.* Translated from Latin and edited by Giorgio Pinton and Margaret Diehl. A volume in **Values in Italian Philosophy.**

105. Judith Presler and Sally J. Scholz, Editors, *Peacemaking: Lessons from the Past, Visions for the Future.* A volume in **Philosophy of Peace.**

106. Dennis Bonnette, *Origin of the Human Species.* A volume in **Studies in the History of Western Philosophy.**

107. Phyllis Chiasson, *Peirce's Pragmatism: The Design for Thinking.* A volume in **Studies in Pragmatism and Values.**

108. Dan Stone, Editor, *Theoretical Interpretations of the Holocaust.* A volume in **Holocaust and Genocide Studies.**

109. Raymond Angelo Belliotti, *What Is the Meaning of Human Life?*

110. Lennart Nordenfelt, *Health, Science, and Ordinary Language*, with Contributions by George Khushf and K. W. M. Fulford.

111. Daryl Koehn, *Local Insights, Global Ethics for Business.* A volume in **Studies in Applied Ethics.**

112. Matti Häyry and Tuija Takala, Editors, *The Future of Value Inquiry.* A volume in **Nordic Value Studies.**

113. Conrad P. Pritscher, *Quantum Learning: Beyond Duality.*

114. Thomas M. Dicken and Rem B. Edwards, *Dialogues on Values and Centers of Value: Old Friends, New Thoughts.* A volume in **Hartman Institute Axiology Studies.**

115. Rem B. Edwards, *What Caused the Big Bang?* A volume in **Philosophy and Religion.**

116. Jon Mills, Editor, *A Pedagogy of Becoming.* A volume in **Philosophy of Education.**

117. Robert T. Radford, *Cicero: A Study in the Origins of Republican Philosophy.* A volume in **Studies in the History of Western Philosophy.**

118. Arleen L. F. Salles and María Julia Bertomeu, Editors, *Bioethics: Latin American Perspectives.* A volume in **Philosophy in Latin America.**

119. Nicola Abbagnano, *The Human Project: The Year 2000,* with an Interview by Guiseppe Grieco. Translated from Italian by Bruno Martini and Nino Langiulli. Edited with an Introduction by Nino Langiulli. A volume in **Studies in the History of Western Philosophy.**

120. Daniel M. Haybron, Editor, *Earth's Abominations: Philosophical Studies of Evil.* A volume in **Personalist Studies.**

121. Anna T. Challenger, *Philosophy and Art in Gurdjieff's* Beelzebub: *A Modern Sufi Odyssey.*